Life Writing and the End of Empire

New Directions in Life Narrative

New Directions in Life Narrative explores the concept of life narrative across the mediums of written work, oral narratives, photography, documentary film, visual art, performance and social media. The series nurtures theoretical, methodological and interpretive innovation in life writing research, supporting projects that apply new combinations of philosophy, critical theory and methodology to the study of life narrative, providing new ways of reading diverse and always evolving forms. It advances interdisciplinary approaches to life narrative, combining the insights of life writing scholarship with those of cognate fields such as art history, history, anthropology, comparative literary studies, law, sociolinguistics, media studies, medicine, philosophy, psychology and sociology. The series strives towards an international scope that mirrors its community, offering a forum for the study of works in translations not previously studied as well as publishing studies of non-Anglophone works.

Series Editors
Kate Douglas, Flinders University, Australia
Anna Poletti, Utrecht University, Netherlands
John Zuern, University of Hawaii, USA

Editorial Advisory Board
Dr Ebony Coletu (Penn State University, USA); Dr Ana Belén Martínez García (University of Navarra, Spain); Associate Professor Claire Lynch (Brunel University, UK); Professor Pramod K Nayar (The University of Hyderabad, India); Dr Nick Tembo (The University of Malawi); Professor Jianling Liu (Shanghai Jiao Tong University, China); Professor Gerardo Necoechea (Instituto Nacional de Antropologia e Historia, Mexico); Dr Laurie McNeill (University of British Columbia, Canada)

Available Titles
Human Rights in Graphic Life Narrative: Reading and Witnessing Violations of the 'Other' in Anglophone Works, Olga Michael
Children and Biography: Reading and Writing Life Stories, Kate Douglas

Forthcoming Titles

The Death Memoir in Contemporary Culture, Claire Nally

Refugee Lives in the Archives: A Pacific Imaginary, Gillian Whitlock

Reading Mediated Life Narratives: Auto/Biographical Agency in the Book, Museum, Social Media, and Archives, Amy Carlson

Life Writing and the Southern Hemisphere: Texts, Spaces, Resonances, edited by Elleke Boehmer and Katherine Collins

Ecological Life Writings from India: Marginalisation, Environmental Justice and Told-to Autobiography, Shalini M. and Moncy Mathew

Life Writing and the End of Empire

Homecoming in Autobiographical Narratives

Emma Parker

BLOOMSBURY ACADEMIC
LONDON • NEW YORK • OXFORD • NEW DELHI • SYDNEY

BLOOMSBURY ACADEMIC
Bloomsbury Publishing Plc, 50 Bedford Square, London, WC1B 3DP, UK
Bloomsbury Publishing Inc, 1359 Broadway, New York, NY 10018, USA
Bloomsbury Publishing Ireland, 29 Earlsfort Terrace, Dublin 2, D02 AY28, Ireland

BLOOMSBURY, BLOOMSBURY ACADEMIC and the Diana logo are trademarks of
Bloomsbury Publishing Plc

First published in Great Britain 2024
Paperback edition published in 2025

Copyright © Emma Parker, 2024

Emma Parker has asserted her right under the Copyright, Designs and Patents Act, 1988,
to be identified as Author of this work.

For legal purposes the Acknowledgements on pp. ix–x constitute an extension of this
copyright page.

Series design by Rebecca Heselton
Cover image courtesy of Lesley Dinsdale and Special Collections,
University of Bristol Library

All rights reserved. No part of this publication may be: i) reproduced or transmitted
in any form, electronic or mechanical, including photocopying, recording or by means
of any information storage or retrieval system without prior permission in writing from
the publishers; or ii) used or reproduced in any way for the training, development or
operation of artificial intelligence (AI) technologies, including generative AI technologies.
The rights holders expressly reserve this publication from the text and data mining
exception as per Article 4(3) of the Digital Single Market Directive (EU) 2019/790.

Bloomsbury Publishing Plc does not have any control over, or responsibility for, any
third-party websites referred to or in this book. All internet addresses given in this
book were correct at the time of going to press. The author and publisher regret any
inconvenience caused if addresses have changed or sites have ceased to exist,
but can accept no responsibility for any such changes.

A catalogue record for this book is available from the British Library.

Library of Congress Cataloging-in-Publication Data
Names: Parker, Emma, 1991– author.
Title: Life writing and the end of empire : homecoming in autobiographical narratives /
Emma Parker.
Description: London ; New York : Bloomsbury Academic, 2024. |
Series: New directions in life narrative | Includes bibliographical references.
Identifiers: LCCN 2023032743 (print) | LCCN 2023032744 (ebook) |
ISBN 9781350353794 (hardback) | ISBN 9781350353800 (pdf) |
ISBN 9781350353817 (epub)
Subjects: LCSH: Autobiography–English authors–History and criticism. |
Imperialism in literature. | Homecoming in literature.
Classification: LCC CT34.G7 P37 2024 (print) | LCC CT34.G7 (ebook) |
DDC 920.009171/241–dc23/eng/20231115
LC record available at https://lccn.loc.gov/2023032743
LC ebook record available at https://lccn.loc.gov/2023032744

ISBN: HB: 978-1-3503-5379-4
PB: 978-1-3503-5383-1
ePDF: 978-1-3503-5380-0
eBook: 978-1-3503-5381-7

Series: New Directions in Life Narrative

Typeset by Newgen KnowledgeWorks Pvt. Ltd., Chennai, India

For product safety related questions contact productsafety@bloomsbury.com.

To find out more about our authors and books visit www.bloomsbury.com
and sign up for our newsletters.

Contents

List of Figures	viii
Acknowledgements	ix
Introduction: Strangers in London: Arriving 'Home' in the Post-War Metropolis	1
1 Double Exposures and Counterfactual Lives in Penelope Lively's Memoirs	25
2 J. G. Ballard's Colonial Uncanny: Settlements, Swimming Pools and Camps	57
3 Back to the Laager: Southern Rhodesia and Doris Lessing's Travel Memoirs	91
4 Possessions, Property and Post-Imperial Melancholia in Janet Frame's Autobiographies	121
5 The Lives of Objects: On Suitcases, Trunks, Tallboys and Dressers	153
Bibliography	179
Index	195

Figures

1.1	Photograph of Bulaq Dakhrur	31
1.2	Photograph of Penelope Lively, three Egyptian children and a donkey	37
2.1	Photograph of the Ballard family home, Shanghai, 1985	58
2.2	Photograph of the original front door of 31a Amherst Avenue, Shanghai, in 1985	64
2.3	Photograph of a drinking station marked as 'Waterloo' in Lunghua camp	78
2.4	Laundry day in the married quarters of Lunghua camp	80
3.1	Photograph of Kermanshah Farm, Doris Lessing's home in Southern Rhodesia	101
4.1	The all-red line of electrical telegraphs linking large swathes of the British Empire from 1902 onwards, public domain	129
4.2	'Fifty-six Eden Street, Oamaru', the former Frame family home	137

Acknowledgements

Thanks are first due to John McLeod, best of teachers, for many years of kindness, good will and excellent advice. For sustaining both me and this project through its early years in Leeds, I am grateful to Bethan Hughes, Nathan Brand, Amber Lascelles, Maddalena Moretti, Clare Fisher, Kate Spowage, Hayley Toth, Rachel Johnson and Adrienne Mortimer. Many colleagues brightened my days in Yorkshire by talking about life writing with me, extending generous invites, and organizing post-conference drinks, especially Haya Alfarhan, Ronnie Barnsley, Alberto Fernández-Carbajal, Andrew Dean, Ed Dodson, Alison Gibbons, Nancy Pedri, Astrid Rasch, Asha Rogers, Amy Rushton, Bill Schwarz and Matt Whittle. Thank you to Elleke Boehmer, for everything, and to Josh Doble and Liam Liburd for our ongoing conversations about post-imperial Britain, all of which shaped the ideas in this book. Sincere thanks to those who edited small excerpts and gave feedback on my ideas in progress, including Nick Bentley, Shirley Chew, Malachi McIntosh, Matthew Taunton and Nonia Williams. Stuart Murray and Marina MacKay asked tough questions and shared brilliant ideas on rewriting a manuscript.

Thank you to Penelope Lively for inviting me to Islington, for tolerating innumerable emails and for granting generous permission to reproduce archival material and interview quotes. Thanks to Homi K. Bhabha and to the estate of Raymond Chandler for permission to quote from published sources, to the Doris Lessing Will Trust for permission to quote from Lessing's letters and to use an image of Kermanshah Farm, and to Susannah Stapleton, Rick McGrath, and my colleagues at the University of Bristol's Special Collections, for all allowing me to reproduce photographs of Shanghai. I am grateful to archivists at the Harry Ransom Center and the University of Otago, the latter particularly for organizing access to the Frame papers which I am regretfully unable to quote from in this book. Thanks also to the staff at the Janet Frame House in Oamaru and Frank Sargeson House in Auckland for my memorable visits, and to the White Rose College of the Arts and Humanities (AHRC) for funding these trips and my doctoral research.

Katie Collins, Mark Lee and Kate Kennedy made me welcome at the Oxford Centre for Life Writing, providing much-needed support and employment after my PhD, and distracting me from the dark months of lockdown. Thank you to all of my brilliant former colleagues at Keele University, especially to Rachel Adcock, David Amigoni, Becky Bowler, Luke Davies, Mariangela Palladino, Hollie Price, and Nick Seager, who supported me during my first academic post, and offered the time, space, and confidence to write. Thank you to the students who took my undergraduate and MA classes in postcolonial literature, especially Jonathan Diaz, Lily Martin and Danny Morris. My new colleagues and students at the University of Bristol welcomed me warmly into their community at the very end of this project, special thanks here to Natalie Ferris, Sian Harris, and Samantha Matthews.

Catherine and Jeremy McIlwaine have cheered me across every finish line, providing courage and good cheer whenever it was needed. Maureen Parker encouraged me to always keep going. While a complete list is impossible, for love, shelter and support thank you to: Jane Barber, Michael Barrington, Alexis Brown, Arabella Currie, Ruth Davies, Simon Davies, David Lawrence, Joe Macmillan, Glenys and Dave Meir, Emily Parsonage, Charlotte and Clark Russell, Chris Williamson, and to Andy, Sandrine and Alice.

Dom Davies arrived on the scene when this project was a single sentence scrawled in a notepad. In the years since he has braved a winter on the South Island pursuing Janet Frame, banished the nagging demons of doubt, cheerfully kept our household running, and provided editorial advice whenever it was needed. He and Olive are always there, whenever I need them. While I have rejected many of Dom's preferred chapter titles (including *You've Been Framed*), I am unspeakably grateful for his wit, wisdom and terrible puns. This book is for him, with love.

Introduction

Strangers in London: Arriving 'Home' in the Post-War Metropolis

Janet Frame arrived in Waterloo station at the end of August 1956. Having endured the difficult, four-week sea crossing from Aotearoa/New Zealand, Frame stood on the concourse and was dismayed to find that London was 'raining and grey and the black taxis looked like hearses'.[1] Despite this ominous first impression, she navigated the hostels and boarding houses which accommodated many other 'strangers in London', making 'long bus journeys to places with haunting names – Ponders End, High Wycombe, Mortlake'.[2] Each time she disembarked 'at a cluster of dreary-looking buildings set in a waste of concrete and brick', she was surprised to see that many of the city's inhabitants 'appeared to be pale, worried and smaller in build than most New Zealanders'.[3] As the September nights grew colder, her damp, rented room near Clapham Common would fill with a thick fog, leaving 'a resulting railway taste' across her tongue.[4] Although Frame's home country had transitioned from a colony to a dominion of the British Empire in 1907, the third volume of her autobiography *The Envoy from Mirror City* (1985) remembers how these imperial legacies 'left a colonial New Zealander overseas without any real identity'.[5]

Arriving in Britain seven years before Frame, Doris Lessing too had undertaken a month-long boat journey from Cape Town, South Africa, in 1949.[6] Her second autobiography, *Walking in the Shade* (1997), recalls her disembarking

---

[1] Janet Frame, *The Envoy from Mirror City*, in *The Complete Autobiography* (London: Women's Press, 1990), pp. 289–435 (p. 299).
[2] Ibid., p. 306.
[3] Ibid.
[4] Ibid., 307.
[5] Ibid., 308.
[6] My thanks to both Robert Bickers and Hayley G. Toth for sending me the passenger lists which record the thirty-year-old Mrs D. Lessing's arrival, and her official classification as a housewife from Southern Rhodesia.

at Southampton and being shocked to see 'white men unloading a ship, doing heavy manual labour'.[7] In Lessing's former home of Southern Rhodesia (now Zimbabwe), such onerous tasks were exclusively carried out by African workers. This disorientating arrival is recorded in several of Lessing's memoirs, where like Frame she remembers how the sinister fogs would envelope bleak, war-damaged streets that were 'stained and cracked and dull and grey'.[8] Just as Frame saw that many Londoners were 'living as if during the days of the Second World War' during the 1950s, Lessing noticed how the psychological traumas of the Blitz were clearly evident in 1949: 'Any conversation tended to drift towards the war, like an animal licking a sore place'.[9] In Southern Rhodesia her parents had regaled their young children with stories of London, remembering evenings spent in music halls and enjoying the glamour of 'the Trocadero and Café Royal'.[10] When their adult daughter found herself in that same metropolis decades later, she discovered that there were few, if any, recognizable coordinates from these stories of 'home'.

Throughout his childhood in 1930s Shanghai – and during his later years in a Japanese internment camp (1943–5) – the young James Ballard listened to similarly nostalgic memories of interwar Britain, where Piccadilly's glimmering lights were 'overlaid by a comfortable Beverley Nichols world of market towns and thatched roofs'.[11] When the SS *Arawa* docked at Southampton in 1946, the teenage Ballard emerged from his sea voyage with high expectations, imagining a soft-focus landscape based on 'J. M. Barrie and [Winnie the Pooh]'.[12] To his astonishment, he discovered that London 'looked like Bucharest with a hangover'.[13] The depleted city was marked by 'heaps of rubble' and inhabited 'by an exhausted ferret-like people defeated by war and deluded by Churchillian rhetoric'.[14] In *Empire of the Sun* (1984), *The Kindness*

---

[7] Doris Lessing, *Walking in the Shade: Volume Two of My Autobiography, 1949–1962* (London: Fourth Estate, 2013), p. 4.
[8] Ibid.
[9] Frame, *The Envoy from Mirror City*, p. 309; Lessing, *Walking in the Shade*, p. 5.
[10] Doris Lessing, *Alfred and Emily* (London: Fourth Estate, 2008), p. 141.
[11] J. G. Ballard, *Miracles of Life: From Shanghai to Shepperton* (London: Fourth Estate, 2008), p. 34.
[12] Although Ballard would always recount his 1946 arrival as if it were his first in Britain, in actuality he had previously visited the UK in 1939. Like Lively (who was also staying in Britain that summer), Ballard hastily departed for China at the outbreak of war. His dubious biographer notes that 'even in his memoirs, Jim never mentioned his pre-war visit to Britain, preferring to date his detestation from his permanent relocation in 1945'. A more generous interpretation might be that Ballard was only nine at the time of his first visit, and was likely to have seen and observed much more when he permanently relocated to Britain as a teenager. – John Baxter, *The Inner Man: The Life of J. G. Ballard* (London: Weidenfeld and Nicolson, 2011), p. 16. Ballard, *Miracles of Life*, p. 34.
[13] J. G. Ballard, 'First Impressions of London', in *A User's Guide to the Millennium: Essays and Reviews* (London: Flamingo, 1997), p. 185.
[14] Ibid.

of Women (1991) and his later autobiography *Miracles of Life* (2008), Ballard developed multiple accounts of life in Shanghai's International Settlement and the sealed confines of the camp. Yet he neither revised nor retracted his early impressions of the British as 'hobbling around [in] a wasteland of poverty, ration books and grotesque social division'.[15] From his adult home in suburban Shepperton, on the outskirts of west London, Ballard always refused to fully embrace the post-imperial island nation as his own, viewing himself as a stranger in a strange land.

The twelve-year old Penelope Lively had arrived in Britain several months before Ballard, travelling from Egypt via Palestine at the tail end of the war in 1945. Raised in a grand mansion on the outskirts of Cairo, Lively had grown up in a protectorate of the British Empire that 'was still effectively run by foreigners and principally by the British'.[16] Having travelled without her immediate family, she was quickly dispatched to live in her grandmother's home on Harley Street, joining a household that was confined to a single, ground floor room (the upper windows 'had been blown out in the Blitz').[17] From there she explored the same bomb-damaged streets that would become familiar to Ballard, Lessing and Frame. While her lodgings were considerably more salubrious than Lessing's bedsits or Frame's fog-filled garden rooms, she shared their first impressions of a blasted landscape wracked by 'the inconceivable cold, [and] the perpetually leaking sky'.[18] Like many arrivals from this period, Lively's colonial education had led her to expect a convivial landscape of 'immutable good weather, gambolling animals and happy laughing folk'.[19] But her memoir *Oleander Jacaranda* (1994) records that, under strict rationing laws, 'the gambolling animals had been turned into offal' and 'the happy laughing folk were transformed into the po-faced raincoat ranks at bus stops'.[20]

Having grown up in the decades after the First World War, this cohort of life writers were raised in colonial, English-speaking households with close ties to the 'mother country', believing that 'not only could the sun never set on the Empire, but it was inconceivable that it would ever do so'.[21] Their respective boat journeys took place during a time of intense transformation in Britain, 'where both workers and intellectuals from the (ex-) colonies migrated to the centre

---

[15] Ibid.
[16] Penelope Lively, *Oleander, Jacaranda: A Childhood Perceived* (London: Penguin, 2006), p. 20.
[17] Ibid., p. 166.
[18] Ibid., p. 165.
[19] Ibid., pp. 173–4.
[20] Ibid., p. 174.
[21] Ibid., p. 59.

in unprecedented numbers'.[22] These writers arrived in London during a pivotal, eleven-year period (1945–56) often described as part of 'the era of dissolution, … the true age of decolonisation'.[23] While it still 'just about made sense' to describe the island nation in 1945 as an 'imperial power', the following decade saw the irreversible decline of British colonial rule across the globe.[24] This seismic shift may have been initially explained by the myth that decolonization was led by Britain – with Winston Churchill committing to 'the eventual abandonment of empire' in exchange for US military support during the war – but the contraction of empire was as much to do with 'anti-colonial revolt', as it was any noble sacrifice on Britain's part.[25] As Priyamvada Gopal and others have demonstrated, 'the crises of insurgency and counterinsurgency in the period immediately following the Second World War', which saw anti-colonial uprisings from Cyprus to British Guiana, were crucial to the disassembly of empire.[26] This cohort of white authors saw how the end of empire not only meant the end of their colonial and settler childhoods, but also that it impacted profoundly on life 'at home', shaping the industrial, social and political landscape of the post-war welfare state.

The uneven process of formal decolonization is often described by a timeline including the Partition of India in 1947, the Mau Mau uprising of the 1950s, the 1956 Suez Crisis and Zimbabwean independence in 1980. Yet as Jordanna Bailkin warns, this history is 'a starting point, rather than a conclusion' for the ongoing configurations of imperial power.[27] For authors whose lives intersected during a critical, post-war period of decolonization, the supposed 'end of empire' in the mid-twentieth century is only the *beginning* of their engagement with colonialism's afterlives. Lively, Ballard, Lessing and Frame would recount their arrivals 'home' across a series of life narratives – published primarily between the 1980s and the early 2000s – which suggest that the end of empire was not a discretely sealed history, confined to a historical era when national

---

[22] Jed Esty, *A Shrinking Island: Modernism and National Culture in England* (Princeton, NJ: Princeton University Press, 2004), p. 165.
[23] John Darwin, *Britain and Decolonisation: The Retreat from Empire in the Post-war World* (Basingstoke: Macmillan Press, 1988), p. 6.
[24] Clair Wills, *Lovers and Strangers: An Immigrant History of Post-War Britain* (London: Penguin, 2018), p. 28.
[25] Camilla Schofield, *Enoch Powell and the Making of Postcolonial Britain* (Cambridge: Cambridge University Press, 2013), pp. 15–16.
[26] Priyamvada Gopal, *Insurgent Empire: Anticolonial Resistance and British Dissent* (London: Verso, 2019), p. 444.
[27] In *The Afterlife of Empire* (2012), Bailkin describes how 'the waning of the formal empire was as much the beginning of a story about the recalibration of British interests as it was an ending of a narrative of domination'. For Bailkin, 'the timeline of the empire's death' is 'hazy and geographically uneven'. – Jordanna Bailkin, *The Afterlife of Empire* (Berkeley: University of California Press, 2012), p. 6.

flags were changed and official maps redrawn.²⁸ Instead these autobiographical texts indicate, to use Derek Gregory's phrase, that 'the treadmill of the colonial present' continues to churn, and that 'the end of empire' remains an ongoing process.²⁹ On the one hand, these life writers responded to decolonization as a particular historical juncture, understanding that there could be no material return to the colonial past. But on the other, their autobiographical writing suggests how 'empire's ruins contour and carve through the psychic and material space in which people live'.³⁰ For all four, the legacies of colonialism continue to linger and coalesce in surprising places.

If the sense of not quite belonging to Britain connects this cohort, this might partly account for their shared autobiographical concern with 'going home' to their memories of colonial territories and former settler colonies.³¹ Yet, as each produced multiple memoirs and autobiographies recording their arrivals as colonial strangers in the metropolis, it would also appear that England was neither the final nor the definitive destination of their life writing.³² Instead they offer first-hand accounts of decolonization which are united by a conflicted, if marked desire to return 'home' to the empire, raising important questions as to

---

²⁸ The clear exception to this book's focus on texts published between the 1980s and the early 2000s is Doris Lessing's early memoir *Going Home* (1957), discussed in Chapter 3 as a prequel to her later travel narrative *African Laughter* (1992). As the author of both the earliest and the latest life narratives discussed in this book, Lessing's final memoir, *Alfred and Emily* (2008), was published three months after Ballard's autobiography, *Miracles of Life* (2008). The chronological range of white life writing at the end of empire (1957–2008) is because these four writers had remarkably long working lives, and it suggests that their memories of empire long outlasted the actual events of formal decolonization in the mid- to late twentieth century.

²⁹ Derek Gregory, *The Colonial Present: Afghanistan, Palestine, Iraq* (Oxford: Wiley-Blackwell, 2004), p. 262.

³⁰ Ann Laura Stoler, 'The Rot Remains: From Ruins to Ruination', in *Imperial Debris: On Ruins and Ruination*, ed. Ann Laura Stoler (Durham: Duke University Press, 2013), pp. 1–38 (p. 2).

³¹ This study uses 'empire' to denote a wide range of colonial practices that, accelerated by the rise of capitalism in Western Europe, led to 'the take-over of territory, appropriation of material resources, [and] exploitation of a labour force' in foreign territories or nations. As Elleke Boehmer and others have argued, empire was 'a textual undertaking' as much as it was an economic or geopolitical venture, and literature – including life writing – contributed to 'the making, definition and clarification' of imperial rule. Ania Loomba, *Colonialism/Postcolonialism* (New York: Routledge, 1998), p. 6; Elleke Boehmer, *Colonial and Postcolonial Literature: Migrant Metaphors*, 2nd edn (Oxford: Oxford University Press, 2005), p. 5.

³² When Paul Gilroy first developed his prescient arguments on 'post-imperial melancholia', he suggested that Britain, and especially England, 'has been dominated by an inability even to face, let alone actually mourn, the profound change in circumstances and moods that followed the end of Empire and consequent loss of imperial prestige'. This rebutted previous arguments – dubbed by historians as the 'minimal impact thesis' – which suggested that 'the broad cultural impact of decolonisation was confined to the colonial periphery' and that the end of empire had 'little influence upon post-war British culture'. Post-imperial melancholia offers one way of considering how the end of empire 'came home' to Britain, profoundly shaping the cultures and politics of the metropole. Paul Gilroy: *After Empire: Melancholia or Convivial Culture?* (Abingdon: Routledge, 2004), p. 98; Stuart Ward, 'Introduction', in *British Culture and the End of Empire* (Manchester: Manchester University Press, 2001), pp. 1–21 (pp. 1, 4).

how white autobiographical subjects remember the colonial past as a new, post-imperial present was coming into view.

In one sense, white life writing at the end of empire exists within a wider autobiographical tradition recording 'the sense of déjà vu which assails colonial travellers on first encountering face-to-face the imperial metropole'.[33] As they disembarked from boats and airplanes, colonial arrivals throughout the twentieth century described their uncanny first impressions of an English landscape which was both familiar and entirely foreign. Several successive generations of life writers who came to Britain – from Jean Rhys and Sarojini Naidu, to Buchi Emecheta, Beryl Gilroy, V. S. Naipaul, Stuart Hall, and Deborah Levy – record a shared sense of 'isolation and loss of identity' after reaching their destination.[34] Emecheta's memoir *Head Above Water* (1986) records how the young Nigerian was taught 'the history of the British Empire and her greatness in school', only to discover that life in 1960s London 'felt like walking into the inside of a grave'.[35] Despite being a citizen of the United Kingdom and Colonies, Emecheta was forced to navigate the official and informal forms of discrimination which deliberately barred many migrant communities from obtaining safe accommodation and secure employment in Britain.[36] It should go without saying that white subjects from colonies, former colonies and overseas territories did not experience the racism endured by many other colonial communities.[37] The relative ease with which Lively, Ballard, Lessing and Frame secured their initial lodgings reveals that they were exempt from a hostile gaze which transformed 'the political body of the immigrant' into a figure 'represent[ing] all the discomforting ambiguities' of empire.[38] And yet these writers also found themselves unable, albeit in less material ways, to make themselves 'at home' in Britain, and were instead repeatedly drawn back to their memories of life on the colonial frontier.

This book considers how the end of empire was witnessed by authors who were unable to conclude their intimate relationships with the colonial past. When it became impossible to return to their settler lives, Lively, Ballard, Lessing

---

[33] Stuart Hall, with Bill Schwarz, *Familiar Stranger: A Life Between Two Islands* (London: Penguin, 2018), pp. 149–50.
[34] Beryl Gilroy, *Black Teacher* (London: Cassel, 1976), p. 115.
[35] Buchi Emecheta, *Head Above Water* (London: Blackrose Press, 1986), pp. 6, 29.
[36] Emecheta's memoir records how migrants 'who lived in London [during the mid-twentieth century] would know the power that landlords had over their tenants. They could throw any tenant out at any time, and few people would think about taking a black family in'. – *Head Above Water*, p. 31.
[37] Chapter 4's discussion of Patrick O'Reilly, an Irish lodger in Janet Frame's third autobiography, explores the precarious 'white' status of Irish immigrant communities in post-war Britain. For further details, see also Noel Ignatiev, *How the Irish Became White*, 2nd edn (Abingdon: Routledge, 2009).
[38] Gilroy, *After Empire*, p. 110.

and Frame each penned multiple memoirs and autobiographies which insist that both imperialism and its afterlives *were never far from home*. In other words, these life narratives register the impact of decolonization through the private spheres of everyday life. If, as Bill Schwarz suggests, settler colonies were often viewed in the UK as an 'idyll of fantasised white home, uncompromised by the complexities and chaos' of modernity, then this study demonstrates how white life writing records the loss of such imaginative dwellings.[39] For the collapse and dismantlement of British colonial power razed not only public systems of colonial governance, but also the spatial imaginaries of home. Life writing offers a chance to nuance contemporary debates as to how, in Ann Laura Stoler's words, imperialism 'continue[s] to carve out the environmental and physic debris in which people live, long after colonial politics have been dismantled'.[40] As we will see, returning 'home' to memories of empire can offer unexpected confrontations with, and provide opportunities to critically consider, life amongst the colonial debris.

The key concerns of this book extend from Stuart Hall's autobiographical reflections that 'in this post-colonial moment, the sensibilities of colonialism are still potent' and we are all 'still its inheritors, still living in its terrifying aftermath'.[41] The five following chapters each grapple, through close textual analysis, with the question of what it means to witness empire's end, only to inherit its afterlives. For Ballard, Lively, Lessing and Frame, 'going home' to the colonial past was a fraught and ultimately unfinished process. This book therefore asks: How do a previously unrecognized cohort of post-war white life writers share overlapping concerns with the legacies of British colonialism? Why did they each create multiple memoirs or autobiographies that rewrite their memories of colonial childhoods over time, and do these texts register the impact of decolonization through experimental narrative forms? In more thematic terms, what are the coordinates of home and belonging for those who have been permanently 'unhoused' from their settler upbringings? Can descriptions of the domestic, and the language of property, offer new understandings of post-imperial identity in the aftermath of empire? By paying especial attention to domestic space, childhood homes and interior worlds, this study's four single-author case studies and fifth comparative chapter ask how the remains of colonialism lodge deep inside everyday life for authors living and working in modern Britain.

---

[39] Bill Schwarz, *The White Man's World (Memories of Empire)* (Oxford: Oxford University Press, 2011), p. 56.
[40] Ann Laura Stoler, *Carnal Knowledge and Imperial Power: Race and the Intimate in Colonial Rule*, 2nd edn (Berkeley: University of California Press, 2010), p. xviii.
[41] Hall, *Familiar Stranger*, p. 21.

It has been suggested elsewhere that 'writers who emerged during the period of post-war decolonisation, many of whom [became] prominent literary figures of the late-twentieth century, have been especially overlooked' in critical assessments of the end of empire.[42] Post-imperial life writing remains an unacknowledged sub-genre within these conversations and the authors discussed here are best known (with the possible exception of Frame) for their fiction. By discussing semi-obscure life narratives alongside well-known autobiographies and memoirs, this book extends Schwarz's argument that 'the transactions between the imperial centre and the overseas possessions were as intense, perhaps more intense, in the dying days of empire as they had been at the height of British imperial rule'.[43] Life writing reveals the full extent – and the lived realities – of these 'intense transactions'. Lively, Ballard, Lessing and Frame may have all traversed the ruined, forbidding streets of post-war London, but their arrivals mark the start of their overlapping, mutual interests in empire and its aftermath. Through extensive life writing projects, these authors probed the relationship between metropole and colony, between autobiography and colonialism, and between the public sphere of formal decolonization and the private recesses of the imperial home.

Life Writing, Postcolonial Studies and Autotheory

This book's focus on autobiographical narrative, whiteness and homecoming, develops from recent, productive intersections between life writing and postcolonial literary analysis.[44] To trace the origins of 'life writing' as both a term and a discreet area of literary studies, we might turn to Virginia Woolf's unfinished memoir, 'A Sketch of the Past' (1939), which reflects on 'the invisible presences who … play so important a part in everyday life' and yet which did not feature in 'those Lives which I so much enjoy reading'.[45] Woolf argued that if

---

[42] Matthew Whittle, *Post-War British Literature and the 'End of Empire'* (London: Palgrave Macmillan, 2016), p. 8.
[43] Schwarz, *The White Man's World*, p. 29.
[44] For recent discussions of postcolonial life writing, see Bart Moore-Gilbert, *Postcolonial Life-Writing: Culture, Politics and Self-Representation* (Abingdon: Routledge, 2009); *Life Writing after Empire*, ed. Astrid Rasch (New York: Routledge, 2018); Gillian Whitlock, *Postcolonial Life Narratives: Testimonial Transactions* (Oxford: Oxford University Press, 2015).
[45] Virginia Woolf, 'A Sketch of the Past', in *Moments of Being: Unpublished Autobiographical Writings* (London: Grafton, 1986), pp. 71–160 (p. 93).

authors did not acknowledge the presence of these spectral forces, 'we know very little of the subject of the memoir; and again how futile life-writing becomes'.[46] In this expression of dissatisfaction with traditional auto/biographical forms (great 'Lives'), Woolf's reference to 'life-writing' anticipates the term's usage – as both a literary genre and a field of study – by almost half a century. As the daughter of Leslie Stephen, editor of the *Dictionary of National Biography*, Woolf was well-placed to critique traditional autobiography as 'a genre that belongs to men, whose public lives it traces'.[47] 'A Sketch of the Past' identifies the exclusionary nature of autobiographical writing *and* inaugurates life writing as a new form of self-representation. Subsequent generations of feminist literary scholars followed Woolf's invitation to look beyond the traditional 'developmental narrative' of autobiography, which ordered 'both time and the personality according to a purpose or goal'.[48] Life writing offered an alternative to the teleological pattern of male development, expanding beyond narratives which retrospectively view an entire or exemplary life.

The numerous memoirs, travel accounts and autobiographies discussed in this book – many of which offer multiple accounts of the same life story – are here broadly defined as life writing, that 'less exclusive genre of personal kinds of writing' including 'autobiography, biography ... letters and diaries'.[49] By the late twentieth century this had become the fluid and 'general term for writing of diverse kinds that takes a life as its subject'.[50] Yet with the advent of a new, digital age, life writing scholars have questioned whether their discipline has surpassed the book, to include 'films, selfies, zines, websites, postcards, and art installations'.[51] While such visual and multi-modal forms of self-expression should indeed be included within future life writing studies, this book insists that there is more to say on the subject of *textual* life narratives, particularly as developed by authors living and working in the southern hemisphere, or

---

[46] Woolf, 'A Sketch of the Past', p. 93.
[47] Shari Benstock, 'Authorising the Autobiographical', in *The Private Self: Theory and Practice of Women's Autobiographical Writings* (Chapel Hill: University of North Carolina Press, 1988), pp. 7–33 (p. 30).
[48] Linda Anderson, *Autobiography*, 2nd edn (New York: Routledge, 2011), p. 8; Sidonie Smith and Julia Watson, *Reading Autobiography: A Guide for Interpreting Life Narratives*, 2nd edn (Minneapolis: University of Minnesota Press, 2010), p. 199.
[49] Marlene Kadar, 'Coming to Terms: Life Writing – from Genre to Critical Practice', in *Essays on Life Writing: From Genre to Critical Practice*, ed. Marlene Kadar (Toronto: University of Toronto Press, 1992), pp. 3–16 (p. 4).
[50] Smith and Watson, *Reading Autobiography*, p. 3.
[51] Anna Poletti, *Stories of the Self: Life Writing After the Book* (New York: New York University Press, 2020), p. 23.

by those who address the entangled legacies of imperialism, slavery and anti-colonial resistance.[52]

It should be noted that the all-encompassing possibilities of life writing have ensured that the term remains partly controversial: Max Saunders suggests that although it covers 'a wide range of texts and forms … it seems, to some, to cover too many'.[53] If life writing could potentially be anything, Saunders implies, perhaps it denotes nothing, indicating only an unstable genre with few discernable boundaries. Such critiques overlook how life writing arises from the inadequacy of 'the term autobiography … to describe the historical range and the diverse genres and practices of life narratives and life narrators'.[54] By breaking from an autobiographical canon dominated by the lives of men, life writing challenges Philippe Lejeune's much-cited definition of autobiography as 'a retrospective prose narrative produced by a real person concerning his own existence … in particular on the development of his personality'.[55] Lejeune's stipulation – along with his argument that the male author, narrator and subject of an autobiography are one and the same – confines autobiography to the promise of 'rendering [a] biographical truth impossible in practice to fulfil'.[56] This argument concedes the inherently fictive nature of autobiographical writing even while it insists upon it.[57] The feminist critique of autobiographical subjectivity as 'rest[ing] upon the Western ideal of an essential and inviolable self' reminds us of the need for life writing's inclusive and ever-expanding parameters.[58] As both a critical and creative practice, life writing offers the opportunity to explore partial and experimental narratives which might be otherwise excluded from traditional autobiographical studies.

This question – of who and what is historically omitted from traditional autobiography – animates the productive and still-developing intersections

---

[52] Gillian Whitlock's scholarship, particularly *Soft Weapons* (Chicago: University of Chicago Press, 2007) and Moore-Gilbert's *Postcolonial Life-Writing* (2009) have both offered important starting points for this much-needed conversation.
[53] Max Saunders, *Self Impression: Life-Writing, Autobiografiction, and the Forms of Modern Literature* (Oxford: Oxford University Press, 2010), p. 4.
[54] Smith and Watson, *Reading Autobiography*, p. 35.
[55] Philippe Lejeune, *On Autobiography*, ed. Paul John Eakin, trans. Katherine Leary (Minneapolis: University of Minnesota Press, 1989), p. 4.
[56] Paul John Eakin, *Touching the World: Reference in Autobiography* (Princeton, NJ: Princeton University Press, 1992), p. 27.
[57] Paul de Man's seminal essay 'AutoBiography as De-facement' troubles the truth value of autobiography even further by suggesting that, through their use of prosopopoeia, all autobiographical narratives can only ever reproduce the very fictions they seek to dispel. – Paul de Man, 'Autobiography as De-facement', *Modern Language Notes*, 94:5 (1979): 919–30.
[58] Bella Brodzki and Celeste Schenck, 'Introduction', in *Life/Lines: Theorising Women's Autobiography*, ed. Bella Brodzki and Celeste Schenck (Cornell: Cornell University Press, 1988), pp. 1–19 (p. 5).

between life writing and postcolonial literary studies. While Edward Said emphasized that postcolonial studies should move 'beyond the asserverations of personal testimony', more contemporary scholarship by Elleke Boehmer, Bart Moore-Gilbert, Gillian Whitlock and others has considered how autobiographical writing specifically develops in colonial and postcolonial contexts.[59] In *Postcolonial Life-Writing* (2009) Moore-Gilbert draws upon Frantz Fanon's autoethnographic descriptions of selfhood, racism, and imperial domination in order to distinguish postcolonial life writing from its Western analogues.[60] Moore-Gilbert's survey study concludes that an 'ambivalent relationship to the concept of Selfhood', an interest in the embodied and psychic consequences of dislocation, and a hybrid approach to autobiographical narrative are all crucial hallmarks of postcolonial life writing.[61] More recently Whitlock has incorporated eighteenth-century slave narratives, frontier memoirs and testimonies from South Africa's Truth and Reconciliation Commission into her own definitions of the genre, creating a history of autobiographical literature which questions 'what it means to be properly human'.[62] Both Whitlock and Moore-Gilbert have expanded postcolonial life writing beyond early assessments of how male leaders, from Nelson Mandela to Jawaharlal Nehru, wrote autobiographically in order to 'embody a new nation's struggle to come into being', entwining their lives with the struggle for postcolonial independence.[63] Yet while these conversations have developed significantly in recent decades, Astrid Rasch is right to suggest that we have only begun to understand how 'life writing provides us with a lens through which to consider the end of empire anew'.[64]

There are two key points to emphasize about existing scholarship which sutures life writing and postcolonial critique. The first is that the considerable number of autobiographies and memoirs by postcolonial theorists are curiously absent from these conversations – with the exception of Said's famous description

---

[59] Edward Said, *Culture and Imperialism* (London: Chatto & Windus, 1993), p. 77.
[60] For further details, see: Fanon's *Black Skin, White Masks* (1952). Moore Gilbert argues that through this pivotal autobiographical text Fanon attempts 'to understand himself as a human being and colonial subject' therefore providing 'a template for so much subsequent postcolonial life-writing'. – Moore-Gilbert, *Postcolonial Life Writing*, p. xxiv.
[61] Moore-Gilbert, *Postcolonial Life Writing*, p. 16.
[62] Whitlock, *Postcolonial Life Narratives*, p. 47.
[63] C. L. Innes, 'Authorising the Self: Postcolonial Autobiographical Writing', in *The Cambridge Introduction to Postcolonial Literatures in English* (Cambridge: Cambridge University Press, 2007), pp. 56–71 (p. 56); Elleke Boehmer has also assessed how postcolonial politicians 'use autobiography to confirm their pre-eminent, form-giving and even dynastic position' in decolonized nations. Elleke Boehmer, *Stories of Women: Gender and Narrative in the Postcolonial Nation* (Manchester: Manchester University Press, 2005), p. 84.
[64] Astrid Rasch, 'Introduction', in *Life Writing After Empire* (New York: Routledge, 2018), pp. 1–6 (p. 1).

of 'myself as a cluster of flowing currents' in *Out of Place* (1999).⁶⁵ This oversight seems all the more perplexing given that academic postcolonial life writing, which should perhaps more accurately be described as postcolonial autotheory, is a flourishing sub-genre of autobiographical narrative. When Sara Suleri described her family history as caught in the 'bewildering streams of people pouring over one brand-new border into another' during Partition, her memoir *Meatless Days* (1989) anticipates not only *Out of Place*, but also Bart Moore-Gilbert's *The Setting Sun* (2014), Benedict Anderson's *A Life Beyond Boundaries* (2016), Stuart Hall's *Familiar Stranger* (2017), and Hazel V. Carby's *Imperial Intimacies* (2019).⁶⁶ When read together, these texts suggest how postcolonial autotheory addresses the ongoing legacies of empire through multi-generational family histories. For Carby, this means exposing British imperialism as an intimate entanglement, one that was 'threaded into [her family's] actions, attitudes and beliefs, ultimately governing even the smallest details of their lives'.⁶⁷ In his own memoir, Moore-Gilbert discovers how fragments from the imperial archive can disrupt the smoothly polished surface of family myths, revealing 'nuances and shades [that are] invisible under the sunny glare of nostalgia'.⁶⁸

So while it is true that life writing scholars have long acknowledged how '"autocriticism" – critique generated by autobiographical experience – plays an important role in the formulation of postcolonial theory', more research is required to address and discuss this distinctive body of life narratives.⁶⁹ If, as Henghameh Soukhani notes, this 'growing class of [autobiographical] literature of empire and its afterlife' combines 'the reflexive abstractions of theoretical discourse with the somatic realities of the critic's life', these texts are rarely – if ever – included in broader studies of autotheory.⁷⁰ There is an urgent need to address the postcolonial dimensions of autotheory, a form of self-representational narrative which, by marking 'the place between criticism and autobiography', explores 'the tenuousness of maintaining illusory separations between art and life'.⁷¹ Postcolonial autotheory has allowed several generations

---

⁶⁵ Edward Said, *Out of Place: A Memoir* (London: Granta, 2000), p. 295.
⁶⁶ Sara Suleri, *Meatless Days* (Chicago: University of Chicago Press, 1989), p. 116.
⁶⁷ Hazel V. Carby, *Imperial Intimacies: A Tale of Two Islands* (London: Verso, 2019), p. 72.
⁶⁸ Bart Moore Gilbert, *The Setting Sun: A Memoir of Empire and Family Secrets* (London: Verso, 2014), p. 272.
⁶⁹ Whitlock, *Postcolonial Life Narratives*, p. 175. See also: David Huddart, *Postcolonial Theory and Autobiography* (New York: Routledge, 2009).
⁷⁰ Henghameh Soukhani, 'Empire, Race, and the Autotheoretical Impulse', *Moving Worlds: A Journal of Transcultural Writing*, 20:2 (2021): 21–36, p. 23.
⁷¹ Lauren Fournier, *Autotheory as Feminist Practice in Art, Writing, and Criticism* (London: MIT Press, 2021), p. 2.

of life writers to trace the connections between the intimate and the imperial, scrutinizing the legacies of empire through personal experience and family history. This autobiographical sub-genre demonstrates not only that life writing is embedded firmly within postcolonial studies, but that postcolonial critics continue to make unrecognized contributions to the development of autotheory, a field read primarily in terms of its feminist genealogies.

The second point to highlight about postcolonial life writing is that previous studies have, with the exception of Whitlock's *The Intimate Empire* (2000), avoided texts concerned with colonial whiteness. There have subsequently been missed opportunities to consider how empire's legacies continue to shape autobiographical accounts of white subjectivity. In one sense this omission is because focusing on settlers and their descendants is, for good reason, considered 'unfashionable in postcolonial criticism'.[72] Previous discussions of colonial memoirs have all too often lapsed into dubious claims of victimhood for white colonial or post-imperial authors, insisting that such writers remain unfairly 'invisible or marginalised' because of postcolonial concerns with subaltern lives and insurgent histories.[73] It is important to be clear: this represents an untenable attempt to elide white writers' beneficial relation to empire and continuing forms of racial violence. This book therefore cautiously suggests an alternative approach by contending that white life writing oscillates between critique of and complicity with Britain's imperial project and that these tense, often contradictory manoeuvres can offer colonial whiteness up for close scrutiny. This means tracing empire's legacies in texts which have not been previously read for their postcolonial concerns; Lively's speculative memoir *Making It Up* (2005), Ballard's autobiographical novel *Empire of the Sun* (1984) and Frame's second autobiography *An Angel at My Table* (1984) have been rarely, if ever, assessed for their imperial dimensions. By establishing the distinct qualities of white life writing after empire, this study develops an approach to reading autobiographical narrative indebted to Said's methodology of contrapuntal reading, drawing out what 'is silent or marginally present' within literary texts.[74] Through contrapuntal analysis this book discusses memoirs, autobiographies and other life narratives which, on the surface, have little to do with white settlement or its consequences.[75] Such readings

---

[72] Whitlock, *The Intimate Empire*, p. 41.
[73] Phyllis Lassner, *Colonial Strangers: Women Writing the End of the British Empire* (New Brunswick: Rutgers University Press, 2004), p. 8.
[74] Said, *Culture and Imperialism*, p. 78.
[75] Edward Dodson has already demonstrated how white Anglophone literature can be productively read through contrapuntal analysis in his exemplary postcolonial readings of novels by Graham

do not exonerate colonial authors for their complicit relationship with British imperialism, but instead ask how these writers share a sustained interest in the afterlives of empire.

In her seminal study of colonial and postcolonial autobiography, Whitlock contends that life writing functions 'as one of the most potent resources for sustaining the settler imaginary'.[76] Yet *Life Writing and the End of Empire* reads autobiographical texts that both sustain *and disrupt* the imagined futures of colonial settlement. Lively's, Ballard's, Lessing's and Frame's life narratives may converge at the site of post-war London, but when read comparatively they offer new perspectives of peripheral or semi-colonial settler societies (Egypt, China, Southern Rhodesia, and Aotearoa/New Zealand) which are usually sidelined in imperial histories and postcolonial literary studies.[77] This book's principle focus is on life narratives which return to the fringes of empire and its metropolitan centres alike, extending a view of British colonialism 'as a series of dynamic and interlocking webs'.[78] When read in concert, these memoirs and autobiographies all emerge as partial representations – the work of writers who created multiple accounts of their early lives. By writing and rewriting their memories of empire, these authors imply that only a politics of the incomplete can represent their relationship with the colonial past; their entanglements with empire and its aftermath could not be concluded by a single or definitive representation. These texts belong to a life writing tradition which pursues fragmentary versions of the self while disputing the sovereign subject of traditional autobiography. By following these acts of writing and rewriting, this book reveals how life narratives can challenge the imaginaries of white settlement, disturb the security of home, and complicate any imaginative or literal attempts to return to the colonial past.

Swift, Julian Barnes, Ian McEwan, Hilary Mantel and others. For full details, see Edward Dodson, 'Postimperial Englishness in the Contemporary White Canon' (unpublished doctoral thesis, University of Oxford, 2018).

[76] Whitlock, *The Intimate Empire*, p. 117.

[77] The reasons for this are partly historical; Egypt's ambiguous status as British protectorate or Aotearoa/New Zealand's role as a dominion could obscure the extent to which 'colonisation and its legacies continue to stand at the heart' of these postcolonial societies. Southern Rhodesia was always 'curiously anachronistic' when compared with other settler states, and Shanghai's International Settlement operated as an informal colony for multiple imperial powers, rather than being solely a British territory. Yet if these locations – and their settler histories – fit awkwardly into wider survey studies of empire, this book demonstrates how white writers from all four can be productively read and discussed through postcolonial scholarship. Dane Kennedy, *Islands of White: Settler Society and Culture in Kenya and Southern Rhodesia, 1890–1939* (Durham: Duke University Press, 1987), p. 8; Tony Ballantyne, *Webs of Empire: Locating New Zealand's Colonial Past* (Vancouver: UCB Press, 2012), p. 13.

[78] Ballantyne, *Webs of Empire*, p. 49. See also: Tony Ballantyne, *Orientalism and Race: Aryanism in the British Empire* (Basingstoke: Palgrave Macmillan, 2002).

Empires of the Home

The initial four case studies in this book discuss Lively, Ballard, Lessing and Frame in the order of their arrival in Britain. By focusing on their memories of home, these readings discuss each author's childhood dwelling as indicative of both the structures *and* the fracture lines of colonial settlement. For Lively, 'home' was the house and gardens of Bulaq Dakhrur, a grand property on the outskirts of Cairo, which 'sat in the landscape like some incongruous island' surrounded by 'the cultivation' of fields, irrigation canals and Egyptian villages.[79] Chapter 1 addresses how her imaginative returns to this 'ur-house' reflect the spatial and ideological structures of colonial whiteness.[80] This then leads to the argument in Chapter 2 that all of Ballard's autobiographical writing returns to 31a Amherst Avenue, a Surrey-stockbroker-style mansion in Shanghai's International Settlement. This location is, I suggest, inseparable from his memories of later living in an internment camp. By reading both the house and the camp as particular kinds of settler enclaves, this case study contends that, through a distinctive imperial unheimlich, Ballard traces the uncanny slippages between that which 'belong[s] to the house' and that which is 'concealed, [or] kept from sight'.[81]

Ballard's enduring connection to the house and camp is matched by Lessing's attachment to the landscape she called 'her myth country', the Rhodesian farm which her parents tried – and ultimately failed – to cultivate in southern Africa.[82] Chapter 3 demonstrates how Lessing's life-long attempts at 'going home' could never conclusively arrive at their destination, and that her returns to the besieged Rhodesian 'laager' (an encircled encampment of settler wagons) results in the contradictory, anti-colonial politics of her life writing. These readings then lead to discussions in Chapter 4 of Frame's transitory homes during her impoverished childhood in Aotearoa/New Zealand, which led her to dismantle the idea of permanent dwelling places altogether. Here Frame's self-described 'homelessness of the self' is read as a critique of settler belonging and white property ownership, as her autobiographies attempt to decouple their subject from both colonial genealogies and the inheritances of empire.[83]

---

[79] Lively, *Oleander, Jacaranda*, p. 9.
[80] Ibid., p. 6.
[81] Sigmund Freud, 'The Uncanny', in *The Complete Psychological Works of Sigmund Freud, Volume XVII, An Infantile Neurosis and Other Works*, trans. James Strachey (London: Hogarth Press, 1955), pp. 219–53 (p. 224).
[82] Doris Lessing, *African Laughter: Four Visits to Zimbabwe* (London: Flamingo, 1993), p. 314.
[83] Janet Frame, *To the Is-Land*, in *The Complete Autobiography* (London: The Women's Press, 1990), pp. 1–140 (p. 110).

As we shall see, the four, respective childhood homes of these life writers – described across multiple memoirs and autobiographies – reveal their tense and ongoing connections to the colonial past, exposing ties that were consistently revised over the course of long writing careers. These houses are much more than physical structures; they are unstable centres which expose the complexity of imperial homecoming long after empire's end. A fifth, comparative chapter offers several, brief autobiographical reflections of my own, before concluding with readings of objects in life writing at the end of empire. These analyze a possession belonging to each of the key authors in this study as both a container for colonial memory, *and* a symbol for the failed promises of empire. Ultimately, none of these material possessions are heirlooms which might be passed down to future generations of settlers. Instead, they herald the end of empire and the odd petrification of the colonial past in a postcolonial present.

If white, post-imperial life writers are consumed by the need to 'go home' to their memories of empire, then the private dwellings which are frequently the intended destination of their autobiographical journeys are crucial to understanding such impossible attempts at return.[84] In his phenomenological study *The Poetics of Space* (1958), Gaston Bachelard suggests that houses – particularly oneiric childhood homes – are 'our corner of the world … our first universe … a real cosmos in every sense of the word'.[85] Here he extends Martin Heidegger's distinction between 'building' and 'dwelling' to interpret 'home' as more than a physical structure.[86] Following Bachelard, subsequent generations of critical geographers have interpreted home as 'a set of intersecting and variable ideas and feelings', becoming both a place (a named site) *and* a series of attachments invested with profound emotional resonance.[87] In one sense, *Life Writing and the End of Empire* follows this critical trajectory, tracing how colonial power was manifest in both the architecture and domestic routines of

---

[84] While Frame alone returned to Aotearoa/New Zealand in 1963 (though not to the confines of her post-settler childhood), she – like each of the life writers discussed in this book – attempted to return to her childhood home and was dismayed to find few traces of her former life in the dilapidated property her parents called 'Willowglen'. Lively returned to Bulaq Dakhrur, Ballard to Lunghua camp, and Lessing to Kermanshah Farm during the late 1980s and early 1990s. None of these life writers record their homecomings as satisfactory but instead discover that these haunting sites cannot become lasting memorials to their colonial childhoods.

[85] Gaston Bachelard, *The Poetics of Space*, trans. Maria Jolas (Boston: New Beacon Press, 1994), p. 4.

[86] In his 1954 essay, Martin Heidegger argues that buildings, as physical constructions, are not automatically dwelling places, explaining: 'The truck driver is at home on the highway, but he does not have his lodgings there; the working woman is at home in the spinning mill, but does not have her dwelling place there; the chief engineer is at home in the power station, but he does not dwell there'. Martin Heidegger, 'Building Dwelling Thinking', in *Basic Writings from Being and Time (1927) to the Task of Thinking* (1964) ed. D. F. Krell (New York: Routledge, 1993), pp. 347–63 (pp. 347–8).

[87] Alison Blunt and Robyn Dowling, *Home*, 2nd edn (Abingdon: Routledge, 2022), p. 9.

white homes across the globe. It expands on earlier arguments that the 'domestic and public interiors of empire [were] significant locations' of colonial rule.[88] Yet these readings advance one stage further, suggesting that not only was domestic space crucial to the consolidation of imperial power but also *that interior worlds became locations for confronting the frailties of white colonial rule.*

As these life writers raise the question of what it means to inherit and imaginatively return to a dismantled empire, their shared concerns might be partially understood through recent historical and literary investigations into 'empires of the home'.[89] These have established that by the turn of the twentieth century – when jingoistic British imperialism had reached its zenith – private dwellings became microcosms for 'the empire in miniature'.[90] The close ties between home and empire are perhaps most explicit in mass-produced nineteenth-century domestic manuals and how-to guides for arriving in the colonies. These texts, aimed primarily at white female settlers, emphasized an ordered, well-run household as central to the imperial enterprise. Popular instruction manuals by writers like Flora Annie Steel suggested that English housewives should view 'the formation of the home' as 'a unit of civilisation', equating the upkeep of domestic standards with direct colonial governance.[91] Lessing records the consequences of these guides when recalling her mother's instructions that, in Rhodesia, 'you will get deathly chills without your binders, bad posture without your liberty bodice, sunstroke without hats that have red linings'.[92] For those living in colonial outposts and frontiers, domestic work – as ordered by white women, yet largely carried out by men and women of colour – was crucial for upholding the tenuous divides of daily life. However, as Rosemary Marangoly George notes, the boundaries between public and private spheres in these societies 'repeatedly broke down and had to be constantly redrawn'.[93] Domestic labour may have been overseen by white women, but it could only

---

[88] Robin D. Jones, *Interiors of Empire: Objects, Space and Identity within the Indian Subcontinent, 1800–1947* (Manchester: Manchester University Press, 2007), p. 21.
[89] For 'empires of the home', see Alison Blunt, *Domicile and Diaspora: Anglo-Indian Women and the Spatial Politics of Home* (Oxford: Blackwell, 2005); Catherine Hall and Sonya O. Rose, eds, *At Home with the Empire: Metropolitan Culture and the Imperial World* (Cambridge: Cambridge University Press, 2006); Rosemary Marangoly George, *The Politics of Home: Postcolonial Relocations and Twentieth-Century Fiction* (Berkeley: University of California Press, 1999).
[90] Marangoly George, *The Politics of Home*, p. 51.
[91] Flora Annie Steel and Grace Gardiner, *The Complete Indian Housekeeper and Cook* (Oxford: Oxford University Press, 2010), p. 16.
[92] Doris Lessing, *Under My Skin: Volume One of My Autobiography to 1949* (New York: HarperCollins, 1994), p. 71.
[93] Marangoly George, *The Politics of Home*, pp. 40–1.

ever bestow on them a form of 'borrowed power'.[94] This context is crucial for understanding how life narratives use domestic space to expose the tenuous and contingent nature of colonial authority. Life writing reveals, and exerts particular kinds of pressure on, narratives of the empire at home.

Cultural studies of imperial homemaking and domestic architecture have previously focused on colonial India or the Dutch Indies.[95] Moreover, any literary analysis they include is drawn from works of fiction.[96] This book therefore develops these conversations both to overlooked regions – Aotearoa/New Zealand, Egypt, Shanghai and Southern Rhodesia – *and* to literary forms beyond the novel. Autobiographical narrative complicates these debates on empires of the home by considering an era of formal decolonization, emphasizing how 'the material and imaginative geographies of home' impacted as much upon the aftermath of empire as they did on its jingoistic, imperial heyday.[97] In retrospective accounts of white colonial life, interior spaces are locations where colonial authority can be scrutinized, challenged and even undone. As Chapter 2 reveals, even the grandest dwellings in the International Settlement were, according to Ballard, only a *facade* of imperial power. Whether in Lessing's Rhodesian farm, Frame's repeated stories of her settler ancestors or Lively's memories of an enclosed, sometimes unsettling colonial garden, life writing at the end of empire imagines home as an imperial centre which cannot hold.

If autobiographical narratives have much to tell us about the construction of the white subject in and through domestic space, then Sara Ahmed offers us a timely reminder that colonialism 'makes the world "white"' and ensures that 'the body-at-home' is 'one that can inhabit whiteness'.[98] Lively, Ballard, Lessing and Frame each question what it means to occupy the unstable residence of white

---

[94] Anne McClintock, *Imperial Leather: Race, Gender, and Sexuality in the Colonial Contest* (Routledge, 1995), p. 6.
[95] For colonial India see: Blunt, *Domicile and Diaspora*; Antoinette Burton, *Dwelling in the Archive: Women Writing House, Home and History in Late Colonial India* (Oxford: Oxford University Press, 2003); Marangoly George, *The Politics of Home*; Robin D. Jones, *Interiors of Empire*. For the Dutch Indies see: Stoler, *Carnal Knowledge and Imperial Power*.
[96] The exception to this novel-based focus is McClintock's *Imperial Leather* (1995), which discusses photography and diaries alongside colonial adventure fiction. Arguably the most influential literary reading of 'empires of the home' is Edward Said's analysis of *Mansfield Park* (1814) in *Culture and Imperialism* (1993), which emphasizes how Sir Thomas needs his Antigua plantations in order to maintain his English estate at home. For Said, *Mansfield Park*'s central 'geographical problematic' is that the Bertram household relies 'for the maintenance of its style on a Caribbean island'. As a result, both the domestic English home and the international trade of the Caribbean plantation uphold a colonial order of 'propriety' and 'law' via territory and possession. Unpicking the threads which connect these twin sites, Said concludes that 'what assures the domestic tranquillity and attractive harmony of one [the house] is the productivity and regulated discipline of the other [the plantation]'. *Culture and Imperialism*, pp. 115, 104.
[97] Blunt and Dowling, *Home*, p. 232.
[98] Sara Ahmed, 'A Phenomenology of Whiteness', *Feminist Theory*, 8:2 (2007): 149–68 (pp. 153–4).

colonial rule. Their returns to particular dwelling places reveal the ambiguities, rather than the certainties, of imperial power. Rather than being shelters or places of refuge, these descriptions of colonial homes illuminate Radhika Mohanram's argument that the 'superiority of whiteness was [always] under siege, under threat, questionable'.[99] In life writing at the end of empire, white colonial identity emerges as an untenable residence. On the one hand, the writers discussed here are indeed, as Ahmed suggests, able 'to inhabit the world as a home', comforted by their own supposed invisibility.[100] The unquestioning gaze with which Lively viewed the brutal contrasts of her colonial childhood – 'I saw it, received it, and did not query' – or Jim Graham's assumption that 'passive and unseeing' Chinese servants do not count as members of his household in *Empire of the Sun*, all offer discomforting forms of supporting evidence.[101] Yet just as Ahmed suggests that we might question 'the "habit" in "in-habit"', these life narratives also render white colonial life as hyper- rather than in- visible, scrutinizing the architectural and emotional structures of colonial whiteness.[102]

To understand how domestic space reveals the contradictions of empire's end, we might turn briefly to Lively's sharp fear of the desert in *Oleander, Jacaranda*, which always seemed to be 'thrust up' in the cellar of her family's house in Cairo, 'just a few feet below the surface of the garden'.[103] The desert represented many things to the young Lively: it was a dangerous, bomb-strewn theatre of war; a wide-ranging mass spreading beyond the national borders of Egypt; an unruly, subterranean force which threatened to undermine the ordered, English-styled interiors of the house above. Her fear of this partially submerged entity reflects the unstable, dual functions of the white colonial home, which in Stoler's words was designed to be both a sealed 'refuge from colonial intrusions' *and* a 'privileged site for colonial surveillance and control'.[104] Ultimately, the desert's presence beneath the house evokes the rising sand of an hourglass, filling steadily as time ran out on British rule. Lively's memoirs, like many life narratives within this book, demonstrate how private homes could not seal their borders to become safe havens of colonial order. They were instead spaces riven by insecurities and imperilled by outside forces. The domestic concerns of these life narratives

[99] Radhika Mohanram, *Imperial White: Race, Diaspora and the British Empire* (Minneapolis: University of Minnesota Press, 2007), p. 46.
[100] Ahmed, 'A Phenomenology of Whiteness', p. 157.
[101] Lively, *Oleander, Jacaranda*, p. 13; J. G. Ballard, *Empire of the Sun* (London: Harper Perennial, 2006), p. 16.
[102] Ahmed, 'A Phenomenology of Whiteness', p. 155.
[103] Lively, *Oleander, Jacaranda*, p. 49.
[104] Stoler, *Carnal Knowledge and Imperial Power*, p. xxi.

indicate the inevitability of empire's end, offering a biblical warning as to the dangers of building a house (or, indeed, a global empire) on sand.

This study's readings of uneasy, even unsettling interiors is attentive to Doreen Massey's warning that any home predicated on an 'apparently reassuring boundedness' is always, inevitably, compromised.[105] The colonial mansions, suburban bungalows and settler farmhouses discussed here are all established, to use Massey's words, 'through negative counterposition with the Other beyond the boundaries'.[106] For Lively, this 'Other' was symbolized by the shifting mass of the Egyptian desert while for Lessing it was the Rhodesian bush – and its inhabitants – which surrounded her family's farmhouse. These properties were never fully sealed enclosures, but instead existed in a complex network of relationships with the landscapes beyond their perimeter. Life writing at the end of empire is replete with private homes and personal archives (including photograph albums, heirlooms and family histories) which act as 'interior frontiers', locations where the dynamics, struggles and inevitable dismantlement of imperial power are laid bare.[107]

Yet it is also important to note that there is more to these autobiographical acts of homecoming than a terrible desire for 'nostos', the hearth or home to which nostalgic memories typically retreat.[108] None of the key authors in this study express a desire to return, straightforwardly, to the colonial past, nor do these life writers long to resurrect the white supremacy of direct colonial rule. Both Ballard and Lessing publicly refused to become a Commander of the British Empire, with Lessing rejecting any title which evoked 'the name of a non-existent Empire' and Ballard voicing suspicion that although 'the dreams of empire [had been] swept away', Britain's 'delusions' of imperial grandeur remained.[109] Although Lively and Frame issued less vocal criticisms of colonialism and its continuing legacies, they too were determined that the racial hierarchies and

---

[105] Doreen Massey, 'A Place Called Home?' in *Space, Place, and Gender* (Minneapolis: University of Minnesota Press, 1994), pp. 157–74 (p. 169).

[106] Massey, 'A Place Called Home?', p. 169.

[107] Stoler, *Carnal Knowledge and Imperial Power*, p. 80.

[108] For a nuanced account of nostalgia in both Doris Lessing's and J. G. Ballard's writing, see Dennis Walder, *Postcolonial Nostalgias: Writing, Representation and Memory* (New York: Routledge, 2011). For a discussion of home and nostalgia in Doris Lessing's writing, see Roberta Rubenstein, *Home Matters: Longing and Belonging, Nostalgia and Mourning in Women's Fiction* (New York: Palgrave, 2001).

[109] For Lessing's and Ballard's respective letters declining their MBEs, see Stephen Adams, 'Doris Lessing Rejected Top Honour', *The Telegraph*, 21 October 2008, https://www.telegraph.co.uk/news/3234807/Doris-Lessing-rejected-top-honour-for-being-in-the-name-of-a-non-existent-Empire.html (accessed 19 February 2023) and Tania Branigan, 'It's a Pantomime Where Tinsel Takes the Place of Substance', *The Guardian*, 22 December 2033, https://www.theguardian.com/politics/2003/dec/22/uk.books (accessed 19 February 2023).

extractive politics of empire should be challenged, critiqued and eventually dismantled.

This shared refusal of colonial nostalgia remains pertinent in the context of contemporary Britain, where resurgent and increasingly outrageous desires for a resuscitated imperial patrimony continue to dominate public and political life. Indeed, the memories of empire were startlingly, even brazenly, manifest in the hyperbolic promises of a 'global Britain' during the referendum to leave the European union, and in the inflated calls for a 'Blitz spirit' which aimed (but eventually failed) to gloss the terrible losses of the Covid-19 pandemic.[110] As post-imperial Britain continues to grapple with the legacies of its colonial past, there is a new urgency to understand nostalgia's place within the imaginaries of empire, imaginaries which Peter Mitchell argues were always suffused 'with a mood of mourning and elegy … already yearning back towards a glorious past' in order to imagine a prosperous future.[111] Against this backdrop, it is important to reiterate that life writing at the end of empire is not confined solely to the context of formal decolonization during the mid-twentieth century. The authors in this study may remember childhoods which took place during the 1920s and 1930s, yet their memories have much – perhaps even more – to teach us about our post-imperial, twenty-first-century present. These life writers belong to a wider body of white, Anglophone literature which can and should be read as offering 'a view of the end of empire animated by something other than nostalgia for lost glories'.[112] Whether in the unheimlich forces which plague Ballard's memories of colonial Shanghai (Chapter 2) or in Frame's critique of home ownership in post-settlement Aotearoa/New Zealand (Chapter 4), these life narratives reject

---

[110] In *British Culture After Empire* (2023) Josh Doble, Liam J. Liburd and I describe the culture and politics of modern Britain as underwritten by the unappeased memories of empire. Here we complicate widespread claims that 'the [2016] EU referendum showed up the last throes of empire-thinking working its way out of the British psyche' and that Britain's contradictory campaign to leave the European Union viewed 'itself simultaneously as a reconstitution of Empire and as an anti-imperial liberation movement'. I remain especially cautious of analyses which imply that the decision to leave the European Union concluded Britain's troubling relationship with its colonial past. Instead, this event – while significant – is part of a much longer continuum regarding the deliberately neglected history of British colonialism. The 2018 Windrush scandal provides one of many tragic examples as to how 'Empire-thinking' remains embedded in British life, after and beyond Brexit. Josh Doble, Liam J. Liburd and Emma Parker, 'Introduction: Rhodesia and the "Rivers of Blood"', in *British Culture after Empire* (Manchester: Manchester University Press, 2023), pp. 1–26; Danny Dorling and Sally Tomlinson, *Rule Britannia: Brexit and the End of Empire* (London: Biteback, 2019), p. 42; Fintan O'Toole, *Heroic Failure: Brexit and the Politics of Pain* (London: Head of Zeus, 2018), p. 81.

[111] Peter Mitchell, *Imperial Nostalgia: How the British Conquered Themselves* (Manchester: Manchester University Press, 2021), p. 57.

[112] John McLeod, 'The Novel and the End of Empire', in *The Oxford History of the Novel in English, Volume Seven: British and Irish Fiction since 1940*, ed. Peter Boxall and Bryan Cheyette (Oxford: Oxford University Press, 2016), pp. 80–93 (p. 82).

nostalgia by emphasizing the contradictions and inconsistencies of Britain's imperial project. This cohort of authors track the anxious processes of becoming which marked colonial identity, showing how these developments shaped everyday life and domestic rituals. Their autobiographical narratives remind us that the stable or sealed settler homestead was an impossible myth, one which obscured the web of imperial relations and the lives of so-called racial Others which it stood in direct relation to.

This book follows Catherine Hall and Sonya O. Rose in insisting that 'the British metropole was [also] an imperial home', a location which existed within the networks of empire rather than apart from it.[113] The continuing importance of this insight has been underscored by a spate of recent attacks from politicians and journalists aimed at researchers who investigate the colonial heritage of public and private homes in Britain.[114] Despite mounting criticisms and personal threats, these collaborative projects have continued to challenge the myth of Britain as an isolated island unaffected by the rise and fall of its vast empire, insisting instead that colonialism was and is embedded 'at home', in the heart of England's vast country estates.[115] For Mitchell, Britain's imagined islandness 'restates on a larger scale the uncomfortable paradoxes of the English country house, as simultaneously a place of retreat from the wider world, and a product of engagement with it'.[116] All of the life writers discussed here were raised in households which either directly mimicked (Lively, Ballard) or contained visual,

---

[113] Catherine Hall and Sonya O. Rose, 'Introduction: Being at home with the Empire', in *At Home with the Empire: Metropolitan Culture and the Imperial World*, ed. Catherine Hall and Sonya O. Rose (Cambridge: Cambridge University Press, 2011), pp. 1–31 (p. 3).

[114] Perhaps the most high-profile of these is the National Trust's 'colonial countryside' project, along with earlier projects at UCL's Centre for the Study of the Legacies of British Slavery. By 2021, public historian David Olusoga commented that researchers who investigated those 'millions who laboured on the plantations, or who resisted British imperial rule' were being portrayed 'not as an expansion of our national history but as a politicised assault upon it'. That same year Corinne Fowler, whose work on the colonial countryside project has been repeatedly maligned by the right-wing press and Conservative Party politicians, estimated that 'there have been at least 135 media articles about my work calling me such things as "halfwit" and attempting to discredit me'. These attacks suggest that the English country or stately home is viewed as a symbol of the nation, and whose defence is mobilized by those who refuse to discuss or even acknowledge Britain's shared colonial past. – David Olusoga, 'Historians Have Become Soft Targets in the Culture Wars. We Should Fight Back', *New Statesman*, 8 December 2021, https://www.newstatesman.com/culture/2021/12/historians-have-become-soft-targets-in-the-culture-wars-we-should-fight-back (accessed 22 November 2022); Corinne Fowler, 'We Need to Defend the Freedom to Research Our Histories in All Their Nuance', *Museums Association*, 16 February 2021, https://www.museumsassociation.org/museums-journal/people/2021/02/qa-we-need-to-defend-the-freedom-to-research-our-histories-in-all-their-nuance/# (accessed 22 November 2022).

[115] The argument that Britain was unaffected by the loss of its empire is known as the 'minimal impact thesis', and is most clearly extended by Bernard Porter in *The Absent-Minded Imperialists* (Oxford: Oxford University Press, 2004).

[116] Mitchell, *Imperial Nostalgia*, p. 89.

depleted reminders of the English country estate (Lessing, Frame). For Lively and Ballard this is echoed in the architecture of 31a Amherst Avenue, and the English-styled gardens of Bulaq Dakhrur. There were more indirect references to this ideal in the Frame family's occasional prized items of Victorian furniture, and in the Liberty-print curtains pinned to the walls of Lessing's Rhodesian farmhouse. In distinct ways, these homes replicate the myth of an isolated island, even while they confirm that such properties could never separate their white inhabitants from the surrounding landscape. Long before stately homes in twenty-first-century Britain were being reappraised by researchers and the general public as part of a shared colonial past, life writers were demonstrating how settler homes could not become inviolate spaces of retreat from imperial power. This cohort of authors were shocked to inhabit unhomely dwelling places after their arrivals in Britain, narrating their early years in basements, bedsits and boarding schools through the imperial myths of their childhoods. Yet their accounts of frustrated homecoming nuance our understanding of empire as 'lived across everyday practices', providing more a specific view of imperialism as working to 'weave itself into the everyday' both during and after colonial rule.[117] By refusing to imagine 'going home' as a nostalgic act, these life writers confront the public, paradoxical histories of colonialism through the private sphere of domestic space.

While each of these writers travelled to London during the post-war period, the socio-economic conditions of their childhoods and later adult lives were markedly different, reflecting the inequalities of life in the metropole and colony alike. Lively may have been educated in an isolated nursery by a live-in nanny while Ballard luxuriated in the grandeur of the Shanghai Cathedral School, but Lessing had only a piecemeal education beneath a leaking thatched roof and shifting mud walls in southern Africa. During her own, impoverished childhood in a succession of railway houses and huts across the South Island, Frame shared a bed with three other siblings. She felt intensely ashamed of being sent to school with 'tide marks of dirt' across her neck and arms.[118] Yet these life writers are drawn into concert with one another by the ways that they explore the ambiguities of white colonial identity in the aftermath of empire. The childhood homes discussed in the first four chapters of this book remind us of these distinctive experiences and geographies; Lively's mansion is not straightforwardly comparable to Frame's cramped living quarters. But despite

---

[117] Hall and Rose, 'Introduction: Being at Home with the Empire', p. 3.
[118] Frame, *To the Is-Land*, p. 39.

their biographical and material distinctions, these life writers each consider what it means to live amongst the bombed-out ruins of empire, to sift through the broken detritus and misplaced heirlooms of settler life, examining genealogies and origin stories rent apart by the legacies of imperialism.

The readings offered here are by no means a complete or comprehensive survey of modern and contemporary life writing which engages with the legacies of empire. Yet these texts do suggest how and why the afterlives of colonialism impacted on writers who, like Lively and Ballard, are usually read and discussed as straightforwardly 'British' or, like Lessing and Frame, whose colonial identities have yet to be fully understood in relation to their life writing. If we were to read the autobiographical oeuvres of these individuals in isolation, it might be possible to interpret their repeated descriptions of colonial childhoods as a personal idiosyncrasy, one which resulted in an unusual number of memoirs and autobiographies. But the multiple acts of life writing and rewriting addressed in this book suggests a more specific phenomenon, one where autobiographical narrative became the principle means for white authors to explore the seismic changes of formal decolonization *and* their own, ongoing connections to empire. By accounting for life amongst the colonial remains, life narratives show us how and why colonialism remains. We have only begun to address how the work of authors who lived and worked in modern Britain is shaped by the nation's colonial past. By turning now to autobiographical texts which repeatedly 'return home' to memories of empire, we will see how life writing endeavours to inhabit, critique and escape from the dwelling places of colonial life.

1

Double Exposures and Counterfactual Lives in Penelope Lively's Memoirs

Introduction: Egypt to England, 'from a world of technicolour to one of black and white'

Penelope Lively's seventh novel, *Moon Tiger* (1987), was initially described by reviewers as the 'housewife's choice', and derided as pedestrian reading material for 'the Harrods and Hatchards market'.[1] Even when it eventually clinched that year's Booker Prize, critics continued to suspect that there 'is something too sheltered' in Lively's postmodern, kaleidoscopic account of a doomed love affair which, they sniffed, did 'nothing to enlarge the sense of the possible for the novel'.[2] While Brian Moore's political thriller *The Colour of Blood* (1987) was the initial favourite to win that year's prize, commentators insisted that Lively's concerns with the interior lives of women were no match for her male contemporaries (this critique strategically ignores *Moon Tiger*'s complex, non-linear narrative structure).[3] The condescending response to her Booker win is indicative of a wider, pervasive suspicion that Lively's writing, despite her many literary prizes and accolades, is middlebrow; although she has retained a loyal – even devoted – readership throughout her long career, her academic reception

---

[1] 'Penelope Lively's Life in Books', *BBC News*, 31 December 2011, https://www.bbc.co.uk/news/entertainment-arts-16362698 (accessed 30 August 2021); W. L. Webb, 'Lively Leaps Off with 15,000 Pounds Booker Prize', *The Guardian*, 30 October 1987.
[2] Penny Perrick, 'Taking the Tiger Lightly by the Tip of the Tail – This Year's Winner of the Best-Known Prize for Fiction', *Sunday Times*, 1 November 1987; 'Lively Leaps Off with 15,000 Pounds Booker Prize'.
[3] Although *Moon Tiger* remains the only text by Lively to have received significant critical appraisal, it is now rightly viewed as a masterpiece of postmodern fiction and has been situated within a wider literary tradition 'of British regionalism and colonial fiction exemplified by … Rudyard Kipling and E. M. Forster'. – Luke Strongman, *The Booker Prize and the Legacy of Empire* (Amsterdam: Rodopi: 2002), p. 117.

continues to be muted, at best.[4] In many ways she continues to be regarded as 'part and parcel of the domestic proficiencies of English fiction' and unworthy of critical scrutiny.[5]

On the one hand, Lively has sustained a remarkably consistent set of literary interests with memory, contingency and – to borrow a phrase from *According to Mark* (1984) – 'the curious ways in which truth can be not so much distorted as multifaceted'.[6] Her characters frequently discover that their stable lives can be altered in a single moment, and many of her novels trace how a brief disruption in the present might permanently reconfigure our established narratives of the past. Typical intrusions include the fleeting violence of a mugging in *How It All Began* (2011) or the discovery of a concealed infidelity in *The Photograph* (2003), both of which trace the rippling consequences of these events to a network of individuals and communities. Beyond her fiction, Lively is a prolific life writer whose five memoirs constitute a significant body of contemporary, experimental life writing. Yet with only a few exceptions, her autobiographical writing remains largely ignored by literary critics.[7] If all of Lively's work has suffered from critical neglect, her accounts of being brought up in Cairo during the 1930s are an especially overlooked area of her oeuvre. Through these accomplished life narratives, Lively has repeatedly articulated how and why her colonial childhood in Egypt continues to influence her life after the formal end of empire.

Lively's life writing includes a memoir of childhood in *Oleander, Jacaranda*; an exploration of her family home Golsoncott in *A House Unlocked* (2001); a collection of speculative life narratives, *Making It Up* (2005); essays on old age in *Ammonites and Leaping Fish* (2013); and a horticultural memoir, *Life in the Garden* (2017).[8] Each of these recalls her childhood and eventual

---

[4] There remains only one book-length study of Lively's writing and, to date, no journal special issue, edited collection or conference has ever been devoted to her work. See: Mary Hurley Moran, *Penelope Lively* (New York: Twayne, 1993).

[5] Dinah Birch, 'Growing Up', *London Review of Books*, 11:8 (1989), https://www.lrb.co.uk/the-paper/v11/n08/dinah-birch/growing-up (accessed 27 January 2021).

[6] Penelope Lively, *According to Mark* (New York: Harper & Row, 1989), p. 212.

[7] For brief critical discussions of Lively's life writing, which largely focus on her first memoir *Oleander, Jacaranda*, see Gillian Whitlock, *The Intimate Empire: Reading Women's Autobiography* (London: Cassell, 2000), pp. 179–92; Huw Marsh, 'Unlearning Empire: Penelope Lively's Moon Tiger', in *End of Empire and the English Novel Since 1945*, ed. Rachael Gilmour and Bill Schwarz (Manchester: Manchester University Press, 2011), pp. 152–65; Nadine Flagel and Anastasia Kozak, 'Excavating the Self: Archeology and Life Writing in Penelope Lively's *Oleander, Jacaranda*', a/b: Auto/Biography Studies, 23:2 (2014): 245–63.

[8] While *Making It Up* has been typically described as a 'fictional memoir' and is generally discussed in the context of Lively's novels, this chapter repositions the text as a vital development in her autobiographical corpus. Maricel Oró-Piqueras, 'When the Personal and the Historical Collide: Reimagining Memory in Penelope Lively's *Making It Up*', *Life Writing*, 14:1 (2017): 57–68 (p. 66).

departure from Egypt during the Second World War, returning to her arrival in Britain at the tail-end of the conflict, when the lonely, homesick child felt alien 'in this place that was apparently the homeland'.⁹ In my own conversations with Lively, she described her younger self as 'having come from a world that was technicolour [to] having moved into one that was black and white', offering a potent metaphor for the sensory shock and emotional losses of this journey.¹⁰ This moment of transition is the point where all of her life narratives converge; *Ammonites and Leaping Fish* remembers the contrast between 'the Middle Eastern world of warmth and colour [and] the chill grey of England', while *Life in the Garden* describes the 'woolly jumpers [and] Chilprufe vests' necessitated by her first English winter.¹¹ These life narratives index a particular moment of post-imperial homecoming to Britain, memorializing Lively's early impressions of an unfamiliar country she had been raised to consider as her own. She may be (mis-)read as a peculiarly English author who rarely ventures beyond the cosy concerns of country houses and domestic routines, yet Lively's life writing is indicative of how public life in modern Britain is underwritten by half-concealed memories of empire. A thorough reappraisal of her prose, and especially her autobiographical writing, is long overdue.

By beginning with a discussion of *Oleander, Jacaranda*, and then focusing on several vignettes in *Making It Up*, this chapter pursues Lively's dual vision of white colonial life. These texts offer a first-person account of the dwelling places which Frantz Fanon attributes to 'settler and native', emphasizing why and how domestic space was crucial for upholding a 'colonial … Manichaean world'.¹² Fanon's scrutiny of the bordered zones 'inhabited by settlers' was informed by his experiences of the Algerian anti-colonial struggle, and his incendiary arguments offer a vital foundation – grounded in the colonial histories of North Africa – for reconsidering Lively's memories of Egypt.¹³ On the one hand, these two memoirs scrutinize her position on a historical hinge, probing what it means to be born into a colonial world, but to bear witness to another, postcolonial age. Yet they also wrestle with the complexities of a dual perspective, oscillating between the child's unquestioning view of

---

⁹ Penelope Lively, *A House Unlocked* (London: Viking, 2001), p. 162.
¹⁰ Penelope Lively and Emma Parker, 'Interview with the Author', 30 August 2017.
¹¹ Penelope Lively, *Ammonites and Leaping Fish: A Life in Time* (London: Fig Tree, 2013), p. 70; Penelope Lively, *Life in the Garden* (London: Fig Tree, 2017), p. 112.
¹² Frantz Fanon, *The Wretched of the Earth* (London: Penguin, 2001), p. 31.
¹³ Ibid., p. 30.

colonial life (the 'world of technicolour') and the adult's critical hindsight. Any homecoming to the colonial past, for Lively, exists in the tension between these layered, oppositional views.

Rather than viewing everyday concerns as confining or limiting Lively's writing, this chapter shows how the 'domestic proficiencies' of her memoirs offer precise and scathing social commentaries. Her doubled gaze brings into sharp focus what Anne McClintock calls the 'ambiguously complicit' social roles of white, colonial women, 'both as colonisers and colonised, privileged and restricted, acted upon and acting'.[14] As we will see, Britain's colonial past seeps into the mundane, everyday aspects of *Oleander, Jacaranda*, lurking in photograph albums, gardens and the furnishings of private homes. The ambiguities of this doubled white gaze later develop into the real and counterfactual lives in *Making It Up*. On the one hand, Caryl Phillips is right to suggest that Lively inhabits a distinctive intersection of the colonial and the postcolonial, and that her work indicates how 'the legacy of empire has produced writing by descendants of the colonisers'.[15] But on the other, her nuanced depictions of empire's spatial divisions and everyday routines have been neither recognized nor fully explored by literary scholars.

Lively's autobiographical returns to Cairo offer a means to interrogate the violent 'ordering of the colonial world'.[16] If Fanon describes the 'compartments' of imperial society as frontiers, dividing private homes and public spaces alike, then Lively's life writing scrutinizes the domestic borders of settler life. These texts reveal the anxieties of maintaining and inhabiting a compartmentalized, colonial world. When she eventually turns to speculative life writing in *Making It Up* (my term for the process where an author rewrites their life with alternative outcomes), her interest in colonial whiteness extends into experiments with autobiographical narrative form. By reading Lively's first and third memoirs, this chapter develops previous arguments made by postcolonial scholars that 'the cult of domesticity' and private, interior worlds were integral to British imperial power.[17] Through her autobiographical 'double exposure' Lively beckons us to re-enter the family's compound in Cairo, that island of white, English culture marooned in the Egyptian landscape.[18] Refusing the progressive, linear chronologies of

---

[14] McClintock, *Imperial Leather*, p. 6.
[15] Caryl Phillips, 'Preface', in *Extravagant Strangers: A Literature of Belonging* (London: Faber & Faber, 1997), pp. x–xii (p. xi).
[16] Fanon, *The Wretched of the Earth*, p. 31.
[17] McClintock, *Imperial Leather*, p. 34.
[18] Lively, *Oleander, Jacaranda*, p. 52.

traditional autobiography, these texts instead circle back to her memories of both colonial life and the end of empire.

Despite the early, gendered dismissals of *Moon Tiger*, Lively is now celebrated as part and parcel of contemporary English literature. As one *New York Times* profile summarizes, '[her] productivity has been so steady and reliable that she is sometimes taken a little for granted' in Britain, viewed as part of the literary establishment, but remaining 'just on the edge of the [critical] radar'.[19] At a time when 'the everyday ties, relations and intricate interdependencies of empire' are being reassessed as key components of a national story, Lively's memoirs powerfully suggest how modern, English life and literature has always been shaped by the legacies of colonialism.[20] For all these reasons, and more, her life narratives are in urgent need of critical appraisal. As Hall and Rose suggest, 'Britain's imperial project affected the everyday [at home] in ways that shaped what was "taken-for-granted"'.[21] Despite her widespread popularity with readers, Lively, like the empire she remembers, is in danger of being overlooked, dismissed as part of the fabric of everyday life. We have barely begun to evaluate her unique contribution to contemporary women's life writing, or how her memoirs address the post-imperial nation. By experimenting with new, autobiographical forms across a formidable number of texts, these life narratives stage a series of restless returns to colonial Egypt, interrogating her position amidst the aftermath of empire.

Gardens and Islands of Whiteness in *Oleander, Jacaranda*

From 1933 to 1945, while living 'on the fringes of Africa', Lively and her family lived in a grand house on the outskirts of Cairo known as Bulaq Dakhrur. Her father, Roger Low, was an employee at the National Bank of Egypt, working as one of many British bureaucrats upholding the country's 'precarious system of foreign administration'.[22] In retrospect it was clear to Lively that although the city's government offices were 'manned by Egyptians', behind each local representative 'stood a British official'.[23] When her parents entertained their European friends

---

[19] Charles McGrath, '"A Writer Writes": Penelope Lively's Fiction Defies the Test of Time', *New York Times*, 4 May 2017, https://www.nytimes.com/2017/05/04/books/review/penelope-lively-profile-purple-swamp-hen.html (accessed 22 April 2021).
[20] Carby, *Imperial Intimacies*, p. 1.
[21] Hall and Rose, 'Introduction: Being at Home with the Empire', p. 21.
[22] Lively, *Oleander, Jacaranda*, p. 22.
[23] Ibid., p. 21.

at home, drinking cocktails on the lawn, the adults unanimously agreed 'that not only could the sun never set on the Empire, it was inconceivable that it would ever do so'.[24] A British 'Protectorate' between 1922 and 1953, Egypt was not an official colony but nevertheless remained 'the foundation of [Britain's] Middle Eastern power' throughout the first half of the twentieth century.[25] For the young Penelope there was a concerning ambiguity about the country's diagonal stripes of pink and white in her child's colonial atlas, its insecure location on the fringes of 'a global rash of pink'.[26] Nor was she consoled by her home school textbooks, which offered fictionalized histories of British glory, featuring 'glossy romantic pictures of national heroes'.[27] Such tales left her with a quiet sense of unease, peering at the images and pondering her own identity as English in Egypt.

Oleander, Jacaranda describes the 'European enclave of three substantial, garden-encircled houses [which] sat in the landscape like some incongruous island' as the centre of Lively's sheltered world.[28] Settled in surrounding fields and canals – known as 'the cultivation' – the house and gardens were an isolated, even embattled domestic space. The green lawns acted as a frontier, separating the property from an unfamiliar agricultural landscape beyond its borders, and Lively would leave to travel 'in to Cairo only once a week', accompanied by her nanny.[29] The gardens of Bulaq Dakhrur belong to the wider context of what Richard Grove terms 'green imperialism', a colonial tradition where naturalists like Joseph Banks developed botanical classificatory systems to order territories across Britain's Empire.[30] The green, enclosed spaces surrounding private homes like Bulaq Dakhrur became microcosmic imperial territories which supported and constructed English colonial identity throughout the nineteenth and early twentieth centuries (Figure 1.1).[31] As a result, the almost-impenetrable hedges of Lively's childhood home marked both the limits of her world and allowed her family to exist in an island of whiteness. These gardens are – perhaps unsurprisingly – the primary location through which *Oleander, Jacaranda* explores the complexities of a colonial upbringing and Lively's identity as a white, English girl living in Egypt.

---

[24] Ibid., p. 59.
[25] Darwin, *Britain and Decolonisation*, p. 206.
[26] Lively, *Oleander, Jacaranda*, p. 18.
[27] Ibid.
[28] Ibid., p. 12.
[29] Ibid., p. 45.
[30] Richard Grove, *Green Imperialism: Colonial Expansion, Tropical Island Edens and the Origins of Environmentalism, 1600–1860* (Cambridge: Cambridge University Press, 1995).
[31] Anne Helmreich, *The English Garden and National Identity: The Competing Styles of Garden Design 1870–1914* (Cambridge: Cambridge University Press, 2002), p. 232.

Figure 1.1 Bulaq Dakhrur. ©Penelope Lively, reproduced with permission of the author.

Life in the Garden remembers the house as an 'alien enclave amid fields of sugarcane … canals and mud-hut villages' that was nevertheless 'a kind of intimate paradise, intensely personal, with private hiding spaces'.[32] The garden is both a lost Eden (the original 'paradise') and an emblem of a colonial settlement (the 'alien enclave'). In *Oleander, Jacaranda*, this location physically shields her family from the Egyptian landscape and its inhabitants while providing a stage for the English social rituals of tea parties and cocktail hours. Lively remembers her mother as always framed within the garden:

> In my mind's eye she is for ever part of a group on a lawn in the glowing light of an early evening, everyone tricked out with white cotton [mosquito] protection tubes on arms and legs so that they look like Michelin men [with] ice-clinking glasses of whisky and soda.[33]

The routines of Cairo's colonial society were barely interrupted by the dangers of the Egyptian climate ('most Europeans in Egypt were mildly ill a good deal

---

[32] Lively, *Life in the Garden*, p. 2.
[33] Lively, *Oleander, Jacaranda*, p. 24.

of the time').[34] In Lively's memories the threat of mosquitoes and malaria is partially disguised by the perennial colonial routine of sundowner drinks. To understand the vital role of this garden, we might turn to Sara Ahmed's arguments – formulated in response to Fanon – that 'bodies are shaped by the histories of colonialism' and that the latter 'makes the world "white"'.[35] If colonialism constructs a world as white, Ahmed suggests, then 'the body-at-home is one that can inhabit whiteness'.[36] Lively's memories of colonial garden parties, with the accoutrements of alcohol and anti-malarial measures, show how the setting of the garden establishes certain bodies as 'at home' in Egypt. She may recall living in an esoteric 'alien enclave', but this habitation is also a shelter, one which reveals broader, imperial ambitions of rendering the world white.

Bulaq Dakhrur's gardens were 'unashamedly English in design, with lawns, lily ponds, pergolas, formal beds and a rose garden'.[37] Lively's mother instructed her servants to cultivate this space as a site for European leisure. Yet *Oleander, Jacaranda* draws our attention to the artifice of this construction, as the garden's 'survival depended, like the surrounding fields, on the periodic release of water from the canal system'.[38] Each month Egyptian servants would breach the property's ditches in an event known as 'the flood' and the rising waters would temporarily confine young Penelope to the verandah. Just as the Suez Canal was crucial to British imperial power, Lively's family relied on local irrigation channels to sustain their personal, green paradise. The tall hedges and water-filled trenches surrounding the family home were porous borders connecting Bulaq Dakhrur to the Egyptian landscape. The garden, after all, relied on the same water supply that served the surrounding farmland; the canal was 'the lifeblood of the agricultural landscape' but it was also an open sewer, a site for laundry, and a source of drinking water.[39] As a child, Lively was repeatedly told that 'to be English was to be amongst the chosen and saved', to be distinguished from all others.[40] Yet the living emblem of an imperial, English identity – the ordered garden surrounding her family home – is an unstable, ambiguous space in *Oleander, Jacaranda*. This leaking, insecure location remains contingent on Egyptian labour, reminding its inhabitants that they are inseparable from the world beyond their property's boundaries.

[34] Ibid., p. 29.
[35] Ahmed, 'A Phenomenology of Whiteness', p. 153.
[36] Ibid.
[37] Lively, *Oleander, Jacaranda*, p. 38.
[38] Ibid., p. 42.
[39] Ibid., p. 10.
[40] Ibid., p. 17.

In an 1870 lecture that would later shape the imperial ambitions of a young Cecil Rhodes, John Ruskin posited that Britain's power as 'mistress of half the earth' relied on the maintenance of 'her enchanted garden' and the ordering of her 'wide and fair' fields.[41] Evoking John Locke's *Second Treatise of Government* (1690), Ruskin justified Britain's overseas colonies through an ideal of cultivation, concluding that seizing foreign lands that were 'fruitful waste ground' would establish the well-ordered English garden-as-nation.[42] Ruskin's celebration of colonial land theft reveals how carefully-tended gardens across Britain's Empire operated as symbolic justifications for imperial expansion. As Lively herself suggests, spaces like the beautifully maintained lawns of Bulaq Dakhrur were also places of leisure, offering Europeans a 'retreat from the strangeness of alien environments' in the colonies.[43] However, in reality, this location offered important opportunities for Lively to subvert the strict, domestic divides of settler life. If the garden was charged with the complex agendas of imperialism, it was also a fluid site which could be used to challenge colonialism's Manichaean divides.

Paying heed to her later warning that gardens are 'not just a background in a story, but ... an essential feature', the garden in *Oleander, Jacaranda* is a colonial contact zone where Lively can temporarily undo the physical and social boundaries of her childhood.[44] The spatial layout inside Bulaq Dakhrur was designed to separate white inhabitants from Egyptian servants; spaces used by the latter, such as the kitchen and pantry, were concealed from view 'behind a screen in the far corner of the hall'.[45] Young Penelope was forbidden from entering the servants' quarters via any internal route inside the house. She would instead reach the circle of cooks and gardeners gossiping at the backdoor by 'creep[ing] through the bushes', sitting 'in fascination, watching and listening'.[46] Lively's excursions into the liminal space of the undergrowth brought her into contact with Ahmed, a twelve-year-old garden boy who later

---

[41] John Ruskin, 'Conclusion to Inaugural Lecture (1870)', in *Empire Writing: An Anthology of Colonial Literature 1870–1918*, ed. Elleke Boehmer (Oxford: Oxford University Press, 2009), pp. 16–20 (p. 19).

[42] Locke's argument stated that property is '*As much Land* as a Man Tills, Plants, Improves, Cultivates and can use the Product of'. This idea of ownership through productivity later served as a justification for European colonialism, and Locke's arguments clearly resound in Ruskin's advocacy of imperialism over 200 years later. John Locke, *Second Treatise of Government and a Letter Concerning Toleration*, ed. Mark Goldie (Oxford: Oxford University Press, 2016), p. 17.

[43] Richard Drayton, *Nature's Government: Science, Imperial Britain and the 'Improvement' of the World* (London: Yale University Press, 2000), p. 183.

[44] Lively, *Life in the Garden*, p. 79.

[45] Lively, *Oleander, Jacaranda*, p. 34.

[46] Ibid.

became her friend. Yet she remembers that her connection to the staff was 'an intimate one, but [it] is also somehow bewildering. I do not know quite where I am'.[47] As Chapter 5 discusses in greater detail, inside the house Lively was banned from entering certain rooms and from touching particular, expensive possessions. The garden was therefore a means of escape from these restrictions, offering an opportunity to become disorientated, and to briefly challenge such rigid domestic arrangements. Her relationship with Ahmed is a tentative, cross-racial friendship, but it also throws into sharp relief their differences; Ahmed is in the garden to work, he is 'employed to fetch and carry', while she is there for recreation.[48] *Oleander, Jacaranda* imagines the garden not just as a reflection of European colonial authority, but also as a dynamic, living space for scrutinizing and challenging that power. It allows Lively to highlight the ambiguities and privileges of her position as a white colonial subject. The intimacies she experienced in the garden punctuated an otherwise solitary existence indoors, where she and Lucy were 'hived off in our upstairs domain', isolated in a small suite of first-floor rooms.[49]

If – as Drayton suggests – colonial gardens represented the imperial 'dream of possessing all nature in a microcosm and understanding its order', then Lively deliberately undermines this codified fantasy.[50] There is a brief moment of solidarity when she and Ahmed find themselves united in their 'flight from authority' (Lively from her nanny, Ahmed from the head gardener) and converge in 'the place behind the bamboo clump'.[51] They wordlessly engage in a dirt-eating contest. The garden's private, shady spaces facilitate such encounters and allow Lively to stage petty acts of sabotage, like the 'snapping off poinsettia heads' which so horrified her mother.[52] Despite subsequent attempts to ban her from the flower beds, these rules were much harder to enact in an outside arena. In *Oleander, Jacaranda*, the white colonial child slips through the insubstantial barriers of flower beds and bushes, discovering new social worlds in the process. She experiences meetings which would be impossible amidst the solid walls and stratified zones of the house. In Lively's autobiographical accounts of late colonial life, the garden is a site charged with the possibilities of social transgression.

On the one hand, Lively's memories of the garden underscore Edward Said's argument that imperialism is 'an act of geographical violence through which

---

[47] Ibid., p. 35.
[48] Ibid., p. 37.
[49] Ibid., p. 22.
[50] Drayton, *Nature's Government*, p. 48.
[51] Lively, *Oleander, Jacaranda*, p. 36.
[52] Ibid.

virtually every space in the world is explored, charted and finally brought under control'.⁵³ As her youthful acts of trespass briefly challenge 'the ordering of the colonial world', the child's perspective in *Oleander, Jacaranda* emphasizes how colonialism might be resisted in private, domestic spaces.⁵⁴ The material and social divisions of Bulaq Dakhrur are unstable when traversed by an inquisitive, garden-loving, mud-eating child. By next turning to the photographs reproduced in the text, we will see how worlds outside the garden are brought into focus by these images. If Lively's view of her colonial childhood is complicated by a so-called double exposure, then these multiple, overlapping realities are revealed through the book's visual, as well as textual, narratives. When read through Lively's photographic metaphor, these images draw our attention to worlds that are excluded from the garden, hovering on the periphery of the memoir.

Photographs and Double Exposures

When Lively, her nanny, and her mother fled Egypt ahead of General Rommel's advancing troops, there was little indication that this departure meant the end of her colonial childhood. Even during the early 1940s, Cairo's European community believed that 'the global British presence' was set to continue indefinitely.⁵⁵ Lively's 'view of things' from this period consequently 'has a double exposure', presenting two overlaid views of empire in which its end is both unthinkable and unavoidable.⁵⁶ Her dual optic is realized not only in the textual narrative but also through the twenty-three black-and-white photographs reproduced in *Oleander, Jacaranda*.⁵⁷ These depict Lively and her family at home in Bulaq Dakhrur, enjoying days out in Cairo and Alexandria, and picnicking in the Egyptian desert. Lively's interest in images and photograph albums spans the entirety of her career; several of her fictional characters discover that photographs can tell their own revelatory truths, 'the alternative stories that lurk beyond the narrative'.⁵⁸ Yet in the context of autobiographical writing, reproduced images are often viewed by critics as a visual supplement which either verifies or directly illustrates events depicted in the text.⁵⁹ By contrast, several of *Oleander,*

---

⁵³ Said, *Culture and Imperialism*, p. 271.
⁵⁴ Fanon, *The Wretched of the Earth*, p. 31.
⁵⁵ Lively, *Oleander, Jacaranda*, p. 59.
⁵⁶ Ibid., p. 52.
⁵⁷ All images discussed here are reproduced in the Penguin Classics edition of *Oleander, Jacaranda*.
⁵⁸ Penelope Lively, *The Photograph* (London: Viking, 2003), p. 23.
⁵⁹ Timothy Dow Adams, *Light Writing and Life Writing: Photography in Autobiography* (Chapel Hill: University of North Carolina Press, 2000).

Jacaranda's photographs disturb the accepted truths of the memoir, taking the reader far beyond the leafy limits of Bulaq Dakhrur. While these photographs do illustrate some episodes from the written memoir, others fill gaps in Lively's life narrative. Through this latter, more nuanced function, several photographs in *Oleander, Jacaranda* echo Jay Prosser's suggestion that autobiographical images are 'chutes into something missing, pointers to a loss that can't be recovered in the text'.[60] They offer not only a counter-narrative which moves beyond the confines of the garden but reveal stories which are otherwise hidden, concealed or repressed in the textual narrative.

The sunny images of colonial life reproduced in *Oleander, Jacaranda* are accompanied by possessions and details which sustain a cultural landscape of Englishness. In these, a tiny Penelope takes afternoon tea behind a table laden with preserves and marmite, reclines in the sunshine amidst her mother's rose garden and leaps into the waters of Alexandria Harbour.[61] The sequence of personal snapshots from Lively's own family album capture the repetitive cultural rituals of imperial life and document the changes to her family's circumstances during the Second World War (in later pictures Lively's mother and her friends exchange tea dresses for khaki uniforms). These latter images are largely historical photographs, selected from the archives of London's Imperial War Museum.[62] One captures a 1943 tea party in Cairo, where repatriated prisoners of war are hosted at the Gezira Sporting Club (a whites-only establishment), and served by 'attendant *suffragis*'.[63] They conclude with a historical shot which loops back to the personal: a full-page spread of the bombed ruins surrounding St Paul's Cathedral in 1941, a site which Lively witnessed first-hand in 1945. The captions describe Lively as 'PL'. As the first-person pronoun 'I' is used sparingly, there is a startling disjuncture between the named girl in the pictures and the author who narrates her story. The selection and presentation of these images illuminates Lively's complicated relationship with her former self, the domestic spaces of her childhood and the history of British colonialism in the Middle East.

---

[60] Jay Prosser, *Light in the Dark Room: Photography and Loss* (Minneapolis: University of Minnesota Press, 2005), p. 9.

[61] Colonial photograph albums have long been discussed by art historians for their capacity to reveal 'as much about the imaginative landscape of imperial culture as ... the physical spaces or people pictured in their frame'. – James R. Ryan, *Picturing Empire: Photography and the Visualisation of the British Empire* (London: Reaktion Books, 1997), p. 20.

[62] Lively's archive at the Harry Ransom Centre confirms the origins of these historical photographs, as her photocopied notes detail that the Imperial War Museum supplied many of the images – Austin, Harry Ransom Center, MS Penelope Lively, 16.4.

[63] Lively, *Oleander, Jacaranda*, n.p.

Yet within the sequence are several personal photographs depicting events that do not feature in the text of the memoir. In one, Lively appears with a baby donkey, standing in the foreground of the shot (see Figure 1.2). She is dressed in a smart overcoat, wearing white cotton socks, buckled leather shoes and her right hand is petting the animal's long ears. This proprietorial interaction between child and animal is reminiscent of British seaside towns, with their ubiquitous donkey rides along the shoreline. It fits seamlessly into the broader visual narrative of Lively's childhood where, surrounded by white family and friends, she enjoys recreational activities across Cairo. However, behind the animal three Egyptian children are also present in the background of the frame. Their bare feet and draped clothes are separated from Lively by the donkey. The four children meet, but do not touch. Unlike other photographs, in which Lively wears light, cotton dresses, this scene appears to be in winter. Her overcoat and

Figure 1.2 Penelope Lively, three Egyptian children and a donkey. ©Penelope Lively, reproduced with permission of the author.

the children's heavy, tightly wrapped scarves imply a chill. Dead twigs and sharp stones litter the path around them. Only one child (Lively) is adequately clothed against the elements. There is a vulnerability to the three who stand with their bare toes pressed into the muddy ground. The donkey is both the focal point and a disturbingly clear barrier in the photograph.[64]

The startling separation between these two worlds is acknowledged in a caption: 'PL with *fellaheen* [peasant] children near Bulaq Dakhrur. A deeply disquieting photo in its brutal contrasts, with the baby donkey as the cosy feature of interest'.[65] The adult who writes this disrupts 'the impervious, accepting eye of childhood', which coolly viewed scenes of Egyptian poverty and dispossession.[66] In the photograph the difference between the children's footwear is emphasized by their mutual interest in the donkey as they cluster around the docile animal. The group is gathered in a semicircle and clearly arranged to face the photographer. The children are both united and separated in a carefully organized scene; it seems unlikely, even impossible, that this was an uncoordinated social interaction. Instead, all four are on display, facing the viewer. Four decades before Lively was positioned in this tableau, curious visitors to the 1889 World Exhibition in Paris flocked to the Rue du Caire, a supposedly 'authentic' (though clearly artificial) Egyptian street scene. Hoping to conjure the exciting energy of a bazaar, the Exhibition's organizers imported fifty donkeys to patrol up and down the street, offering rides to young visitors.[67] The donkey photograph in *Oleander, Jacaranda* therefore restages an earlier European imitation of Cairo, one where this animal was inseparable from Egypt in the imperial imagination, becoming entertainment for a colonial gaze. While any echo of the 1889 Exhibition is likely unintentional, it reveals how a family photograph can be a spectacle of imperial order, a curated scene for a colonial audience, as well as a snapshot of family life.

Unlike the previous photos of Lively amidst rose pergolas and grand fountains, this photograph of four children is not taken in Bulaq Dakhrur's gardens, with their manicured lawns and English artifice. We are *near to* but no longer *inside* the boundaries of the property. Here the screen provided by the garden's high hedges and irrigation ditches briefly falls away, revealing colonial

---

[64] In her brief discussion of this photograph, Gillian Whitlock suggests that it is 'an exemplar for colonial discourse analysis, in particular that most elementary trope of the "self" and the "other", with the British child defined in and through the fellaheen'. Whitlock, *The Intimate Empire*, p. 185.
[65] Lively, *Oleander, Jacaranda*, n.p.
[66] Ibid., pp. 10–11.
[67] For a full description of this spectacle at the 1889 World Exhibition, see chapter 1 of Timothy Mitchell's *Colonising Egypt* (1991).

subjects who inhabit a landscape beyond the garden walls. As this photograph witnesses an encounter absent from the main text of *Oleander, Jacaranda* it becomes, to use Prosser's phrase, a 'shute into something missing', a reality omitted from the narrative.[68] Although Lively recalls playdates with a handful of (European) friends, she 'was distinctly short on companionship'.[69] There are no encounters with Egyptian children in the textual narrative (excepting her dirt-eating competition with Ahmed). Yet there is also nothing accidental about this snapshot's position in a sequence of sunny images from a colonial childhood. By embedding this in the visual record of her upbringing, Lively gestures towards lives that are omitted both from the family photograph album and her own written account. In Fanon's terms, this photograph tells us who, exactly, is excluded from 'the forbidden quarters' of the settler's town.[70]

This photograph, nestled amongst familial and historical images, irrevocably alters the meaning of every subsequent and preceding picture in *Oleander, Jacaranda*. Without it, the black-and-white images of Lively's family on the beach, or eating sandwiches and clutching thermos flasks in the desert, are marooned in a decontextualized, domestic world. The isolation of her childhood, where 'for the most part I was significantly alone', risks obscuring the racial inequalities and consequences of British colonial rule.[71] Yet if we look carefully, there are brief traces of life outside the garden in other photographs. One depicts a European WREN (a Women's Royal Naval Service member) and her companion strolling through Cairo while on leave. To the sharply dressed WREN's right, a small shoeless child follows in her wake. In the crowd behind her are several barefooted children, their eyes focused on the smart couple. There is also the disturbing depiction of segregated white POWs enjoying their afternoon tea at the Gezira Sporting Club, waited upon by Egyptian staff. But these photographs are from historical archives held by the Imperial War Museum or the Hulton Deutsch Collection (now owned by Getty Images). They do not feature Lively herself, nor do they take place in the domestic confines of her childhood world. In the full-page image of the children and the donkey, the shocking results of empire's racial hierarchies are laid bare *and* positioned in close proximity to the author herself. This is a single glimpse of a reality that exists just beyond the representative frames of *Oleander, Jacaranda*.

---

[68] Prosser, *Light in the Dark Room*, p. 9.
[69] Lively, *Oleander, Jacaranda*, p. 40.
[70] Fanon, *The Wretched of the Earth*, p. 31.
[71] Lively, *Oleander, Jacaranda*, p. 41.

On a final note, the gleaming reflection of still water to the left of the children implies that this photograph was captured next to water, most likely the canal that was responsible for the annual flood and which lay just beyond the boundaries of Bulaq Dakhrur. The image is literally and metaphorically close to home, existing just out of sight when Lively describes long afternoons playing amidst the flower beds. Evoking Ahmed's conceptualization of whiteness once more, the three children cannot be bodies-at-home in Bulaq Dakhrur. They inhabit neither the forbidding interior of the house, nor its well-tended gardens. Ahmed reminds us that to be at home in a world oriented around whiteness means inhabiting this 'absent centre' as 'a form of positive residence'.[72] The unnamed Egyptian subjects in the background of the photograph are excluded from a property which served and soothed a colonial gaze. Bulaq Dakhrur's gardens are not only a frontier for the house as an island of whiteness; they mark the limitations and the boundaries of the memoir itself.

Rather than viewing the reproduced photographs in *Oleander, Jacaranda* as a sequence illustrating the text, these pictures create a complex, visual counter-narrative. As the memoir is structured around a series of memories narrated in the present tense, followed by retrospective reflections from Lively, it becomes a series of snapshots arranged like a photograph album. Annette Kuhn suggests that 'in the process of using – producing, selecting, ordering, displaying – photographs [for an album] the family is actually in the process of making itself'.[73] For Susan Sontag, the family album is a 'portrait-chronicle', a portable selection of images whose owners can take 'an imaginary possession of a past that is unreal'.[74] These arguments suggest how the written and textual snapshots in Lively's first memoir are a form of collective self-representation, an arrangement which highlights the limits of any white, colonial 'portrait-chronicle'. The first photograph album which contained many of these pictures fulfilled the purposes of Lively's parents, its original contributors. But when they are reproduced, these photographs allow Lively to scrutinize the narratives and counter-narratives of her colonial childhood. *Oleander, Jacaranda*'s written and visual elements are snapshots with a double exposure, charged with the dual meanings and contradictions of a colonial childhood on the fringes of empire. Here Lively develops a bifocal optic by connecting England and Egypt, text and photograph, and a colonial garden to the 'wilderness' beyond. By turning next to

---

[72] Ahmed, 'A Phenomenology of Whiteness', p. 154.
[73] Annette Kuhn, *Family Secrets: Acts of Memory and Imagination* (London: Verso, 2002), p. 19.
[74] Susan Sontag, *On Photography* (London: Penguin Books, 1979), pp. 8–9.

her third memoir, *Making It Up*, we will see how these dual visions are extended by her experiments with actual and counterfactual lives. Rather than escaping from this imperial enclave, Lively's alternative lives again return to Cairo, asking what it means to outlive the rose-shaded cartographies of colonial rule and instead face a future that extends after empire.

On Speculative Life Writing

In his 2019 study, *Counterfactuals: Paths of the Might Have Been*, Christopher Prendergast describes 'the weird temporal cartwheel of the counterfactual' where narratives exploring 'what if' flip 'between the "before" and "after"' in a manner that disconcerts but can also illuminate'.[75] The revelatory power of the counterfactual is perhaps most typically evident in historical fiction which revisits the lives of famous men, reimagining alternative outcomes to decisions made on the battlefield or in high political office.[76] Yet alternative narratives can do more than revise the lives of princes and politicians, as thinking counterfactually temporarily halts the forward movement of time. In Catherine Gallagher's words, returning to the past to imagine alternative outcomes 'take[s] a 360-degree survey of a particular moment' allowing us to 'recover and explore history's cul-de-sacs and unfinished projects'.[77] Indeed, counterfactuals may foreground 'aspects of "the way it was" that are often overlooked in unilinear histories', returning to possibilities that lie, forgotten, on the fringes of the official record.[78] Here, counterfactual thought is one means of guarding against historical amnesia, asking what might have been in order to illuminate, more clearly, what was.

While counterfactual histories tend to cluster around moments of crisis (an imagined victory for the Axis powers remains a perennial favourite), alternative narratives also hold a possible revelatory power for individuals.[79] If, as Michael Wood suggests, we tend to 'pass forks in the road and forget them' when

---

[75] Christopher Prendergast, *Counterfactuals: Paths of the Might Have Been* (London: Bloomsbury, 2019), p. 13.
[76] J. C. Squire's influential anthology *If It Had Happened Otherwise* (1931) exemplifies this tendency, with essays that include Winston Churchill's 'If Lee Had Not Won the Battle of Gettysburg' and Emil Ludwig's 'If the Emperor Fredrick Had Not Had Cancer'.
[77] Catherine Gallagher, *Telling It Like It Wasn't: The Counterfactual Imagination in History and Fiction* (Chicago: University of Chicago Press, 2018), p. 47.
[78] Ibid.
[79] For examples of counterfactual Axis victories, see *SS-GB* (1978) by Len Deighton, Philip K. Dick's *The Man in the High Castle* (1962), and *Fatherland* (1992) by Robert Harris.

reading narrative fiction, then recent memoirs, including Lively's *Making It Up*, Lessing's *Alfred and Emily* (discussed in Chapter 5), and even Ruth Prawer Jhabvala's *My Nine Lives* (2004) have explored the roads that each author did not take.[80] These experimental life narratives issue a challenge to the certainty of traditional, linear autobiography, which offers a chronological account of an individual's development from birth to the present. Just as Wood reads the crossroads – that symbolic site of deliberation and dilemma – as 'a haunted place' in literary fiction, 'where the taken and untaken … stretch out in front of us', diverging paths are clearly *also fertile ground for life writers*.[81] By pursuing alternative possibilities, counterfactual lives disrupt the forward propulsion of autobiographical narrative, allowing authors like Lively and Lessing to return to the dismantlement of Britain's imperial power, surveying the overlooked details and 'cul-de-sacs' of formal decolonization. In their autobiographical experiments both expand the boundaries of their long life writing projects. Indeed, as the latter half of this chapter explores, counterfactual thought allows Lively to complicate and extend the bifocal view of her colonial childhood in *Oleander, Jacaranda*.

Making It Up comprises eight counterfactual stories which explore alternative outcomes to Lively's own life, jeopardizing the biographical truths established in her earlier memoirs. These expand on an interest – first expressed in *A House Unlocked* – in returning to pivotal moments when her life might 'have spun off in different directions'.[82] Through a sequence of semi-autobiographical vignettes, *Making It Up* hones 'in upon the rocks, the rapids, the whirlpools, and … the alternative stories', looking back on climactic decisions and events 'when things might have gone differently'.[83] Each tale begins with an italicized explanation of how the counterfactual life relates to Lively's real memories, from her departure from Cairo in the early 1940s to her marriage and later experiences of motherhood. Each speculative life is therefore tethered to real experiences, several of which have already been recorded in her previous memoirs. Yet as three of the eight vignettes return to Cairo, *Making It Up* also offers counterfactual narratives that destabilize the certainty of empire's end. By

---

[80] Michael Wood, *The Road to Delphi: The Life and Afterlife of Oracles* (New York: Farrar, Straus and Giroux, 2003), p. 65.

[81] Ibid.; In chapter four of *Counterfactuals* (2019), Prendergast reflects on the importance of the crossroads to counterfactual thought, noting that this location raises 'both routes and futures, those possible alternatives, the "paths" both literal and figurative that will feature as part of the life journey and those that won't but might have.' Prendergast, *Counterfactuals*, p. 90.

[82] Lively, *A House Unlocked*, p. 176.

[83] Lively, *Making It Up*, pp. 1–2.

experimenting with alternative endings Lively not only returns to her memories of a colonial world on the brink of collapse but also asks 'what if' her own life did not continue after empire.

Making It Up is emblematic of what I term 'speculative life writing', a previously unrecognized autobiographical sub-genre where authors reimagine key episodes from their lives with alternative outcomes.[84] Speculative life narratives cannot be satisfactorily classed as fictions because they pursue diversionary routes established in a writer's previous autobiographies.[85] In other words, speculative life writing involves the rewriting of earlier life narratives. As *Making It Up* was published in the same decade as *Alfred and Emily* and *My Nine Lives*, it forms part of a modest, post-2000 autobiographical practice that followed the 'memoir boom' of the 1980s and 1990s.[86] After the turn of the new millennium, as burgeoning sales of memoirs in both Britain and the United States expanded the market for life writing, authors like Lessing and Lively published rewritten versions of their earlier life narratives. Viewing speculative life writing as a specific autobiographical practice joins a wider critical conversation surrounding autofiction, a term coined by Serge Doubrovsky and later summarized by Catherine Cusset as 'fiction, of strictly real events and facts'.[87] Autofiction experiments 'with the definite limits of the self', entertaining speculative concerns which transcend 'the slavish recapitulation of known biographical facts'.[88] Speculative life writing similarly attributes the author's

---

[84] Speculative life writing remains distinct from Donna Lee Brien and Kiera Lindsey's coinage of 'speculative biography', a process where biographers go beyond archival evidence and verifiable sources to hypothesize about a subject's 'emotional responses, thoughts and motivations'. 'Speculative biography' names the process of creative invention and highlights the inevitable artifice of biographical reconstruction. My specific criteria for speculative life writing as an *autobiographical* act of self-representation which rewrites previous life stories remains distinct from these otherwise intriguing conversations, including James Worner's discussion of novels as 'speculative autobiography'. – Donna Lee Brien, 'The Facts Formed a Line', in *Speculative Biography: Experiments, Opportunities and Provocations*, ed. Donna Lee Brien and Kiera Lindsey (New York: Routledge, 2021), p. 4; James Worner, '*Why Not Tell?*: Eddie Samuels, 'The Authentic Self and the Novel as Speculative Autobiography', in *Speculative Biography: Experiments, Opportunities and Provocations*, ed. Donna Lee Brien and Kiera Lindsey (New York: Routledge, 2021), pp. 287–305.

[85] My attempt to define the parametres of this term differs from other, brief references to 'speculative memoirs' as a means to discuss novels. For examples, see Keith McDonald, 'Days of Past Futures: Kazuo Ishiguro's *Never Let Me Go* as "Speculative Memoir"', *Biography*, 30:1 (2007): 74–83; and Sanna Lehtonen, 'Experiments with Identity and Speculative Life Writing in Twilight Fan Fiction', *Fafnir: Nordic Journal of Science Fiction and Fantasy Research*, 2:2 (2015): 7–18.

[86] See G. Thomas Couser's *Memoir: An Introduction* (2012) for a full account of this 'boom', which Couser notes was 'not confined to Anglophone countries'. Examples like Marjane Satrapi's best-selling *Persepolis* (2000) or Azar Nafisi's *Reading Lolita in Teheran* (2003) suggest, for Couser, 'that memoir [now] rivals the novel as a medium of expression on the international stage'. G. Thomas Couser, *Memoir: An Introduction* (Oxford: Oxford University Press, 2012), p. 142.

[87] Catherine Cusset, 'The Limits of Autofiction' (Unpublished Conference Paper, 2012), www.catherinecusset.co.uk/wp-content/uploads/2013/02/the-limits-of-autofiction.pdf (accessed 27 April 2021).

[88] Hywel Dix, 'Introduction: Autofiction in English: The Story So Far', in *Autofiction in English*, ed. Hywel Dix (New York: Palgrave, 2018), pp. 1–23 (p. 4).

name to a fictionalized, counterfactual self. Yet it is, by my definition, a more specific response to a writer's previous memoirs and autobiographies which answers back to earlier texts, rather than debunking or dismissing them entirely.

Because *Making It Up* and *Alfred and Emily* were created in the latter decades of long writing careers, both disrupt established biographical truths.[89] Yet rather than being solely an autofictional experiment, or the result of an increased market for memoirs, both of these life narratives reflect their respective authors' late style. In his discussions of artistic lateness, Edward Said identifies that 'sort of deliberately unproductive productiveness' which answers back to an artist's earlier work.[90] Here Said extends Theodor Adorno's formulation of late style 'as process, but not as development', offering both a challenge to and a reworking of what came before.[91] Reading speculative life writing as late style suggests that – in the final decades of their careers – both Lively and Lessing sought new autobiographical forms which could articulate their memories of empire *and* break from the expected confines of old-age narratives. By embracing the counterfactual, these speculative texts reject a presumptive, progressive narratives of ageing which, as Helen Small notes, can only end in 'the terminal event' of death.[92] *Making It Up* demonstrates how Lively's late style responds to the Saidian/Adornian model of late productivity by disrupting her previous memoirs. Speculative life writing sees her circle back to the subject of colonial life, thus interrupting an established timeline of ageing as inevitable deterioration.

When Lively and Lessing use speculative life writing to re-examine their memories of empire, they question the closure of imperial history.[93] There are two key points to stress about their comparative forms of late style, the first being that this shared counterfactual impulse draws closer parallels and exchanges between their autobiographical writing than has ever previously

---

[89] While Lessing died in 2013, Lively announced her retirement as an author in 2022. See 'Penelope Lively Put Down Her Pen after a Life in Books', *The Times*, 16 May 2022, https://www.thetimes.co.uk/article/penelope-lively-puts-down-her-pen-after-a-life-in-books-m9qjqb375#:~:text=Dame%20Penelope%20Lively%20has%20vowed,time%20to%20%E2%80%9Cbow%20out%E2%80%9D (accessed 12 January 2023).

[90] Edward Said, *On Late Style: Literature and Music Against the Grain* (New York: Pantheon Books, 2006), p. 7.

[91] Theodor Adorno, 'On Late Style in Beethoven (1937)', in *Essays on Music*, ed. Richard Leppert, trans. Susan H. Gillespie (Berkeley: University of California Press, 2002), pp. 564–8 (p. 567).

[92] Helen Small, *The Long Life* (Oxford: Oxford University Press, 2007), p. 105.

[93] Prawer Jhabvala describes *My Nine Lives* as a potential autobiography, an experiment in 'alternative destinies' where the central 'I' of each chapter is the author, albeit in changed circumstances. Because this text does not rewrite previous memoirs, *My Nine Lives* is adjacent to my understanding of speculative life writing. It remains an important reference point to these discussions, as a post-2000 experiment in counterfactual thought. Ruth Prawer Jhabvala, *My Nine Lives: Chapters of a Possible Past* (London: John Murray, 2004), p. vii.

been recognized.[94] The second is that speculation allows both life writers to track empire's unfolding legacies, insisting that colonial history cannot be neatly sealed within an increasingly distant twentieth century. Speculative life writing may have gone unnoticed in literary discussions of both counterfactual literature and autofiction, but as the remainder of this chapter demonstrates, it marks an important development in Lively's autobiographical corpus.[95] The eight alternative stories in *Making It Up* extend the dual perspective of *Oleander, Jacaranda* by returning to, rather than escaping from, her memories of a confined home in colonial Egypt. As her third memoir disassembles a sovereign or stable autobiographical subject, Lively explores 'a series of past incarnations' who haunt her in the present.[96] While both Ballard and Frame experimented with different kinds of autofictional writing throughout their career, speculative life writing is an autobiographical practice that remains particular to Lively and Lessing. It nevertheless pursues the same thematic concerns with homecoming and memory shared by all of the post-imperial life writers discussed here, offering a further autobiographical route for white authors attempting to 'go home' to the colonial past.

Counterfactual Lives in *Making It Up*: 'Mozambique Channel' and 'Comet'

In her first drafts of *Making It Up*, Lively experimented with various titles that could convey the book's counterfactual content. 'Forking paths', 'life as fiction' and 'confabulation' are all jotted down in her handwritten notebooks from the early 2000s, now held in the archives of the Harry Ransom Center.[97] Correspondence with her editor during this period expresses a shared concern with how to describe (and market) a book that was eventually pitched as an 'anti-memoir'.[98] The archive suggests that, in *Making It Up*, Lively was experimenting

---

[94] For previous comparative readings of Lively and Lessing, see Whitlock's *The Intimate Empire* and Susan Watkin's article '"Summoning Your Youth at Will": Memory, Time and Ageing in the Work of Penelope Lively, Margaret Atwood and Doris Lessing', *Frontiers: A Journal of Women Studies*, 34:2 (2013): 222–44.
[95] Speculative life writing remains an unexplored area for studies of autofiction, *Making It Up* having been entirely overlooked by this burgeoning field, while Lessing's *Alfred and Emily* is mentioned once, in a footnote, of *Contemporary Autofiction in English* (2018).
[96] Penelope Lively, 'Late Style', *BBC Radio 3*, 18 April 2017, http://www.bbc.co.uk/programmes/b08n2 442 (accessed 3 December 2022).
[97] Harry Ransom Center, MS Penelope Lively, 11.6.
[98] Lively, *Making It Up*, p. 2.

with a kind of autobiographical narrative which did not, in 2005, belong to an identifiable literary genre. The handwritten list of potential titles in her spiral bound notebooks might initially appear inconsequential, yet they reveal a serious attempt to expand the horizons of the memoir form at the turn of a new millennium. The book's final, published title suggests both reconciliation and invention, while revealing little of its central, counterfactual impulse.

Far from being an 'anti-memoir' *Making It Up* is, from the outset, anchored to the real events of Lively's life. The first story 'Mozambique Channel' begins with an autobiographical preface that could be taken directly from *Oleander, Jacaranda*, outlining how this counterfactual narrative has its origins in a 'garden [that] was in Egypt … but its furnishings were English – ponds and pergolas and rose-beds'.[99] Returning to the heart of her childhood world, Lively recalls the 'fields of sugar-cane [and] mud villages' that encircled her former home, noting that 'beyond the rim of this known landscape was the desert'.[100] So far, so familiar, at least for the readers of her previous life narratives. From the outset this text marshals a dual perspective, combining the actual and the counterfactual to look beyond the enclosed garden. Yet the italicized explanation preceding 'Mozambique Channel' describes, in greater detail than *Oleander, Jacaranda*, her expulsion from Bulaq Dakhrur. Lively recalls how, in 1942, a German assault on Cairo was increasingly likely and the anticipated invasion prompted the burning of 'files at the British Embassy and GHQ' which sent 'charred paper raining down on the streets'.[101] The banks were besieged by panicked British residents, and as the main transport routes out of Egypt became crowded, travel options were increasingly limited. Although Allied forces halted General Rommel's troops that summer, many of the city's inhabitants believed that the Axis powers could soon seize Egypt.

As Gallagher reminds us, counterfactual history is the pursuit of an 'explicit or implicit past-tense, hypothetical, conditional conjecture' even when 'the antecedent condition is known to be contrary to fact'.[102] Given the historical context of wartime Egypt outlined in Lively's italicized preface, the most obvious hypothetical alternative for 'Mozambique Channel' would be: What if the advancing German forces *did* successfully invade Cairo in 1942, rather than being halted at the second battle of El Alamein? While the first story in *Making It Up* does roughly adhere to Gallagher's definition, it does not focus on the traditional

[99] Lively, *Making It Up*, p. 3.
[100] Ibid.
[101] Ibid., p. 4.
[102] Gallagher, *Telling It Like It Wasn't*, p. 16.

military (and masculine) concerns of counterfactual history. Instead it pursues an alternative ending to Lively's life, outlining a hypothetical scenario where her alter ego, Jean Leech, flees Egypt for South Africa along with her mother and nanny (in reality Lively left Egypt via Palestine before eventually travelling to Britain). In 'Mozambique Channel', the eight-year-old Jean dies before reaching her destination on the South African Cape. The story is therefore narrated from the perspective of Shirley, a fictional figure inspired by a combination of Lively's actual nanny and her memories of another nursemaid from Cairo. 'Mozambique Channel' breaks out of Lively's former life in the garden while reimagining her real memories. The result is an alternative view of a colonial childhood at the end of empire.

At the heart of 'Mozambique Channel' is Shirley's ambiguous relationship with white society. She remembers that, upon her first arrival in Egypt

> she'd been shocked by the beggars and the droves of children ... the women up to their elbows in muck ... the babies with flies crawling all over their eyes. How could people live like this? But they did, and after a while you got used to it. You seemed to be shut away on the other side of a glass screen, where things were done in the way that you knew, and out there was their world in which everything was otherwise, but it was none of your business.[103]

Although both Shirley and her employers abhor overt expressions of racism from the British community in Cairo, this passage reflects how they nevertheless accept the screened domesticity of colonial life. For Shirley, this involves locking herself within a comfortable existence supported by rampant social inequality and racial segregation. 'Their world' – that of the dispossessed Egyptian population – is carefully distinguished from 'our world', as Shirley's daily life is confined to the exclusive, central district of Zamalek, located on Gezira Island in the middle of the Nile River. As home to the fictional Leech family, Zamalek was, in reality, the neighbourhood of choice for many British families living in interwar Cairo (Lively's parents took the relatively unusual choice to *not* settle there). Shirley is encouraged to view the city – and especially its Egyptian inhabitants, like a visitor staring at a museum exhibit, echoing Fanon's diagnosis of 'the colonial world [as] a world cut in two'.[104] Rather than witnessing a dynamic society on the verge of decolonization, Shirley insists that the lives of agricultural labourers, street vendors and Egyptian housewives are nothing more than a static scene to

---

[103] Lively, *Making It Up*, p. 18.
[104] Fanon, *The Wretched of the Earth*, p. 29.

be collected, arranged and exhibited for a European imperial gaze. Rather than dwelling on her initial, sensory responses to heat, poverty and dirt ('the beggars … the droves … the muck') she tries to sever the causal linkages which connect her privileged life on Zamalek to the poverty of 'their world'. Restaging a classic European encounter with the Orient, Shirley's confined existence is predicated on the majority of the Egyptian population being confined to a separate sphere 'in which everything was otherwise'. But, as the photograph of four children and a donkey in *Oleander, Jacaranda* has already demonstrated, the boundaries between home – a life inside the garden – and the unfamiliar world of 'out there', are never stable in Lively's life writing.

'Mozambique Channel' reports the banal details of Shirley's life, including regular attempts to protect hers and Jean's bodies against the 'daily perils of dirt, disease, sun'.[105] Similar precautions against sunstroke, poisonous flora and disease are the mainstays of many colonial memoirs; Lessing remembers that, after her family arrived in Southern Rhodesia, her mother was afraid of 'snakes … scorpions … mosquitoes', dosing her children with quinine and wrapping them 'in tight binders that were supposed to prevent chills on the liver'.[106] Yet threaded through the mundane descriptions of imperilled white bodies in 'Mozambique Channel' is a carefully crafted vision of colonial malaise. Shirley tells herself that her own identity is assured – rephrasing a line from *Oleander, Jacaranda*, she states that 'one was English' – yet she struggles to remember her childhood home in Pinner, suburban London.[107] The distinctions between home and the unfamiliar begin to destabilize once she realizes that she 'couldn't remember England very well', that 'somehow a shutter had dropped down between that time and this, so that the norm was now heat, dust'.[108] Rather than becoming a dispassionate observer of Cairo-as-an-exhibition, Shirley has become trapped on the other side of the 'glass screen', a colonial subject in jeopardy of losing her national identity. As she attempts to confine herself and Jean from the potential dangers of Egypt, 'Mozambique Channel' suggests that this quarantine destabilizes their sense of Englishness. Their confinement is manifest in spatial, as well as psychological, terms, as their lives are largely limited to the island of Zamalek. This story is a counterfactual which rewrites Lively's earlier accounts of

---

[105] Lively, *Making It Up*, p. 10.
[106] Lessing, *Under My Skin*, pp. 70–1.
[107] In *Oleander, Jacaranda*, this declaration is uttered in more personal terms: 'We were English. I was English … so far as I was concerned England was a place a long way away which was nothing much to do with me, except in some mysterious and solemn way it was, and don't you forget about it.' Lively, *Oleander, Jacaranda*, p. 9.
[108] Lively, *Making It Up*, p. 10.

life on the 'incongruous island' of Bulaq Dakhrur.[109] Yet the narrative's relocation only further emphasizes *Oleander Jacaranda*'s central proposition: that colonial life itself is a kind of marooning. Both Lively and her counterfactual creations, eventually realize that this isolated, untenable existence can only partially obscure its close connections to the surrounding landscape.

Shirley's vague memories of England conjure up 'an unreal and unreachable place, much like the time that was unattainable: before the war'.[110] On her previous visits to Pinner, 'she had [even] begun to feel a bit strange with her family. Distanced'.[111] Shirley's familial bonds, her sense of national belonging and her personal memories are slackened by a perpetual present and a repeated sense of being out of time. The escalating list of negative prefixes – 'unreal', 'unreachable', 'unattainable' – become expressions of absence, a loss of self. But while she loses the accent which rooted her to a local community, Shirley is still unable to enter the upper-middle-class world of the Leeches. She is therefore stranded, caught in a doubly liminal position as both a white woman and a working-class employee of high colonial society. By reworking her own, boundaried upbringing through the perspective of a nanny (a woman who was, in reality, her only companion), Lively scrutinizes her colonial childhood anew. Far from being able to dispassionately gaze at an ordered exhibit of Cairo through a glass screen, Shirley is instead forced to grapple with her own reflection, becoming fundamentally displaced by her experience of white, colonial life.

Embedded in Lively's speculative life writing is a concern with both endings and the end of empire. Shirley is surrounded by indicators that the world she lives in is coming to a close. These include the ageing Thomas Cook travel posters she glimpses at the docks, which advertise the shipping of 'Polo Ponies, at the best rates' from Egypt to Britain.[112] Shirley knows that the age of colonial administrators (and their polo ponies) in the Middle East is coming to an end. Yet Lively's choice of Cape Town as an alternative destination for the fleeing Leech family is not only so that Japanese U-boats can provide the requisite narrative tension, and eventually cause Jean's death. Instead, the South African Cape offers them a safe haven of white minority rule.[113] After all, Shirley's fellow nannies

---

[109] Lively, *Oleander, Jacaranda*, p. 12.
[110] Lively, *Making It Up*, p. 11.
[111] Ibid.
[112] Ibid., p. 6.
[113] In 1942, the route to Cape Town down the Red Sea and into the Mozambique Channel was far more likely to result in an encounter with Japanese U-boats than Lively's real trip to Palestine. For details on the historical events that inspired this counterfactual tale, see Penelope Lively, 'The View from Elsewhere: Egypt', in *Discourses of Empire and Commonwealth*, ed. Alastair Niven and Sandra Robinson (Leiden: Brill Rodolpi, 2016), pp. 153–8.

note with relief that, in Cape Town, 'they don't let the natives' in to cinemas when white women are present.[114] Jean's mother can barely contain her excitement at the prospect of living in a city she perceives as being 'quite English really'.[115] In Cairo, despite living surrounded by the Nile, Shirley and Jean are confined to 'the house, Gezira Sporting Club … and the YMCA', reflecting the partitions of a city under British rule.[116] But Cape Town promises a more formalized system of segregation, a society where the racial logic of empire disciplined every detail of daily life, from familial relationships to the changing layout of the city. Shirley's fantasies of living in a developing apartheid state repositions Lively's memories of the end of empire in a broader geopolitical context. In Cairo, the age of polo ponies might be ending, but the self-governing colony of South Africa was implementing new laws in support of white supremacy during the 1940s, extending the reach of empire long into the twentieth century.

At the close of 'Mozambique Channel' Shirley sits with 'Jean's cold little body across her knees' and faces an uncertain future.[117] In the first vignette of *Making It Up*, Lively's counterfactual life never progresses after empire. She refuses to let her alter ego experience a time beyond decolonization, as Jean never escapes from her confined, colonial existence. Jean is one of several alternative selves in this collection who evoke Lively's memories of Egypt, but are killed before they leave Cairo. In the sixth story, 'Comet', a character called Penelope returns to the Middle East just when 'the Suez crisis was starting to rumble … anti-British feeling on the up'.[118] Against these clear indicators of imperial decline, Penelope (who was raised, like Lively, in Egypt) walks the streets of Cairo, visiting the familiar sights of the Gezira Sporting Club and Groppis.[119] However, she expresses a sense of unease, having imagined that this 'would be a sort of homecoming and it wasn't'.[120] Penelope's colonial childhood has left her stranded in time, unable to return to the past yet equally incapable of adapting to the present. Decades after Penelope is killed in a plane crash while departing Egypt in the mid-1950s, the remains of her British passport are found on a hillside. All

---

[114] Lively, *Making It Up*, p. 12.
[115] Ibid., p. 6.
[116] Ibid., pp. 11–12.
[117] Ibid., p. 43.
[118] Ibid., p. 196.
[119] Robert Gildea, and innumerable imperial historians, have noted that 'for both France and Britain, the Suez intervention [quickly known as the Suez Crisis] was a desperate attempt to shore up their empires'. The loss of Egypt as a strategic site for maintaining British imperial influence in the Middle East involved losing control of the Suez Canal, a vital route connecting Britain and its remaining colonies on the African continent. Robert Gildea, *Empires of the Mind: The Colonial Past and the Politics of the Present* (Cambridge: Cambridge University Press, 2019), p. 87.
[120] Lively, *Making It Up*, p. 182.

that remains is her formal signifier of British citizenship, the ghostly trace of an identifying photograph being concealed 'somewhere in this wodge of matter'.[121] It is important to state that the Egyptian settings of vignettes like 'Comet' and 'Mozambique Channel' are not an exercise in wish-fulfilment, where Lively returns to a lost Eden. Instead, these speculative life stories turn to the counterfactual to embrace 'history's unfinished projects'.[122] Empire, for Lively, is neither concluded nor finished. The untimely deaths of Jean and Penelope confirm that there is no life after colonial rule in these speculative life narratives.

By rewriting her own memories, Lively highlights that her colonial upbringing cannot be resolved with alternative outcomes (there are few happy or final endings to the vignettes in *Making It Up*). Indeed, this collection of speculative lives questions all endings, especially the end of empire. Through the 'temporal cartwheel' of the counterfactual, these stories blur the distinctions between colonial rule and its aftermath.[123] When the Leech family make for Cape Town, or Penelope boards her ill-fated flight out of Egypt, *Making It Up* extends the autobiographical 'double exposure' first developed in *Oleander, Jacaranda*. By making speculation a key component of her late style, Lively returns to what Fanon calls 'the settler's town', and works her way back into the shuttered heart of domestic, colonial life.[124] In so doing she is able to explore a world predicated on 'the fact of belonging to or not belonging to a given race', scrutinizing its dividing lines and interior frontiers from a new perspective.[125] The untaken roads of Lively's speculative life writing consequently lead not away from empire, or out of Egypt, but back into the thicket of white, English identity in an age of imperial decline. Her experiments with counterfactuals mark an important expansion of her life writing project, developing her abiding, autobiographical concerns with life in the aftermath of empire.

Conclusion: Wastelands and Willowherb

Oleander, Jacaranda ends with Lively's memories of exploring 'the bomb-flattened area around St Paul's [Cathedral]' in 1945, describing how the building 'rose from a wasteland of rubble, cropped walls and sunken lakes of willowherb'.[126]

---

[121] Ibid., p. 168.
[122] Gallagher, *Telling It Like It Wasn't*, p. 47.
[123] Prendergast, *Counterfactuals*, p. 13.
[124] Fanon, *The Wretched of the Earth*, p. 30.
[125] Ibid., p. 31.
[126] Lively, *Oleander, Jacaranda*, p. 178.

The city's Roman foundations had been exposed by German bombs, and the twelve-year-old Lively peered down into a strata of history usually concealed beneath the pavement. *Oleander, Jacaranda* is neither the first nor the last rehearsal of this pivotal memory, which is recorded in both Lively's first work of nonfiction – *The Presence of the Past* (1976) – and her most recent memoir *Life in the Garden*. Even her unpublished teenage diary dated 1951 and held at the Harry Ransom Center describes this scene, suggesting the remarkable threads of continuity which span Lively's writing career.[127] In *Oleander, Jacaranda* the image of St Paul's concludes both the visual and the textual narrative of the memoir; a historic image of the cathedral surrounded by rubble in 1941 closes the book's sequence of black-and-white photographs. The famous white, towering dome rises high in the background of the shot, while the foreground is a wasteland of splintered buildings and rubble. Dotted in the ruinous landscape are small, human figures as Royal Engineers traverse the bomb craters, attempting to clear the area. The cathedral is the obvious landmark in this image, as a symbol of Britain which emerged largely intact from the blitz. The caption notes that when Lively saw this landscape four years later, the debris may have been cleared 'and the willowherb had grown but the effect was much the same'.[128]

In each rendition of this memory, the image of ruins covered with willowherb marks the end of Lively's childhood.[129] The fast-growing plant (sometimes known as fireweed) flourishes in soil recently exposed to heat and was a familiar sight in Britain's bomb-damaged cities both during and immediately after the Second World War. What *Life in the Garden* calls 'the sea of purple [flowers] in every bomb site' might ostensibly symbolise both fiery destruction and verdant rebirth.[130] The flowers transformed the ruined streets into scenes 'of tranquil decay, like some ruined site of antiquity'.[131] Lively's repeated descriptions of these vivid, magenta fronds waving in the breeze might suggest that both she, and the British nation, were emerging triumphantly into a post-war era, ready to thrive in a radically altered landscape.

---

[127] Austin, Harry Ransom Center, MS Penelope Lively, 15.5.
[128] Lively, *Oleander, Jacaranda*, n.p.
[129] In *Reading the Ruins* (2011) Leo Mellor explains that many London bomb-sites were sites of interest for naturalists during the war years; by 1941 ruined buildings were 'luxuriant spaces where ruins and ashes were shaded by the energetic growth of leaves and flowers'. Willowherb/fireweed became the emblematic plant of this devastated landscape, and its distinctive pink flowers appear in both Elizabeth Bowen's and Rose Macaulay's blitz literature. Lively was one of many post-war writers to be entranced by the plant, whose bright colours and fast-growing qualities suggested a phoenix-like regeneration for London. Leo Mellor, *Reading the Ruins: Modernism, Bombsites and British Culture* (Cambridge: Cambridge University Press, 2011), p. 166.
[130] Lively, *Life in the Garden*, p. 124.
[131] Lively, *Oleander, Jacaranda*, p. 178.

However, both the photograph and the written description of St Paul's in *Oleander, Jacaranda* emphasises how the colonial past underpins Lively's present in Britain. The memoir recalls that she was, in 1945, a trespasser in the city who ignored the official signs of 'Danger! Keep out!', only to be halted by the startling discovery of a Roman bastion near to the cathedral:

> What did this mean? We had Romans down in Egypt. Had Romans, time was. I knew about Romans. They came from Rome and Italy and surged all over Egypt and Palestine … They had dropped their money everywhere. … So how could there be Romans, right up here, in England?[132]

The presence of these Roman remains reconfigures the coordinates of Lively's colonial education, which had taught her all about 'the finer moments of the [British] rise to pink glory' through recommended books such as *Our Island Story* (1905).[133] She 'knew' all about Romans from these textbooks, and by visiting various archaeological digs (where she witnessed ancient coins being unearthed from the Egyptian desert). After arriving in Britain, Lively was blindsided by the confusing social mores and the unwelcoming climate of her island home, which bore little resemblance to the idealized nation she had read about in Egypt. This encounter with the Roman ruins beneath St Paul's allows her to find common ground in the familiar histories of antiquity. But crucially the concealed Roman foundations also allow her to view 1940s Britain, which was then (still just) the centre of a global empire, in a wider network of imperial histories. The damaged streets of wartime London connect to a historical narrative leading back to the ancient world. This Roman bastion proved to Lively that not only were ancient peoples 'right up here, in England', but that Britain itself was once the colonial outpost of another empire, its inhabitants subject to a foreign imperial power.

It is no coincidence that this totemic memory is set in the City of London shortly after the blitz. As Robert Gildea explains, 'the [famous] photograph of the dome of St Paul's Cathedral rising above the smoke, published in the *Daily Mail* on 31 October 1940, came to symbolise Britain "standing alone" against Nazi Germany'.[134] However, this image also partially concealed Britain's 'imperial crisis' that was well underway during the early 1940s. The singular triumphant building, emblematic of an imperial nation, obscured the anti-colonial movements which were gathering apace across the British Empire,

---

[132] Ibid., p. 173.
[133] Ibid., p. 19.
[134] Gildea, *Empires of the Mind*, p. 53.

including in Egypt. Just as importantly, the myth of a solitary nation standing strong against its Nazi foe was a falsehood: Britain's reliance on troops from its dominions, colonies and allies demonstrates, as Gildea notes, that 'if it had stood alone, it would have crumbled'.[135]

The cathedral is key to understanding Lively's nuanced account of empire and its legacies in her life writing. Her repeated descriptions of St Paul's focus not on the single dome which towers high above the London skyline, but on what lies beneath it, on the layers of history exposed in its foundations. The Roman coins reveal an alternative, more varied story of multiple empires than the surface-level presentation of imperial grandeur. Texts like *Oleander, Jacaranda* and *Making It Up* appear to deliver emblems of colonial nostalgia, such as the enclaved white mansion, or the English colonial garden, but Lively subjects these to a double exposure. By excavating their multiple meanings she unsettles grand narratives of empire and imperial prowess. Her turn to speculation and counterfactuals is an extension of this subversive practice. The recollection of a London cathedral standing alone amongst the rubble, and her memories of living on an island of whiteness in Cairo are archetypal images of imperialism, both 'out there' in the colonies and 'at home' in Britain. Yet Lively repeatedly draws our attention to what lies beyond the boundaries of these narratives: the Egyptian landscapes and subjects just beyond the borders of Bulaq Dakhrur, or the strata of histories buried beneath street level. As readers, we are invited to peer at what lies behind or beyond these facades of imperial power.

When *Oleander, Jacaranda* closes with Lively gazing into London's foundations, she realizes that 'the patriotic rantings of *Our Island Story*' cannot account for the rich, complex landscape beneath her feet.[136] This is, perhaps, no surprise. Henrietta Elizabeth Marshall's bestselling children's book *Our Island Story* spans one thousand years of British history, while neatly sidestepping the violent, extractive politics of Britain's Empire. One particularly egregious episode describes Australia as an island 'inhabited only by scattered groups of natives', glossing the widespread massacres of Aboriginal people by implying that they conveniently disappeared after the arrival of European settlers.[137] Even as a child, the book's jingoistic national myths left Lively 'with a whisper of unease'.[138] Amidst the ruins of London, she realizes that nationalist histories – which supported the myth of a self-contained island, unmarked by its colonial

---

[135] Ibid.
[136] Lively, *Oleander, Jacaranda*, p. 179.
[137] Marshall, *Our Island Story*, p. 446.
[138] Lively, *Oleander, Jacaranda*, p. 18.

past – could not account for the complex, interwoven legacies of empire in Britain.

In 2010, six decades after Lively's revelation amongst the rubble, then British prime minister David Cameron proudly declared that *Our Island Story* had been his most treasured book as a child. Newspapers reported Cameron's claim that it had 'really captured my imagination and … nurtured my interest in the history of our great nation'.[139] During Lively's upbringing in the 1930s, this book was already anachronistic, representing a worldview that was 'not exactly up-to-date'.[140] Cameron's claim reveals how *Our Island Story* has been re-mobilized in a new century to service a broader, amnesiac account of Britain's colonial past. Such fantasies continue to view Britain as the undiminished centre of a global empire, attempting to paper the cracks in an increasingly strained national identity.[141] *Our Island Story* demonstrates why Lively's memories of empire raise a series of politically and culturally urgent inquiries, positioning her early life on an island of whiteness in a broader set of island stories. If, as Paul Gilroy so presciently argues, twenty-first-century Britain is unable 'to even face, never mind actually mourn' the end of empire 'and consequent loss of imperial prestige', then the dual vision of Lively's life writing encourages us to look closer at these entangled histories.[142] Returning to her years in Bulaq Dakhrur, she asks what it means to be at home in the colonial past, examining how the memories of this former dwelling place orientate her later habitations in London. While Lively's early critics viewed her writing as too sheltered or myopic – confined to the 'domestic proficiencies of English fiction' – these life narratives demonstrate how such interior worlds might continue to challenge the narratives of post-imperial Britain.[143]

---

[139] Andrew Hough, 'Revealed: David Cameron's Favourite Childhood Book Is *Our Island Story*', *The Telegraph*, 29 October 2010, https://www.telegraph.co.uk/culture/books/booknews/8094333/Revealed-David-Camerons-favourite-childhood-book-is-Our-Island-Story.html (accessed 27 January 2021).

[140] Lively, *Oleander, Jacaranda*, p. 101.

[141] It is no coincidence that Cameron's love of the 'world-beating' British history in *Our Island Story* was announced in October 2010. This complemented the education reforms proposed (and later implemented) by then-secretary of state for education Michael Gove, who delivered a speech at that year's Conservative Party conference entitled 'All pupils will learn our island story'. When Gove revealed his redesigned national curriculum in 2013, the history sections of this program were decried as 'depressingly narrow' and 'resolutely insular' by historian and Oxford professor David Priestland. Michael Gove, 'All Pupils Will Learn Our Island Story', *Conservative Party Speeches*, 5 October 2010, https://conservative-speeches.sayit.mysociety.org/speech/601441 (accessed 1 December 2022); David Priestland et al., 'Michael Gove's New Curriculum: What the Experts Say', *The Guardian*, 12 February 2012, https://www.theguardian.com/commentisfree/2013/feb/12/round-table-draft-national-curriculum (accessed 1 December 2022).

[142] Gilroy, *After Empire*, p. 98.

[143] Birch, 'Growing Up'.

2

J. G. Ballard's Colonial Uncanny: Settlements, Swimming Pools and Camps

The unhomely is a paradigmatic colonial and post-colonial condition.[1]
– Homi K. Bhabha

Nothing ever looks emptier than an empty swimming pool.[2]
– Raymond Chandler

Introduction: Shanghai's Bright Lights and Hard Pavements

Born in 1930 within the confines of Shanghai's International Settlement, James Ballard grew up in a Surrey-stockbroker-style house at 31a Amherst Avenue (Figure 2.1), living in an enclave that 'was not a British colony' but nevertheless a distinctly colonial space.[3] Inside the high walls of their compound, his family's suburban lives were supported by a host of servants, including the 'No. 1 boy', 'Nos. 1 and 2 Coolie', a cook, several 'amahs' and a Russian nanny. Ballard recalled how, during his early years,

---

[1] Homi K. Bhabha, *The Location of Culture* (Abingdon: Routledge, 2004), p. 13.
[2] Raymond Chandler, *The Long Goodbye* (New York: Ballantine Books, 1971), p. 104.
[3] Ballard, *Miracles of Life*, p. 4; Shanghai was one of the five Chinese cities to receive treaty port status in the 1842 Treaty of Nanjing, allowing British merchants to claim residence and set up trading partnerships. British residents of Shanghai were subject to their own, domestic laws even while they lived on Chinese soil. The result was a form of informal imperialism (amongst competing colonial powers) that began during the First Opium War and was dismantled following Japan's invasion of China during the Second World War. As Isabella Jackson notes, both the creation of a French Concession and the American presence in Shanghai reveals that, 'while the British were dominant economically and politically ... other colonial and transnational forces' shaped informal imperialism in China during this period. Isabella Jackson, *Shaping Modern Shanghai: Colonialism in China's Global City* (Cambridge: Cambridge University Press, 2018), p. 2.

Figure 2.1 The former Ballard family home at 31a Amherst Avenue, Shanghai, in 1985. ©Peter Brigg, reproduced with permission of Rick McGrath.

partying, cholera and smallpox somehow coexisted with a small English boy's excited trips in the family Buick to the country club swimming pool. [My] fierce earaches from the infected water were assuaged by unlimited Coca-Cola and ice cream, and the promise that the chauffeur would stop on the way back to Amherst Avenue to buy the latest American comics.[4]

Yet the glamorous world of white society in Shanghai was little more than a facade maintained through exclusive, bordered zones including chauffeured cars, private members' clubs and elite schools. From these locations Ballard both observed and was separated from the seething metropolis of urban life, cloistered in a privileged colonial world which was on the brink of collapse. In the series of texts now termed his 'life trilogy' – *Empire of the Sun*, *The Kindness of Women* and *Miracles of Life* – he records this upbringing through a blend of semi-fictionalized protagonists and first-person narrators.[5] When read together, these present an uneven and recursive autobiographical narrative plotting a route from his birth in China, his incarceration during the Second World War, his adult life in the English suburb of Shepperton and his eventual diagnosis of terminal cancer in 2006.

Ballard's inclusion in this book is principally because these life narratives all return to a colonial childhood – and an imperial city – which was marked by brutal contrasts. While the 'uniquely transnational form of colonial authority' in the International Settlement was different from British territories such as Singapore or Hong Kong, 'the hegemonic position of its settler community' was comparable to other colonial societies.[6] The inequalities of informal imperialism were illustrated by the British trucks that toured Ballard's neighbourhood each morning, removing the bodies of Chinese beggars who had died from starvation the night before. Watching their progress, the young boy quickly concluded that 'if Shanghai's neon lights were the world's brightest, its pavements were the hardest'.[7] To both Ballard and his contemporaries like J. G. Farrell, the city was 'a harsh world' that existed both in and 'outside the limits of British rule'.[8]

---

[4] Ballard, *Miracles of Life*, p. 5.
[5] Umberto Rossi, 'Mind Is the Battlefield: Reading Ballard's "Life Trilogy" as War Literature', in *J. G. Ballard: Contemporary Critical Perspectives*, ed. Jeannette Baxter (London: Continuum, 2008), pp. 66–78 (p. 66); Although his collected non-fiction is rarely included in this cohort of life narratives, Ballard's essays, collected in *A User's Guide to the New Millennium* (1996), also frequently returned to his memories of China.
[6] Jackson, *Shaping Modern Shanghai*, p. 250; Robert Bickers, *Britain in China: Community, Culture, and Colonialism 1900–1949* (Manchester: Manchester University Press, 1999), p. 68.
[7] J. G. Ballard, 'The End of My War', in *A User's Guide to the Millennium: Essays and Reviews* (London: Flamingo, 1997), pp. 283–94 (p. 287).
[8] J. G. Farrell, *The Singapore Grip* (London: Orion Books, 2010), p. 82.

Throughout his life writing trilogy, Ballard remembers living in close proximity to extreme poverty, while his family enjoyed 'race meetings at the Shanghai Racecourse ... and patriotic gatherings at the British Embassy on the Bund'.[9] Yet two years after the 1941 Japanese seizure of Shanghai, the Ballards were forced to enter Lunghua Civilian Assembly Centre, a forty-two-acre internment camp that housed two thousand Europeans and Americans until the end of the war. Like Lively's family in Cairo, the Ballards believed, during the early years of the conflict, that the Axis powers 'would be no match for the British Empire and the Royal Navy'.[10] This changed after the fall of Hong Kong (1941) and the surrender of Singapore (1942). In the psychological limbo of Lunghua, Ballard witnessed the adult community around him 'los[ing] faith in themselves' amidst the end of empire.[11] His autobiographical alter ego Jamie (the protagonist in *The Kindness of Women*) traces this inertia to an insecure, post-imperial identity; the camp's adults were too keen to impose 'a mythology of slogans, a parade of patriotic flags that sealed the past away forever, far from any searching eye'.[12] Like Janet Frame (discussed in Chapter 4), Ballard saw how new mythologies of British identity during the Second World War were mobilized to obscure the loss of imperial power. This chapter demonstrates that, by recording his childhood and internment, Ballard's life writing witnesses the decline of British imperialism through a series of enclosed domestic spaces, from his former family home in Shanghai to Lunghua camp. These texts track the end of empire through a series of increasingly unhomely dwelling places, developing what I term a colonial and later a post-imperial unheimlich. By repeatedly returning to the International Settlement and the camp, Ballard's life writing exposes how the memories of empire lodge in everyday life long after formal decolonization.

The dwelling places of Ballard's life writing, particularly those from his childhood in Shanghai, are fundamentally uncanny – evoking that 'class of the terrifying which leads back to something ... once very familiar'.[13] For Ballard, colonial life at the end of empire was a disturbing, unheimlich world. Throughout his life writing Shanghai is both an originary location which captures his imagination and a recurrent, unsettling home to which he cannot permanently return. For Freud, the uncanny denotes not just the unfamiliar, but a more specific transition in which the familiar turns upon its former owners. In

---

[9] Ballard, *Miracles of Life*, p. 8.
[10] Ballard, 'The End of My War', p. 289.
[11] J. G. Ballard, 'Memories of Internment', in *A User's Guide to the Millennium: Essays and Reviews* (London: Flamingo, 1997), pp. 251–2 (p. 251).
[12] J. G. Ballard, *The Kindness of Women* (London: Harper Perennial, 2008), p. 94.
[13] Freud, 'The Uncanny', p. 220.

a famous 1919 essay, he explains how this process is marked etymologically, in the sequence or slippage through which the heimlich, 'the idea of homelike … belonging to the house', also comes to mean that which is 'concealed, kept from sight'.[14] Eventually it meets with its apparent antonym, the unheimlich, becoming the 'eerie' and the 'uneasy'.[15] As Anthony Vidler notes, Freud's 'slow unfolding of homely into the unhomely' addressed a haunted, twentieth-century modernity through the language of domestic life.[16] If the uncanny disturbs our sense of home, then this interruption is expressed through the language of property and private dwellings. For Ballard, the banalities of ordinary life are marked (and marred) by the uncanny, and his unheimlich homes offer a crucial means for understanding the end of empire.

The uncanny is predicated on a lack of orientation, it results from 'something new, foreign, and hostile invading an old, familiar, customary world'.[17] Ballard's childhood homes were both literally and metaphorically invaded by the violent events of the Second World War. It is during this conflict that Jim in *Empire of the Sun*, Jamie in *The Kindness of Women* and the retrospective narrator of Ballard's autobiography, *Miracles of Life*, all witness the collapse of British colonial power. The legacies of war and imperial decline exert a particular pressure on these autobiographical narratives, which return to the familiar coordinates of Shanghai and Lunghua, only to become disorientated. On the one hand, this is symptomatic of the post-war and post-imperial perspective from which Ballard recorded all of his life narratives; from a contemporary vantage point, it is perhaps inevitable that the once-familiar colonial past becomes an unfamiliar memory. Indeed, Ken Gelder and Jane M. Jacobs have already suggested that the uncanny is 'consistent with postcoloniality as a contemporary moment' where subjects must 'remain within the structures of colonialism even as one is somehow located beyond or "after" them'.[18] Straddling this dual time both during and after empire, Ballard's life writing naturally attests to the double, uncanny realities of the postcolonial present.

But on the other hand, the unsettling dwelling places of Ballard's life writing suggest that the familiar confines of a colonial home – like his family mansion at 31a Amherst Avenue (Figure 2.2) – always anticipated historical decolonization

---

[14] Ibid., pp. 224–5.
[15] Ibid., p. 222.
[16] Anthony Vidler, *The Architectural Uncanny: Essays in the Modern Unhomely* (Cambridge, MA: MIT Press, 1992), p. 25.
[17] Ibid., p. 23.
[18] Ken Gelder and Jane M. Jacobs, *Uncanny Australia: Sacredness and Identity in the Postcolonial Nation* (Melbourne: Melbourne University Publishing, 1994), p. 24.

as an invading force. What Vidler calls that 'old familiar, customary world' of the colonial heimlich is, for Ballard, firmly connected to the disorientating qualities of the unheimlich.[19] In his autobiographical writing, late colonial life is troubled by a combination of the strange and the familiar. Despite their relatively similar post-war journeys by boat to the imperial metropole, no other author in this study experienced a transition comparable to Ballard's move from a wealthy suburban home to the deprivations of Lunghua camp. This sharp rupture, which marked the abrupt end of his colonial childhood, remains unique amongst his peers. Yet this chapter traces how the haunted spaces of the camp and the house at Amherst Avenue are more closely connected than they might first appear. In both of these enclaves colonial life is unsettled by a series of repetitions, marking both the final years of empire and the advent of formal decolonization.

Ballard's descriptions of his childhood homes suggest that white colonial life was defined by doubled figures and uncanny repetitions (not least in the blurred boundaries between Jim, Jamie and 'I'). In *Empire of the Sun*, for example, the well-fed inhabitants of Amherst Avenue live surrounded by luxurious possessions, yet the property's outer boundaries are marked by a beggar who holds only 'an empty Craven A [tobacco] tin which he shook at passers-by'.[20] If the uncanny indicates a slippage between that which 'belong[s] to the house' and that which is 'concealed, kept from sight', then Ballard's life writing draws our gaze always towards the dichotomies between visible/concealed, property/dispossession and familiar/unsettling.[21] As a result, the abandoned family home in *Empire of the Sun* – and the archetypal Ballardian image of the empty swimming pool – finds its uncanny double or repetition in Lunghua camp, described in both *The Kindness of Women* and *Miracles of Life*. The house and the camp exchange what Freud describes as 'that constant recurrence of the same thing', creating a series of mirrored spaces and selves.[22] When Ballard turns to domestic space, late colonial life emerges as a fragile world, existing always in anticipation of its demise. These cross-textual readings uncover how the familiar routines of race meetings on the Bund and afternoons at home are never as reassuring or as stable as they might appear. Instead uncanny dwellings emerge as the hallmark of Ballard's life writing, an autobiographical project which eventually turns the

---

[19] Vidler, *The Architectural Uncanny*, p. 23.
[20] Ballard, *Empire of the Sun*, p. 21.
[21] Freud, 'The Uncanny', p. 224.
[22] Ibid., p. 234.

interiors of his colonial childhood inside out, bearing witness to the end of empire through a series of unsettling and disassembled homes.

31a Amherst Avenue: Abandoned Homes and Empty Swimming Pools

In the opening chapters of *Empire of the Sun*, Jim Graham watches from a waterfront hotel window as the Japanese army arrive in Shanghai. He and his parents have temporarily relocated to the French Concession for safety, abandoning their home at Amherst Avenue. After watching the sinking of the *HMS Petrel* in the city's harbour, and losing his parents in the ensuing chaos, Jim realizes he is 'witnessing the complete humiliation of the Allied powers by the Empire of Japan', and follows the blood-soaked tramlines home to the International Settlement, hoping to find his family.[23] As this is the first full description of the house at Amherst Avenue, the interior of Jim's (which is also Ballard's) childhood home is revealed only after its abandonment, once it has been hastily emptied of its former inhabitants. Jim navigates the property's guarded defences by first scaling the high perimeter walls topped with broken glass, then clambering through the 'scythe-like blades' of the garbage disposal chute.[24] The house's fortifications may now appear like bared teeth, but 'the enclosed and silent garden' was previously 'more Jim's true home than the house itself'.[25] After the Japanese invasion the untended lawns where he once spent endless afternoons playing war games seem 'to grow darker [...] wilder' in the family's absence.[26] Without the attention of servants, the grounds become an unhomely and threatening space, transformed from a safe enclosure to a wilderness in a few days, and full of half-recognized details. As the discussions of *Oleander, Jacaranda* in Chapter 1 demonstrate, the garden is a key location in life writing at the end of empire. For both Lively and Ballard, English-styled green spaces can reveal the borders and precarities of colonial life. These life writers suggest that gardens, which were intended to act as a buffer between white households and the 'foreign landscape' beyond their boundaries, can only ever offer insecure perimeters.

[23] Ballard, *Empire of the Sun*, p. 52.
[24] Ibid., p. 62.
[25] Ibid., p. 61.
[26] Ibid.

Figure 2.2 The real entrance to 31a Amherst Avenue, Shanghai: The original front door, in 1985. ©Peter Brigg, reproduced with permission of Rick McGrath.

In *Empire of the Sun*, Jim crosses the thickening grass of the uncut lawn only to discover that the swimming pool where he spent many summer afternoons 'had fallen by almost three feet, draping a scummy curtain on the sides'.[27] A packet of Chinese cigarettes bob under the diving board and the frightening imprints of heavy army boots inside the house suggest his parents' hurried eviction from the property. Jim notes that the shoe prints of Japanese soldiers are disconcertingly focused around his mother's bedroom, where they are outlined in a spilled bottle of talcum powder. Unable to fully decipher this altered domestic world, he ponders whether the chaotic markings mean that his mother was teaching Japanese soldiers a foxtrot in her bedroom. In the aftermath of implied sexual violence, there is a marked contrast between 'his mother's bare feet whirling' and the 'clear images of heavy boots'.[28] These movements invert the usual harmony of a dance routine through the intrusion of militarized masculinity. As Vron Ware notes in *Beyond the Pale* (1992), 'real or imagined violence towards white women' across the British Empire was firmly associated 'with the most dangerous form of [anti-colonial] insubordination'.[29] Protecting the 'virtue' of wives and daughters was a common rationale for acts of colonial suppression, and the security of the white female body – vital for reproducing the next generation of settlers – was viewed as inseparable from the prosperity of the British Empire.[30] While Jim's interpretation of this scene remains ambiguous, the talcum-powder markings imply that his mother is an extension of the ransacked house. Inscribed on the bedroom floor is a colonial set piece (even a collective nightmare) which reminds the reader that 'white women provided a symbol of the most valuable property known to white man'.[31]

The colonial world of Jim's childhood is never described in *Empire of the Sun* as a functioning reality. It is instead presented as an empty set (and most likely a crime scene) whose main participants have recently departed, leaving behind only traces of their lives through footprints and discarded possessions. The

---

[27] Ibid., p. 62.
[28] Ibid.
[29] Vron Ware, *Beyond the Pale: White Women, Racism, and History* (London: Verso, 1992), p. 39.
[30] Ware cites the stories of General Wheeler's murdered daughters, which circulated after the Indian Rebellion of 1857, as illustrative of 'the dynamics of colonial repression in which the Englishwoman symbolised all that was most dear in British civilisation'. In more literary terms, when Lessing depicts the killing of Mary Turner at the hands of her Black servant, Moses, in *The Grass Is Singing* (1950), she traces the unease this crime causes amongst the settler community, who feel that 'their livelihood, their wives and families, their way of living, [are] at stake' following Mary's death. In both instances the violated white female body provides both a rationale for colonial vengeance *and* a discomforting reminder of settler society's fragility. Ware, *Beyond the Pale*, p. 40; Doris Lessing, *The Grass Is Singing* (Oxford: Heinemann, 1973), p. 12.
[31] Ware, *Beyond the Pale*, p. 38.

abandoned house offers both pleasure and peril for Jim, who rides his bicycle gleefully through the empty rooms of formal furniture – 'something he had always longed to do' – yet remains uneasy in a property which appears to be 'withdrawing from him'.[32] Jim eventually pauses in his mother's bedroom

> Facing the star-like image of himself that radiated from the centre of the mirror. A heavy object had been driven into the full-length glass, and pieces of himself seemed to fly across the room, scattered through the empty house. He fell asleep at the foot of his mother's bed ... below this jewelled icon of a small exploding boy.[33]

These multiple and partial reflections are an apt entry point for the hall of mirrors or *mise en abyme* of Ballard's life writing. Jim Graham is one of many alter egos who parade through the multiple renderings of his Shanghai childhood. For Andrzej Gasiorek, this scene establishes *Empire of the Sun* as a quest narrative in which Jim 'sets about re-assembling himself out of the broken shards of his pre-war identity'.[34] Yet I suggest that Jim cannot reform his shattered self, nor can he return to the colonial world of his pre-war life. Instead, the exploding boy in *Empire of the Sun* marks a key transition, the reflective surface acting as a threshold or portal through which Jim steps from the enclosed world of his childhood into the multiple possibilities of his post-imperial, adult existence.[35] The abandoned rooms and increasingly unkempt garden suggest that white life in Amherst Avenue – and across the former British Empire more broadly – was only ever a front, one guarded by heavily fortified perimeters and requiring constant maintenance by gardeners and other domestic staff. By refusing to show Jim comfortably at home in this setting, *Empire of the Sun* depicts colonial life as an illusion, a hall of mirrors which is now shattered. This is reflected in the rapid degradation of the house and its grounds; within a few days the food in the large kitchen begins to rot, the garden is overgrown and the swimming pool outside quietly secretes its liquid contexts.

---

[32] Ballard, *Empire of the Sun*, p. 66.
[33] Ibid., p. 63.
[34] Andrzej Gasiorek, *J. G. Ballard* (Manchester: Manchester University Press, 2005), p. 146.
[35] This scene echoes the beginning of Ballard's earlier novel *Concrete Island* (1974) in which the shattered windscreen of Robert Maitland's car studs his clothes with 'fragments like a suit of lights'. Like Maitland, Jim experiences an event (the home invasion) whose violence shatters the reflective surface of his established world and offers him a doorway into another dimension or existence altogether. As Jim appears 'star-like' after his experiences, mirroring Maitland's 'suit of lights', both of these scenes indicate the infamous allure of violence in Ballard's oeuvre, which often appears as transcendent, even celestial. My thanks to Dominic Davies for pointing out the correlations between these two scenes. J. G. Ballard, *Concrete Island* (New York: Farrar, Straus and Giroux, 1974), p. 7.

If Jim's return to Amherst Avenue witnesses the aftermath of a violent home invasion, this extraordinary event rearranges the interior world of his childhood and renders it sinister. However, this upturned scene also captures an imperial domesticity that is permanently interrupted at the end of empire, a microcosmic view of English colonial culture during its dismantlement. In her study of white colonial life in Asia, Ann Laura Stoler reads imperial homes as 'interior frontiers', postulating that intimate, private spaces across former European empires functioned as charged public domains.[36] For Stoler, 'a cordon sanitaire surrounded European enclaves, was wrapped around mind and body, around each European man and his home'.[37] Here domestic space was not only used to maintain imperial power, but it was enclosed by boundary markers designed to maintain a quarantined, white colonial identity. The high walls of 31a Amherst Avenue, topped with broken glass, suggest how literal this cordon sanitaire could be. But Jim's altered perspective of his surroundings – in which the familiar becomes disconcerting, even unsettling – also reveals how the barriers of his white, imperial childhood, once 'wrapped around [his] mind and body', have been breached and their defences overcome.

From the beginning of *Empire of the Sun*, Jim fantasizes about enjoying an 'empty' home, imagining himself as ruling the roost while his parents are out. He qualifies this by noting that of course 'the nine Chinese servants would be there [in the house] but in Jim's mind, and in those of the other British children, they remained as passive and unseeing as the furniture'.[38] Jim's refusal to view the family's employees as fellow inhabitants reveals how the house at Amherst Avenue functions as an interior frontier of empire. But contrary to the shared beliefs of Shanghai's British children, servants *were* present within their homes, and are frequently visible at the edges of the novel. When Jim first returns after the sinking of the *Petrel*, what strikes him is the silence of the house: 'There was no sound of the amahs arguing over the laundry vat in the servants' quarters, or the clip-clip of the gardener trimming the lawn.'[39] The noisy labour carried out on the spatial fringes of the property (in the servants' laundry room, or in the garden) defines Jim's colonial childhood. The stark absence of this background work reveals how his boundaried, white world was supported always by the labour of so-called racial others. If late colonial life is a hall of mirrors, reflecting an endlessly repeating image of comfortable prosperity, its smooth surface has

[36] Stoler, *Carnal Knowledge and Imperial Power*, p. 80.
[37] Ibid., p. 77.
[38] Ballard, *Empire of the Sun*, p. 16.
[39] Ibid., p. 60.

been broken by the onset of war and the decline of British imperial power across Asia. Jim experiences the consequences of this rupture first-hand when he receives a violent, stinging slap from an unnamed 'amah' while looking for his parents. Clutching his stinging face, Jim suspects that the amahs 'were paying him back' for something that he, or his community 'had done to them'.[40] This exchange forces him to interrogate his belief in the passivity of Chinese servants, suggesting that the family's employees have seen and remembered more than he initially realized. As an act which continues the unsettling disruptions of the abandoned home, the amah's slap issues a visceral challenge to the logic of Jim's colonial existence. If, as Stoler suggests, European empires arranged domestic space to represent 'the racial cleavages between "us" and "them"', then the interior frontiers of Jim's childhood home are fatally undone in these early scenes.[41]

For Freud, the uncanny marks a revelatory process where 'everything that ought to have remained … secret and hidden… has come to light'.[42] In Jim's temporary return to a house which now unnerves him, the contradictions of his quarantined white life are uncovered. Jim is never depicted as comfortably at home in Amherst Avenue: *Empire of the Sun* explores the internal details of his colonial childhood *only once* they become 'odd and unsettling' to him.[43] As a result, the distinctions between his family inside the house, their 'unseeing' servants living on the property's outer limits and the beggars rattling their tobacco tins on the pavement outside, have been unequivocally challenged. Indeed, as the footprints in his mother's bedroom suggest, the dwelling place which previously sheltered them from the city has now become a perilous space. While the garden turns back into wilderness, and Jim becomes increasingly hungry across his four days 'at home', the tenuous colonial order of the International Settlement is overthrown. His frustrated attempt to return develops a distinctive form of colonial uncanny in *Empire of the Sun*; by scrutinizing the fundamental anxieties and inconsistencies of white colonial life, Ballard extends what Freud describes as 'that class of the frightening which leads back to what is … long familiar'.[44] As a result, Amherst Avenue can be neither a secure nor a homely location in his first autobiographical novel. Instead it stands both in and for the ruins of empire, a half-disassembled replica of a hallucinatory imperial power.

[40] Ibid., p. 68.
[41] Stoler, *Carnal Knowledge and Imperial Power*, p. 77.
[42] Freud, 'The Uncanny', p. 224.
[43] Ballard, *Empire of the Sun*, p. 66.
[44] Freud, 'The Uncanny', p. 220.

But it is the site of the drained swimming pool in the garden which instils an archetypal Freudian vision of 'dread and horror' and provides a disturbing epicentre to the scene of Jim's return.⁴⁵ In an autobiographical aside to his 1919 essay, Freud explains the uncanny is partly manifest in the compulsion to repeat, citing his own experiences of being lost in 'a provincial town in Italy' where he finds himself returning, over and over, to the same neighbourhood of 'painted women'.⁴⁶ From his supposedly involuntary journeys back 'to one and the same spot', Freud connects the uncanny to the disorientating idea of the double, represented in those recurrent similarities (or locations) from which he could not escape.⁴⁷ There are numerous sites which recur across Ballard's oeuvre, including derelict shopping malls, abandoned hotels and crashed cars. Roger Luckhurst describes these as part of a distinctive 'textual signature' which is 'immediately recognisable' to the reader.⁴⁸ Ballard himself claimed that such near-obsessive fictional returns were an 'attempt to invert and reverse the commonplace'.⁴⁹ However, none symbolize the ideal of 'the Ballardian' quite like that of the drained swimming pool, a motif which first appears in his 1960 short story, 'The Voices of Time', and recurs throughout his writing.⁵⁰ In *High-Rise* (1975), the dropping water levels of a community pool chart one apartment building's social collapse, and the novel concludes with the drained tank transformed into a mass grave, filled with 'skulls, bones, and dismembered limbs'.⁵¹ During the final decade of his career Ballard was still plumbing these exposed depths, with *Cocaine Nights* (1997) describing an empty pool as 'a sunken altar' in the neo-colonial setting of the Estrella de Mar resort.⁵² As Edward Dodson notes, this text 'envisions expatriate life on the Costa del Sol as an intra-European form of neocolonialism', satirically depicting late-twentieth-century English culture – both at home and abroad – as entangled

---

⁴⁵ Ibid., p. 219.
⁴⁶ Ibid., p. 237.
⁴⁷ Ibid.
⁴⁸ Roger Luckhurst, *'The Angle between Two Walls': The Fiction of J. G. Ballard* (Liverpool: Liverpool University Press, 1997), p. 168.
⁴⁹ Thomas Frick and J. G. Ballard, 'The Art of Fiction', in *Extreme Metaphors: Interviews with J. G. Ballard, 1967–2008*, ed. Simon Sellers and Dan O'Hara (London: Fourth Estate, 2012), pp. 181–99 (p. 184).
⁵⁰ Innumerable readers and critics have suggested that 'the most iconic of Ballardian images' is the swimming pool. By tracing the exact origins of this motif, Rowland Wymer notes that Ballard's short story 'The Voices of Time' 'marks the first appearance of a number of his favourite images' including the drained pool. Rossi, 'Mind is the Battlefield', p. 73; Rowland Wymer, 'Ballard's Story of O: "The Voices of Time" and the Quest for (Non)Identity', in *J. G. Ballard: Visions and Revisions*, ed. Jeannette Baxter and Rowland Wyler (Basingstoke: Palgrave Macmillan, 2012), pp. 19–34 (p. 19).
⁵¹ J. G. Ballard, *High-Rise* (London: Fourth Estate, 2016), p. 243.
⁵² J. G. Ballard, *Cocaine Nights* (London: Flamingo, 1997), p. 178.

in the legacies of empire.[53] The empty tank in *Empire of the Sun* therefore belongs to this broader network of signs. For Ballard, the pool is a recurring site symbolizing both transience and loss, a void exposing the ruins of British imperial power, and a stark (even brash) psychoanalytic warning regarding the dangers of uncovered, subterranean depths.

Miracles of Life traces the biographical origins of this distinctive image to wartime Shanghai; Ballard remembers living in a temporary rented property inside the French Concession where an empty tank occupied 'the garden like a mysterious empty presence'.[54] Soon it became possible to identify other abandoned homes by their similarly vacant swimming pools (unlike the Ballards, many of Shanghai's European residents fled to other British colonies and dominions ahead of the advancing Japanese army). Ballard notes that, in retrospect, these contained 'the obvious symbolism that British power was ebbing away' despite 'faith in the British Empire [being] at its jingoistic height'.[55] While Freud found himself circling back to an insalubrious Italian street corner, Ballard's interest in the dry pool returns to the site of British imperial decline. David Ian Paddy rightly cautions against any all-encompassing explanation for the drained tanks that reappear throughout Ballard's oeuvre, yet in *Empire of the Sun*, Jim's encounter with the empty pool interrupts the commonplace of his Shanghai childhood.[56] Once he enters this subterranean space, the certainty of British imperial identity is revealed to be nothing more than a hollow, disconcerting absence.

During Jim's brief stay in the house and gardens, only 'the water level almost imperceptibly falling in the swimming-pool' marks the passing days.[57] Inside, a layer of dust over the furnishings creates an illusion that 'time had stopped', and that his childhood home has become petrified.[58] But outside, in the garden, the days are marked by the increasing exposure of the pool's tiled depths. Feeling curious, Jim jumps into the shallow end, cuts his knee on the tiles and begins to explore:

---

[53] Edward Dodson, 'Postimperial Englishness in the Contemporary White Canon', p. 58.
[54] Ballard, *Miracles of Life*, p. 23.
[55] Ibid.
[56] Paddy rightly states that Ballard's offer of 'the drained pool as "obvious symbolism" of British imperial decline is enticing ... but the obvious should be met with caution'. While the empty pool has a specific function in Ballard's life writing, Paddy questions whether this repeated, fictional motif has always indicated back to a singular, biographical origin in his wider oeuvre. – David Ian Paddy, 'Empires of the Mind: Autobiography and Anti-Imperialism in the Work of J. G. Ballard', in *J. G. Ballard: Visions and Revisions*, ed. Jeannette Baxter and Rowland Wymer (London: Continuum, 2012), pp. 179–97 (p. 186).
[57] Ballard, *Empire of the Sun*, p. 65.
[58] Ibid., p. 64.

Around the brass vent at the deep end lay a small museum of past summers – a pair of his mother's sunglasses, Vera's hair clip, a wine glass, and an English half-crown which his father had thrown into the pool for him. ... Jim pocketed the coin and peered up at the damp walls. There was something sinister about a drained swimming pool, and he tried to imagine what purpose it could have if it were not filled with water. It reminded him of the concrete bunkers in Tsingtao, and the bloody handprints of the maddened German gunners on the caisson walls. Perhaps murder was about to be committed in all the swimming pools of Shanghai, and their walls were tiled so that the blood could be washed away.[59]

In this scene each of the key adults in Jim's Shanghai childhood (mother, father and nanny) leave a totemic object for him to discover in the pool's deepest recess, which he views as a revealed exhibit. These items – sunglasses, hair clip, half-crown – are redolent of summer evenings at home, indicating pleasure and easy living. Yet like T. S. Eliot's 'testimony of summer nights' (the empty bottles and forgotten handkerchiefs abandoned beside a riverbank in *The Waste Land*), Ballard's found objects suggest that the good times have long passed.[60] The accessories and loose change that Jim sees in the pool are now rearranged in an empty space which he identifies as sinister. Only the English half-crown offers any utility value (and indeed, this is the sole object that Jim takes on his journey, only to be later pickpocketed). His fear of the drained tank initially stems from its gaping absence, which appears like a grave. This location emphasizes that, as his own colonial childhood comes to an end, Jim cannot join and replicate the luxurious world of his parents on the surface. Instead the empty pool fulfils a similar function to its twin, the smashed mirror; it is a portal through which Jim enters another dimension, an alternative, not-quite underwater world where the coordinates of his old life appear as a distorted reflection, matching the 'star-like image' of a fractured boy inside the house.[61] As the cavernous sides of the tank loom high above, Jim's new perspective transforms the once-familiar remnants of his colonial childhood into an unfamiliar, disconcerting future.

---

[59] Ibid., p. 66.
[60] T. S. Eliot, 'The Waste Land', in *Selected Poems* (London: Faber and Faber, 2002), pp. 51–68 (p. 58).
[61] While this reading is specific to the colonial context of *Empire of the Sun*, I suggest that the upside world reached through a portal is one of Ballard's principle, if unrecognized, textual signatures. Whether his novels are set in the London commuter belt, or in the fantastical rice paddies of a 'drowned world', they frequently offer distorted reflections of mundane realities. Entry into these realms often takes place through a reflective surface. From the dead dog which sends ripples across a communal pool in *High Rise*, to Robert Maitland's smashed windscreen in *Concrete Island*, fractured surfaces are thresholds in Ballard's novels. When characters step across them, the violent realities they encounter in these new worlds are as terrifying as they are recognizable.

Yet there is a further twist: in the exposed depths of the pool, the unsettling private exhibition of Jim's former life is transformed and fused to the public histories of the First World War. His association with 'concrete bunkers' remembers the siege of Tsingtao, a bloody 1914 clash between Japanese-British forces and a German garrison, just north of Shanghai in modern Qingdao.[62] The smear of blood left by Jim's grazed knee finds its uncanny echo in the handprints of the maddened German gunners. In the pool, histories of violence repeat and are layered one atop the other, with the Second World War evoking the First. Through this palimpsestual space, the swimming pool becomes a bunker and potentially – in Jim's vivid imagination – a slaughterhouse. It is both the container of previous conflicts and the site of future massacres, where all signs of the past, present and future bloodshed can be sluiced away.

In response to Freud's formulation of the uncanny, Homi K. Bhabha describes how 'the intimate recesses of domestic space [can] become sites for history's most intricate invasions', concluding that 'the unhomely is the shock of recognition of the world-in-the-home, and the home-in-the-world'.[63] When Jim cuts his knee while entering the empty pool, this mark leaves a genealogy on the tiled surface, connecting him to both the bloodied German handprints in 1914 and to the footprints left by his mother in the talcum powder upstairs. These bodily markings fuse public histories to private memories, creating a record of violence (the death of the German gunners, his mother's implied assault) that could be quickly erased, washed down the pool's brass vent.[64] As the vital coordinates of his childhood home are invaded by these unsettling global events, he is left disorientated and vulnerable. Yet as Bhabha suggests, when such domestic boundaries are breached and 'the private and public become part of one another', the unhomely ensures that 'another world becomes visible'.[65] Jim returns to the International Settlement only to discover a series of banal, everyday objects – the mirror, the hair clip, the wine glass – which are rearranged into an unfamiliar configuration. They subsequently appear to turn on their former owners. To use Bhabha's phrase, when Jim encounters the unhomely in this submerged tank,

---

[62] *Miracles of Life* recalls Ballard's summer holidays in Tsingtao, 'a pretty, almost Riviera-style beach resort' which had been a naval base during the First World War. During his childhood tours of the abandoned German forts, 'the Chinese guides were very proud of the bloody handprints which they claimed were those of the German gunners driven mad by the British bombardment'. Ballard, *Miracles of Life*, p. 43.

[63] Homi K. Bhabha, 'The World and the Home', *Social Text*, 31 (1992): 141–53 (p. 141).

[64] In Steven Spielberg's 1987 adaptation of *Empire of the Sun*, Jim returns home to Amherst Avenue and witnesses the talcum powder footprints left by his mother and the Japanese soldiers blown away in an ominous breeze.

[65] Bhabha, 'The World and the Home', p. 141.

another world is revealed both behind and beyond Amherst Avenue. Deep inside his former home, the violent histories of imperial Shanghai emerge. If Jim's return to the property is marked by a distinctive form of the unheimlich, then Ballard's descriptions of an abandoned house and its empty swimming pool narrate the end of empire *and* reveal that colonial life itself is a temporary, unsettling illusion. Jim's descent down into the damp interior of the tank suggests how the end of British colonial power literally comes home in *Empire of the Sun*.

In the latter half of the novel Jim is interned in Lunghua only to leave the camp as part of a Japanese-led evacuation in early August 1945. Walking at the front of an exhausted column of internees, he trudges towards the docklands of Nantao through 'a landscape of hallucination'.[66] Having been imprisoned for over two years, the once-distant buildings of Shanghai appear to Jim 'like a mirage' rising from the watery landscape of paddy fields and canals.[67] Those who survive the punishing journey eventually reach a dilapidated stadium built by Madame Chiang as part of a failed 1930s Olympic Games bid, now repurposed as a storage facility for Japanese troops and 'used as an open-air warehouse'.[68] The heavily fortified perimeter of the complex, surrounded by 'damaged army vehicles parked in neat rows', implicitly evokes the International Settlement, which was encircled by the Japanese army during the early 1940s and hemmed in by borders of barbed wire and checkpoints.[69] Inside this bizarre recreation of the city's British enclave, Jim and the remaining survivors enter an uncanny space where the familiar artificial trappings of their former lives are made strange. As Mr Maxted (a former friend from Shanghai) lies dying on the stadium floor, Jim realizes that the arena is filled with

> [D]ozens of black-wood cabinets and mahogany tables and hundreds of dining-room chairs [that] were packed together as if in the loft of a furniture depository. Bedsteads and wardrobes, refrigerators and air-conditioning units were stacked above each other, rising in a slope towards the sky.[70]

Gazing at American cars similar to those his parents used to cruise around the city, Jim looks for his family's Packard and wonders where the chauffeurs were, who 'should have been waiting … as they always did outside the country club'.[71] The luxuries of life at Amherst Avenue are multiplied in this cavernous

---

[66] Ballard, *Empire of the Sun*, p. 242.
[67] Ibid., p. 244.
[68] Ibid., p. 262.
[69] Ibid.
[70] Ibid.
[71] Ibid.

display; the tiered stands of the stadium resemble a department store, with wares tantalizingly displayed in order to tempt a sale. However, the produce is clearly spoiled: 'rolls of Persian and Turkish carpets, hastily wrapped in tarpaulins, lay on the concrete steps, water dripping through them as if from a pile of rotting pipes'.[72] Inside this inversion of the settlement, there are no customers to bid for the ruined goods, nor are any drivers waiting to whisk the dead and dying back to their former existence at the country club. Instead these luxurious commodities resemble crumbling infrastructure (evoking water or sewage pipes) which underscore the end of colonial life.

The interiors of Jim's childhood home are turned inside out in this scene. The crowded tiers of the galleries, and the dead bodies which lie between rusting bedsteads, confirm that there is no future among such remnants of the imperial past. These material goods, once indicators of prosperity and security, are of little comfort or use to those dying on the stadium floor. Vidler explains that, for Freud, the unhomely was 'more than a simple sense of not belonging, it was the fundamental propensity of the familiar to turn on its owners'.[73] Jim wishes that many of the ailing prisoners from Lunghua would 'die, surrounded by their rotting carpets and cocktail cabinets'.[74] Yet even if they are not *directly killed by* the material excesses of their former lives, the carpets and cocktail cabinets are implied co-conspirators in their deaths (they uncannily, to use Vidler's phrase, 'turn on their former owners').[75] In the stadium Jim witnesses the end of empire. As owners perish before their possessions, the private world of Amherst Avenue *and* the public age of British imperialism – the collective 'lives of the colonial British' – stutters to an end.[76] If interior frontiers across European colonies functioned, according to Stoler, as indictors of 'respectability, domesticity and a carefully segregated use of space', then the intimate attachments between individuals and their possessions are undone in the stadium.[77] If Freud's original reflections on the unhomely developed out of 'the no man's land between the trenches or the field of ruins left after bombardment' during the First World War, then Ballard's colonial uncanny emerges at a later historical moment: the collapse of British imperial power.[78] Yet as we will see, the abandoned house at Amherst Avenue, the empty pool, and the crowded tiers of the Olympic stadium

---

[72] Ibid.
[73] Vidler, *The Architectural Uncanny*, p. 7.
[74] Ballard, *Empire of the Sun*, p. 266.
[75] Vidler, *The Architectural Uncanny*, p. 7.
[76] Ballard, *Empire of the Sun*, p. 267.
[77] Stoler, *Carnal Knowledge and Imperial Power*, p. 77.
[78] Vidler, *The Architectural Uncanny*, p. 7.

do not mark the end of unhomely dwelling places in Ballard's life writing. Instead, the interiors of his childhood home in the Settlement find their uncanny, recurrent double – and their logical conclusion – in the site of Lunghua camp.

Lunghua Camp: *The Kindness of Women* and *Miracles of Life*

Empire of the Sun had been available in Britain's bookstores for just four weeks when the first letters from readers arrived at Ballard's home in Shepperton. Many were from men and women who had also been imprisoned in Japanese-run camps during the war. While some former internees expressed admiration for how Ballard captured the enclosed world of Lunghua, others picked up their pens in outrage, contradicting the novel's insistence that low morale, British apathy and the threat of violence defined daily life. They viewed Jim's confession that 'the years in Lunghua' had not given him 'a high opinion of the British' as tantamount to treason.[79] One incensed missive demanded that he remove the term 'autobiographical' from the book's cover altogether.[80] Another from a Dr Ransom (a fellow inmate of Lunghua and perhaps the inspiration for the fictional Dr Ransome) accused him of outright lies. The real doctor angrily protested that – contrary to Ballard's descriptions of malaria and malaise – many British inhabitants worked hard to make the camp sanitary and safe.[81] These complaints demonstrate how the fantasy of the white cordon sanitaire, which Stoler identifies as crucial to colonial rule, extended far beyond the International Settlement.

While Lunghua was home to various Dutch, Belgian and American citizens, the controversies surrounding the camp's representation in *Empire of the Sun* largely centred on its descriptions of the camp's British community. Lunghua has been broadly read by Ballard scholars as 'the traumatic kernel for the alienation, violence, dehumanisation and psychological terror that flares up again and again in his fiction'.[82] If the term 'Ballardian' evokes a self-mythologizing corpus, filled with empty pools, abandoned airfields, crashed cars and urban dystopias, then the camp occupies a central position in this complex web.[83] *Miracles of*

---

[79] Ballard, *Empire of the Sun*, p. 168.
[80] British Library, Add MS 88938/2/1/6.
[81] Ibid.
[82] D. Harlan Wilson, *J. G. Ballard* (Urbana: University of Illinois Press, 2017), p. 18.
[83] The editors of the *Collins English Dictionary* installed the term 'Ballardian' to denote anything 'resembling or suggestive of the conditions described in Ballard's novels and stories, especially dystopian modernity, bleak man-made landscapes, and the psychological effects of technological, social or environmental developments'. – 'Ballardian' in *The Collins English Dictionary* [online]

Life describes Ballard's transition from the International Settlement to Lunghua as the beginning of a life-long suspicion 'that reality itself was a stage set that could be dismantled at any moment'.[84] In the camp he discovered that global empires and the gleaming edifices of modernity 'could be swept aside' with little notice, swiftly relegated 'into the debris of the past'.[85] Yet during his first return journey in the 1990s – accompanied by a BBC film crew – Ballard stood in his former room in G-block and announced that 'this was where I was happiest and most at home, despite … living under the threat of an early death'.[86] During his internment Ballard was relatively free from social and familial ties, roaming the camp's fortified edges, admiring the Japanese guards' kendo armour and creating vegetable gardens with his father. This all came to an end during the second week of August 1945 (following the bombing of Hiroshima and Nagasaki), when Lunghua's inmates awoke 'to find that the Japanese guards had disappeared during the night'.[87]

In *The Kindness of Women*, Jamie emerges from the camp, returns to Shanghai and is shocked to discover that life had 'resumed without a pause, as if the war had never occurred'.[88] In reality, several months after their release, Ballard, his mother and his sister boarded the *SS Arawa*, arriving in Britain during early 1946. When Jim steps aboard the ship in *Empire of the Sun*, he claims to be 'setting out for a small, strange country on the other side of the world that he had never visited, but that was nominally "home" '.[89] This departure comes with the caveat that 'only part of his mind would leave Shanghai'.[90] If the bordered zones of the camp and the settlement are the defining coordinates in Ballard's life writing trilogy, then throughout these life narratives 'Jim', 'Jamie' or the autobiographical 'I' moves from one boundaried world to another. He lives in the sealed world of Amherst Avenue and the International Settlement, learns to survive in the camp and is later transplanted to post-war England, an unfamiliar home from which he will always feel estranged.[91]

---

https://www.collinsdictionary.com/dictionary/english/ballardian#:~:text=(b%C3%A6l%CB%88%C9%91%CB%90d%C9%AA%C9%99n%20),technological%2C%20social%2C%20or%20environmental%20developments (accessed 3 May 2023).

[84] Ballard, *Miracles of Life*, p. 58.
[85] Ibid.
[86] Ballard, 'The End of My War', p. 294.
[87] Ibid., p. 283.
[88] Ballard, *The Kindness of Women*, p. 65.
[89] Ballard, *Empire of the Sun*, p. 351.
[90] Ibid.
[91] By his own admission, these early experiences led Ballard to identify 'as a lifelong outsider', scrutinizing the peculiarities of post-imperial Britain from his suburban home in Shepperton. Ballard, *Miracles of Life*, p. 127.

Despite Ballard's insistently positive recollections of his war years, life at Lunghua was harsh and undoubtedly marked by deprivations.[92] Only eight miles from their former home on Amherst Avenue, Ballard lived with his parents and sister inside a single 45-square-foot room in G-block, within a complex of poorly constructed dormitories, assembly halls, kitchens and bathrooms.[93] Residents made signs naming 'the drinking-water stations that boiled our water [as] "Waterloo" and "Bubbling Well Road"' imaginatively connecting the great imperial metropolises of London and Shanghai (see Figure 2.3).[94] In *The Kindness of Women* Jamie describes 'the hunger reveries into which I often slipped', depicting a closed world where 'small favours were the secret currency' used to mitigate the daily hardships.[95] Throughout *Empire of the Sun* Jim, too, is frequently 'light-headed with hunger', forcing himself to eat the weevils in his daily ration (six spoons of cracked wheat), in a desperate attempt to obtain extra protein.[96] Reading these descriptions alongside official reports from Lunghua, held in the British Library's archives confirms that, by 1944, starvation seemed possible to many of the camp's inmates. One minuted conversation between internees, including Ballard's own father and the Commandant Tomohiko Hayashi, reports how conditions were rapidly deteriorating due to insufficient rations and a lack of healthcare.[97] By the end of that year, Lunghua's minimal food stores were depleted and there were repeated malaria epidemics. During the winter there were neither enough shoes nor enough clothes to go around.[98] The documented realities of camp life therefore – for the most part – tally with Ballard's semi-fictional descriptions of 'unheated cement buildings [which] seemed arctic' and the stresses of ever-decreasing rations.[99] Despite the outraged letters challenging *Empire of the Sun* –which have prompted numerous literary critics to since declare Ballard 'an unreliable witness' regarding his years in the camp – his descriptions of hunger and low morale do have a basis, at least, in

---

[92] As *Miracles of Life* recalls, William Braidwood chaired a committee of internees overseeing the camp's administration. Several decades after the war his wife, Margaret Braidwood, shared their records of camp life with Ballard, including a cache of documents that detailed the sharp decline of 'the daily calorie count in 1944', confirming his memories of hunger and malnourishment. Ballard, *Miracles of Life*, p. 76.

[93] Archives at the British Library detail the precise layout of each camp building, with G-block containing some of the most cramped conditions for families of internees. British Library, Add. MS 88938/2/1/7/4.

[94] Ballard, *Miracles of Life*, p. 66.

[95] Ballard, *The Kindness of Women*, pp. 39–40.

[96] Ballard, *Empire of the Sun*, pp. 182–3.

[97] British Library, Add. MS 88938/2/1/7/4.

[98] Ibid.

[99] Ballard, 'The End of My War', p. 291.

Figure 2.3 Drinking station marked as 'Waterloo' in Lunghua camp. Photograph by Oscar Seepol. Image courtesy of Susannah Stapleton and Special Collections, University of Bristol Library (www.hpcbristol.net).

historical reality.[100] The complaints Ballard received reflect not only the vagaries of memory, but also a peculiar brand of post-imperial British nationalism which accused him of lying because he fails to embrace a survival narrative of heroic failure.[101]

Published six years after *Empire of the Sun*, *The Kindness of Women* extends and revises Ballard's account of his internment. As Luckhurst explains, these

---

[100] Matthew Hart is rightly cautious of the archived correspondence disproving *Empire of the Sun*'s vision of Lunghua, but acknowledges that these letters 'provide grounds for speculation about what [Ballard's] enclave settings mean for the historicity of his fiction'. For Jeannette Baxter, the complaints Ballard received suggest that he 'shifted the parameters of historical fact so considerably that his fellow prisoners cannot possibly locate themselves within his text'. I would note that firstly, many life narratives induce the wrath of those they depict; all autobiographical texts are, after all, a subjective and individual account. Jenny Diski's *In Gratitude* (2016), for example, 'writes back' to the previous memoirs of her adoptive mother (Doris Lessing) and criticizes Lessing's habit of claiming that she 'had no memory' of particular, painful incidents from their time together. Second, reader's letters to Ballard frequently complain that his account of Lunghua is illegitimate because it was unpatriotic. The text's reception was undoubtedly entangled not only with wider issues surrounding the viability of 'truth' in autobiographical writing but also with debates on post-imperial British nationalism. Neither of these complications should lead us to dismiss Lunghua's representation in *Empire of the Sun* and *The Kindness of Women* as invalid. – Matthew Hart, *Extraterritorial: A Political Geography of Contemporary Fiction* (New York: Columbia University Press, 2020), p. 219; Jeannette Baxter, *J. G. Ballard's Surrealist Imagination: Spectacular Authorship* (Farnham: Ashgate, 2009), p. 137; Jenny Diski, *In Gratitude* (London: Bloomsbury, 2016), p. 102.

[101] For the relationship between narratives of 'heroic failure' and Britain's imperial past, see: Fintan O'Toole, *Heroic Failure: Brexit and the Politics of Pain* (London: Apollo, 2018).

autobiographical novels were viewed as a turning point in a career which had previously been defined by 'the derogatory appellation of science fiction'; critics were delighted to see Ballard turn to a more 'honourable "confessional" mode' of writing.[102] The early readers' letters in the British Library's archive make clear that this development into 'confessional' writing brought new expectations of autobiographical truth. Therefore, it seems important to state: Despite their grounding in historical reality, neither novel is a straightforward rendition of Ballard's life. Conspicuously, both depict Jim/Jamie as unaccompanied in Lunghua, yet in actuality Ballard spent the war years interned with his family. When explaining this omission, he would describe how a 'gradual estrangement began in Lunghua' and that it was therefore 'truer to present myself as alone … [as] there was a separation between me and my parents in the camp'.[103]

Clearly, then, Ballard's life writing experiments with the unstable relationship between 'Jim' (*Empire*), 'Jamie' (*Kindness*) and the authorial 'I' (*Miracles*). As *The Kindness of Women* rewrites and embellishes scenes from *Empire of the Sun*, neither text ultimately offers a stable nor wholly truthful timeline of the author's life. For his part, Ballard viewed both as 'literally true half the time' and 'psychologically true the whole of the time'.[104] The remainder of this chapter now turns to the descriptions of Lunghua in *The Kindness of Women* and *Miracles of Life*. Rather than being mired in distinctions between truth and falsehood, or the autobiographical and the fictive, these readings ask how the confined enclave of the camp is an *unheimlich* successor to the sealed world of Amherst Avenue. In her discussions of prison-camp literature, Marina MacKay notes that both Jim and Jamie 'must scavenge from the ruins' of their old lives, 'and the ruined lives of others' in the uncompromising world of Lunghua.[105] Extending these readings of life amongst the wreckage, Ballard's depictions of the camp are discussed here for what they reveal about an irrevocably broken British imperial identity. Both Jamie and the autobiographical 'I' realize that there can be no return to their enclaved life in either the house or the camp, even if the latter is a distorted double or reflection of the former. Lunghua is repeatedly described in Ballard's autobiographical writing as 'my real home', but it is

---

[102] Roger Luckhurst, 'Petition, Repetition and "Autobiography": J. G. Ballard's *Empire of the Sun* and *The Kindness of Women*, *Contemporary Literature*, 35:4 (1994): 688–708 (p. 690).
[103] Ballard, *Miracles of Life*, p. 82; Lynn Barber and J. G. Ballard, 'Alien at Home', *Sunday Review*, 15 September 1991, https://www.jgballard.ca/media/1991_sept15_independent_sunday_review.html (accessed 29 June 2022).
[104] Barber and Ballard, 'Alien At Home'.
[105] Marina MacKay, *Ian Watt: The Novel and the Wartime Critic* (Oxford: Oxford University Press, 2018), p. 75.

Figure 2.4 Laundry day in the married quarters of Lunghua camp. Photograph by Oscar Seepol. Image courtesy of Susannah Stapleton and Special Collections, University of Bristol Library (www.hpcbristol.net).

defined by the same post-imperial unheimlich which characterizes all of his life writing.[106] Like Lessing, who was always trying to get back to 'her real home' on the kopje (discussed in Chapter 3), or Lively's inability to return to her beloved house at Bulaq Dakhrur (see Chapter 1), Ballard's life writing reveals always the impossibility of returning to key coordinates of the colonial past. Through the twinned dwelling places of camp and mansion, he explores his own position as an unhoused colonial subject at the end of empire.

The Cave Inside a Camp

Part one of *The Kindness of Women* describes Jamie's wartime years, reworking Ballard's memories of both the International Settlement and Lunghua. Across its three opening chapters the novel depicts life in Amherst Avenue during 1937, returns to the community of the camp in 1943 when 'the war had begun to turn against the Japanese',[107] before concluding in August 1945, when Jamie ventures 'beyond the fence' of Lunghua and into the 'different world' of

---

[106] Ballard, *The Kindness of Women*, p. 53.
[107] Ibid., p. 36.

post-war Shanghai.¹⁰⁸ Accompanied by his (fictional) friend, the fourteen-year-old internee Peggy Gardner, Jamie's greatest fear is not the imminent threat of starvation 'but that Lunghua ... which had become my entire world, might degenerate into anarchy' if the Japanese guards stop providing rations.¹⁰⁹ Jamie understands (in comments echoed by Ballard in interviews) that he has been indelibly 'shaped by the camp' and that he 'found a special freedom [there] which I had never known in Shanghai'.¹¹⁰ Yet Lunghua also marks Jamie's fraught relationship with Englishness and the class divisions of English society. When his father warns him, in 1945, that after the war he would be schooled 'at home', he worries 'that the England I visited ... would be a larger version of Lunghua camp, with all its snobberies and social divisions, its "best" families with their strangled talk of "London town"' (see Figure 2.4).¹¹¹ His fear is not that England will be strange, but that it will be recognizable as a simulacrum of the camp (which itself replicates the confined world of the settlement). Lunghua is therefore a paradox for Jamie; it ostensibly functions as a respite from the claustrophobia of his former life, and yet it is also a sealed microcosm of colonial English identity, with established social codes and inflexible boundaries. Jamie observes the other internees as an outsider, noting the hubris of this strange imperial community 'whose armies in Singapore had surrendered without a fight but [who] nonetheless acted as if they had won the war'.¹¹²

Inside Lunghua Jamie realises that 'British power had waned, sinking like the torpedoed hulks of the *Repulse* and the *Prince of Wales*'.¹¹³ He extends this hypothesis by observing the behaviour of the adults around him who are deeply sunken 'in their torpor', concluding that this is because 'the British had nothing to which they looked forward, unlike the Americans, whose world was always filled with possibilities'.¹¹⁴. Viewing the widespread depression and general languor at Lunghua as a microcosm of imperial decline, Jamie sees the war as 'the first revolt by the colonized nations of the east against the imperial west'.¹¹⁵ He develops a personal thesis regarding the depressive impact of formal decolonization on this enclosed community. Yet ultimately Jamie's response to the British adults who seem incapable of mobilizing around or even imagining

[108] Ibid., p. 52.
[109] Ibid., p. 37.
[110] Ibid., p. 48.
[111] Ibid., p. 41.
[112] Ibid., p. 35.
[113] Ibid., p. 53.
[114] Ibid., pp. 40–1.
[115] Ibid.

their futures after war and empire, is to stage a curious journey into the heart of Lunghua – and by extension, to the core of British imperial identity. If the Freudian uncanny contrasts 'a secure and homely interior [with] the fearful invasion of an alien presence', Jim's attempts to build a home at the centre of Lunghua ultimately reveal the impossibility of permanently dwelling in this unheimlich world.[116]

The Kindness of Women's second chapter takes place during a single night in 1943, when a gang of male internees attempt to break out of the camp under cover of darkness. As they launch this daring escape (which eventually fails), the ever-hungry Jamie stages his own parallel act of re-entry, chiselling into the communal kitchens where the camp's coveted food store, containing '[our] food supply for the week', is kept.[117] As the other internees scale the external fence, Jamie is engrossed in his internal journey:

> I pulled bricks from the soft mortar, steadily enlarging the aperture. The distant lights of the airfield threw silhouettes of the perimeter fence-posts on to the wall above my head. A straw sack filled most of the opening, but in the sweeping searchlight I could see the airless interior of the store-room, a mysterious inner world like the dwarfs' cottage in Snow White. The heavy sacks slumbered against the walls, their comforting bulk reminded me of a family of dozing bears. My few doubts about stealing the food were forgotten. Already I thought of crawling into the store-room and sealing the wall behind me. Peggy and I would sleep there, out of the cold, safe among the great drowsing sacks.[118]

In a sequence which evokes and inverts Plato's allegory of the cave, Jamie faces away from the lights of the airfield and towards a vista of shadows, the 'silhouettes' of the perimeter fence cast onto a brick wall. Rather than looking to escape through the camp's boundaries, Jamie turns away from the realities of war and the escapees who are scaling the barbed wire, determined to reach the International Settlement. Instead, he moves towards a shadow play in the camp's interior, burrowing deeper into the storeroom and seeking the inner recesses of the camp. In Plato's allegory, the fettered prisoners can only interpret the world through shadows cast on a wall by firelight, 'deem[ing] reality to be nothing else than the shadows of the artificial objects'.[119] Any prisoner who escaped and perceived actual objects in the sunlight outside would, 'if he recalled to mind

---

[116] Vidler, *The Architectural Uncanny*, p. 3.
[117] Ballard, *The Kindness of Women*, p. 43.
[118] Ibid., pp. 43–4.
[119] Plato, 'Republic: VII', in *The Collected Dialogues of Plato*, ed. Edith Hamilton and Huntington Cairns, trans. Paul Shorey (Princeton, NJ: Princeton University Press, 1961), pp. 747–72 (p. 748).

his first habitation', realize 'that what he had seen before was all a cheat and an illusion'.[120] But unlike the allegorical prisoner who is freed from the bondage of his first home, and who will subsequently refuse to descend again into the illusory, underground world, Jamie desperately seeks access to the dark recesses of the storeroom. The result is a scene which reverses a Platonic pursuit of knowledge, as Ballard's autobiographical alter ego attempts to re-enter these fictions of the interior. Unlike Plato's allegorical prisoners, Jamie cannot escape into daylight beyond; his only option is to join the escapees in the dark airfield, attempting to avoid the glare of Lunghua's harsh searchlights.[121]

Once inside the storeroom, Jamie discovers not a permanent home or sanctuary, but the return of several, partially remembered figures from childhood. These include the 1937 film *Snow White and the Seven Dwarves* – which *Miracles of Life* recalls as Ballard's first cinematic experience – where the heroine's discovery of a dwarves' cottage leads her into a gloomy, almost subterranean domestic space.[122] Jamie connects this to Robert Southey's 1837 fairy tale in which a distempered woman – subsequently renamed Goldilocks – invades a home belonging to three bears. Like Jamie, the woman is ostensibly searching for food and shelter.[123] In *The Kindness of Women*, the store room is therefore tempting not only because it contains sacks of sweet potatoes (easily the most appealing option in Lunghua's daily menu of weevil-infested porridge) but also because it returns to the fictions of life in Amherst Avenue. Together these form a genealogy of melancholic returns to unwelcoming homes in European and Western literature. These familiar stories cannot offer any real comfort, because none can offer Jamie a secure dwelling place. In Walt Disney's animation Snow White consumes the infamous poisoned apple and collapses on the cottage floor;

---

[120] Plato, 'Republic: VII', p. 749.
[121] *Miracles of Life* recounts how Ballard – like Jamie – would search for pieces of coal on the ash-tips outside Lunghua's furnaces, 'poking with a bent piece of wire through the dust and clinkers'. One evening 'I led Bobby Henderson [another young internee] to the rear wall of the coal store behind the kitchens, and used the bayonet to scrape away the mortar. After removing two of the bricks, I drew out several handfuls of coal'. He uses the fuel to make his mother a cup of tea, while the young Henderson, who is alone in Lunghua, stood 'in the darkness, hurling the pieces into a deep pond beyond the perimeter fence'. In this memory of the storeroom, Ballard attempts to bring comfort to his family but compromises both his and his father's moral principles through the theft. The futility of Henderson's gesture articulates a despair felt, but rarely verbalized, by Lunghua's other inmates. Ballard, *Miracles of Life*, pp. 93–5.
[122] "The first film I saw [in a cinema] was *Snow White*, which frightened the wits out of me. The wicked Queen … reminded me too much of my friends' mothers when they tired of me rearranging their furniture.' Ballard, *Miracles of Life*, p. 19.
[123] Iona and Peter Opie note the distinct parallels between these fairy tales, which both depict an intruder who discovers their 'a new home' (in actuality the dwelling place of dwarves and bears), before consuming food, claiming a bed and being later disturbed by the original inhabitants. Iona and Peter Opie, 'Goldilocks and the Three Bears', in *Classic Fairy Tales*, compiled by Iona and Peter Opie (Oxford: Oxford University Press, 1980), pp. 260–3 (p. 262).

Southey's tale ends with the terrified female intruder jumping from a window to escape the bears, and either breaking 'her neck in the fall', or being 'sent to the House of Correction for [being] a vagrant'.[124] The folk stories which converge in the storeroom offer no more security than Plato's flickering shadows on a wall. Instead they evoke unhomely and ultimately dangerous domestic spaces, where intruders are punished for their acts of trespass, children are threatened by malicious adults, and all refuge is temporary.

Importantly, when Jamie turns to the 'mysterious, inner world' and the 'airless interior of the store room', he realizes that he cannot return to his former home, (perhaps explaining why he is unwilling to join the escape attempt heading for the settlement).[125] While he is initially described as a thief intent on 'stealing food', he is actually appraising the space as possible living quarters. Later he will acknowledge that, 'far from wanting to escape from the camp' like the other prisoners, he had been looking to move 'ever more deeply into its heart'.[126] He attempts to seal himself within the tomb-like 'airless interior' of an enclave which is 'a small version of England'.[127] Once inside, Jamie is faced with the suffocating realities and blank absences of English colonial identity. His journey into the interior replicates the archetypal colonial trajectory of Charles Marlow's voyage in *Heart of Darkness* (1899). Jamie may later attempt to construct 'a small hutch' in his sleeping bunk which emulates the storeroom's 'peaceful' setting, but this attempt to excavate the heart of Lunghua-as-England is ultimately unsuccessful.[128] Like Marlow, his intrepid explorations are doomed to failure.

Following Japan's surrender in August 1945, Jamie leaves the camp and returns to the surreal, 'quiet suburban roads' of the International Settlement.[129] When he arrives at Amherst Avenue he explores the unaltered rooms of the preserved property, noting that 'the heavy leather furniture and dark walls reminded me of the food store'.[130] The expensive leather furnishings obviously bear little resemblance to the depleted sacks and brick walls of the latter, but Jamie now understands that both spaces reconstruct an imaginative England. He concludes that neither can shelter him from the volatile end of colonial rule. If Amherst Avenue is the central setting of Ballard's colonial upbringing – one

---

[124] Robert Southey, 'The Story of the Three Bears', in *Classic Fairy Tales*, compiled by Iona and Peter Opie (Oxford: Oxford University Press, 1980), pp. 264–9 (p. 268).
[125] Ballard, *The Kindness of Women*, p. 43.
[126] Ibid.
[127] Ibid., p. 69.
[128] Ibid., p. 48.
[129] Ibid., p. 62.
[130] Ibid., p. 63.

returned to in *Kindness* and *Miracles* – then the storeroom at Lunghua eventually emerges as its double, becoming both its uncanny replica and logical conclusion. These repetitions fulfil and extend the post-imperial *unheimlich* first developed in *Empire*. Jim attempts to return to the state of Plato's allegorical prisoners, who know nothing 'except the shadows cast from the fire on the wall of the cave', because his former life in Amherst Avenue is predicated upon a similar falsehood.[131] The property's dark walls and heavy furniture can barely screen the realities of war and imperial decline at the end of empire.

In the months immediately after the war, Jamie is disorientated by the feeling that 'I had landed in an unfamiliar future'.[132] He believes that 'I had mislaid part of my mind somewhere between Lunghua and Shanghai'.[133] While again demonstrating the close ties between the camp and his childhood home, this description also suggests that, if colonial life was a phantasm, then a world after empire is also an impossible proposition, offering an 'unfamiliar', almost speculative, future. Jamie finds himself homeless in this post-war landscape, unable to return to his past, and equally uneasy in the post-imperial present (a sensation that intensifies throughout his first decade in England). Ballard's autobiographical writing moves ever inwards, from the hollow dwelling places of an abandoned house to an empty swimming pool, before arriving in an airless room at the heart of an internment camp.

If *Miracles of Life* largely offers an abbreviated account of events previously recorded in autofictional novels and essays, the autobiography nevertheless provides new details of the years leading up to *and* following Ballard's internment at Lunghua. Offering the only chronological account of Ballard's childhood from birth to his departure on the *Arawa*, it recounts how, as the war progressed during the late 1930s, the landscape of everyday life in Shanghai became physically and psychologically smaller. Once Japanese forces entered the International Settlement, seizing control of the city and the Whangpoo River, 'all foreign cars were confiscated', leaving Ballard and his father to cross checkpoints and barbed wire on foot, or by bicycle.[134] The family's limited mobility reflected wider geopolitical events, including 'the capture of the Philippines and the threat to India and Australia', which marked the impending collapse of Britain's imperial authority. It was, in Ballard's words, 'the end of a way of life'.[135] During

---

[131] Plato, 'Republic: VII', p. 747.
[132] Ballard, *The Kindness of Women*, p. 65.
[133] Ibid.
[134] Ballard, *Miracles of Life*, p. 55.
[135] Ibid., p. 56.

the early years of the war, his younger self 'could see that the British Empire had failed', and he 'began to look at A. A. Milne and the Chums annuals [filled with patriotic tales of imperial derring-do] with a far more sceptical eye'.[136] While interrogating the romantic fictions of British imperialism, *Miracles of Life* provides a clear outline of the late 1930s and early 1940s (a period largely absent from Ballard's previous life narratives), when his family were left in a rapidly emptying settlement. As the final inhabitants of a shrinking island, they watched the familiar coordinates of their imperial lives being steadily dismantled.

Yet the autobiography also contains an explicit, spatial understanding of Ballard's colonial childhood as a kind of marooning or imprisonment, suggesting the extent to which his life in the settlement anticipated his later years in the camp. It explains how full-scale internment began in 1943, when many British civilians were taken to sites which – unlike Lunghua – were in the city's pre-existing suburbs. These included the 'well-guarded residential estates' which had been home to European residents.[137] Former gated suburbs were ideal complexes for incarceration, because 'the security measures that kept intruders out worked just as well at keeping their former residents in'.[138] Looking back, Ballard acknowledges that, in the pre-war years, 'my insulation from Chinese life was almost complete', despite his attempts to navigate Shanghai on his bicycle.[139] While neither *Empire* nor *Kindness* explore, in any detail, Jim's/Jamie's life before the war, *Miracles of Life* gives a vital account of Shanghai *before* the Japanese occupation, making clear that Lunghua is an unheimlich repetition of his childhood. Despite the camp's obvious deprivations, it fulfilled the logic of an isolated colonial settlement. The distinctions between 'intruders out/residents in' are no more stable, Ballard's autobiography suggests, than the slippery distinctions between the homely and the unhomely.[140] In this final life narrative the camp and the settlement are at their most explicitly inseparable, offering different forms of life inside a sealed white enclave.

---

[136] Ibid.
[137] Ibid., p. 59.
[138] Ibid., p. 60.
[139] Ibid., p. 33.
[140] *The Kindness of Women* draws a more oblique connection between the initial Japanese occupation of Shanghai 'ringing the International Settlement with their tanks and machine-gun[s]' and the camp sentries who would 'close the gates with a set of heavy padlocks' at the first sign of an escape attempt. In both instances the British community inside were trapped and isolated from the Chinese landscape, but they existed in comparative 'haven[s] of affluence', filled with 'cricket bats and tennis rackets'. Such luxuries came in stark contrast with the deprivations suffered by many Chinese peasant communities. Ballard, *Kindness of Women*, pp. 27, 31.

Miracles of Life also offers a singularly detailed account of Ballard's arrival in England and his time at Cambridge during the post-war years. In a reversal of the usual colonial 'journey in', Ballard viewed Britain as a colonial backwater, describing himself as being 'stuck in a deeply provincial outpost'.[141] The 'shabby streets and bomb sites' were startling to a teenager who noted a contrast between the bleak realities of post-war life, and widespread collective delusions regarding 'Britain's [central] place in the world'.[142] During the holidays Ballard was left with his grandparents in the Black Country, where 'some of the most ill-housed and poorly educated people in western Europe [were] still giving their lives after the war to maintain an empire that had never been of the least benefit to them'.[143] Languishing in a centre that was also, therefore, a colonial periphery, he viewed post-imperial and post-war England as 'deeply repressed and ready to be laid on the analyst's couch'.[144] Although he remained intensely homesick for his former life, by 1948 he had realized 'that I would never go back to Shanghai. Lunghua Camp and the International Settlement would be swept away ... the locks had been changed'.[145] In Lunghua, Ballard had traversed 'the earth and cinder road-tracks named Oxford Street and Piccadilly', navigating the social mores of an isolated Anglo-community who were trapped in an extreme rendition of their former, enclosed lives. If both Lunghua and the International Settlement allowed Ballard to explore the compelling, contradictory, specifics of English colonial identity, *Miracles of Life* suggests that this continued during his adult years in Britain. The twinned locations of his childhood might have been 'swept away' amidst the rising tide of Chinese communism, but in post-imperial England Ballard lapses once again into the language of domestic confinement; he speaks of the colonial past being hidden behind locked doors, of feeling 'stuck' in the mid-twentieth century and finding himself trapped in a gloomy society 'where none of the lights would come on'.[146] In the autobiography he articulates how the global changes brought about by decolonization and the rise of Mao Tse-tung shut the door on his colonial upbringing and indelibly shaped his adult life in Britain. More so, then, than any of Ballard's previous life narratives, *Miracles of Life* charts the end of his domestic, imperial world and laments the impossibility of return.

---

[141] Ballard, *Miracles of Life*, p. 133.
[142] Ibid., pp. 126–7.
[143] Ibid., p. 131.
[144] Ibid., p. 138.
[145] Ibid., p. 134.
[146] Ibid., p. 132.

Conclusion: Britain in the Home

By the early twentieth century, the combined land of Shanghai's International Settlement and the French Concession spread across thirty-three square kilometres, creating what Matthew Hart terms a 'double-natured' and 'bordered zone of foreign impunity'.[147] Yet while these extraterritorial spaces were never defined as Crown Colonies – like Hong Kong or Singapore – the International Settlement and the French Concession employed social 'mechanisms familiar from colonial societies in South-east Asia and East Africa'.[148] Publicly these included the racial segregation of shared amenities and the protection of white inhabitants' financial interests, while in private the settlement's British, female inhabitants – including Ballard's mother – were tasked with 'the duty of recreating Britain in the home'.[149] In this context, domestic space was both designed for relaxation and intended to be 'a statement of [colonial] identity and purpose'.[150] As we will next see in Chapter 3, such distinguishing factors of public and private colonial life would have been broadly familiar to Doris Lessing, growing up over 11,000 kilometres away on the colonial frontier of Southern Rhodesia. There too, the private homes of white-owned farmers were literal and ideological battlegrounds where the future of white supremacy might be secured. Yet in Shanghai, the city's 'settlers lacked the absolute certainties of formal colonialism', relying instead on informal imperialism.[151] The result was a society which lacked the rigid practices (i.e. colonial laws or full territorial recognition) which could categorically protect an enshrined 'British identity from dilution or deterioration'.[152]

On the one hand, the autobiographical narratives discussed throughout this book suggest that white life across Britain's colonies, protectorates and dominions was always shot with the fear of 'dilution or deterioration'. The high garden walls which surrounded Amherst Avenue, or the thick hedges of Bulaq Dakhrur, reveal that late colonial life was an embattled existence, tenuously maintained by the labour of servants and repeated social rituals of white families. Yet on the other, Ballard's life writing responds to the particular, insecure conditions of the International Settlement as a semi-colonial enclave.

---

[147] Hart, *Extraterritorial*, p. 197.
[148] Bickers, *Britain in China*, p. 222.
[149] Ibid., p. 89.
[150] Ibid.
[151] Ibid., p. 222.
[152] Ibid.

The sites which recur throughout his autobiographical writing – the house at Amherst Avenue, the drained pool and the confined interiors of Lunghua camp – allow him to reflect on the fragility of colonial rule and the tenuous nature of settler hegemony in ways that are specific to imperial Shanghai. Ballard's development of a colonial and later a post-imperial uncanny reflects the similarities and distinctions between Shanghai and other British settler colonies.

As Britain was recreated in households across the International Settlement, Ballard's autobiographical unheimlich allows him to disturb the propriety of colonial property. In this sense Ballard's life writings intersect with Janet Frame's own challenges to settler home ownership in Aotearoa/New Zealand (discussed in Chapter 4). His descriptions of private, disconcerting spaces depict British imperial identity as permanently unsettled both during colonial rule and at the end of empire. For Freud, the uncanny was revealed by a process of repetition, of 'recurrent similarities' wherein 'every endeavour to find the marked or familiar path ends again and again in a return to the same spot'.[153] Ballard too would find himself returning, over and over, to the house and the camp, a pair of twinned 'x' which mark the spot of his imperial childhood. His life writing not only depicts a kind of besieged whiteness – a familiar crisis enacted in many memoirs of colonial life – but also repeatedly circles back to his memories of empire's end and his two, interconnected 'homes'. The stark shift in his living conditions during the Second World War, and his determination to return imaginatively to these dwelling places, complicates Bhabha's suggestion that the unhomely can connect the 'ambivalences of a personal, psychic history to the wider disjunctions of political existence'.[154] It is through interior spaces and lost dwelling places that Ballard forges new pathways between the individual subject at the end of empire (the 'personal psychic history') and a post-war era where the colonial past appeared drastically out of joint. In these autobiographical texts formal decolonization is partially acknowledged through geopolitical events, but it manifests primarily in his memories of home. By returning to the doubled, unhomely locations of camp and house, Ballard bears witness to empire's collapse, and records the many, stuttering ends to 'the lives of the colonial British'.[155]

---

[153] Freud, 'The Uncanny', pp. 236–7.
[154] Bhabha, 'The World and the Home', p. 144.
[155] Ballard, *Empire of the Sun*, p. 267.

3

Back to the Laager: Southern Rhodesia and Doris Lessing's Travel Memoirs

Thank you for offering me this honour: I am very pleased. But for some time now I have been wondering, 'But where is this British Empire?' Surely there isn't one. And now I see that I am not the only one saying the same.
— Doris Lessing's letter to Alex Allan, declining her Damehood

I have lived in over sixty different houses, flats and rented rooms ... and not in one of them have I felt at home. ... The fact is I don't live anywhere; I never have since I left that first house on the kopje.
— Doris Lessing, *Going Home*

Introduction: Life in the Laager

In his 2015 memoir *Dispatcher*, Mark Gevisser tracks the vital coordinates of a Johannesburg childhood, overlaid with his later experience of a violent home invasion in the city's northern suburbs. One of the connecting threads between these past and present lives in southern Africa is the idea of 'the laager', a nineteenth-century Afrikaner term for a circle of settler wagons. In the traumatic aftermath of his assault, Gevisser reflects that the laager is central to the collective unconscious of those 'raised white in apartheid South Africa':

> The violation of one's home and hearth is the primal settler anxiety, deeply embedded in white South African consciousness, epitomised by the image of the ox-wagon laager corralled against the savages beyond. It is at the foundation

of Mau-Mau anxiety; it is what happened in Kenya, it is what happened in Zimbabwe, and now, look, it's happening to *us*.[1]

Gevisser's own childhood took place within 'a leafy suburban laager', an enclosed white existence built from the blueprints of defensive, circular encampments used by early white settlers in both South Africa and Southern Rhodesia/Zimbabwe.[2] Over a century after the first ringed wagons sought protection from Zulu warriors, their memory was preserved to support fictions of racial difference, upholding both South African apartheid and the Rhodesian colour bar.[3] Fearing the 'violation of one's home and hearth', white home owners built their own personal laagers, erecting barbed wire fences and elaborate home security around their farmhouses and suburban bungalows.[4] By the mid-twentieth century this embattled circle of settlement was the shared ideological project of two, neighbouring apartheid states. As Gevisser explains, both Southern Rhodesia and South Africa were 'dedicated to defining some people into the laager, such as my Jewish immigrant antecedents, while defining the black majority out'.[5] Yet the troubling events of *Dispatcher* confirm that these only ensured a permanent phenomenon of home (in)security in settler society.

This chapter explores the frustrated attempts at homecoming in Doris Lessing's two African travel memoirs, *Going Home* and *African Laughter*, demonstrating that both ultimately expose the limits of the white 'laager' in southern Africa. While the two are rarely read in concert, they map Lessing's attempts to both criticize and get back to the colonial past in her life writing. As we will see *Going Home* (her first memoir, published in 1957) is ultimately compromised by these contradictory impulses of escape and return. Yet the fragmentary, often frustrating form of her later travel narrative *African Laughter*, published in the early 1990s, responds to its predecessor's limitations by

---

[1] Mark Gevisser, *Dispatcher: Lost and Found in Johannesburg* (London: Granta Books, 2015), p. 269.
[2] Ibid., p. 312.
[3] Dickson A. Mungazi attributes widespread use of the term 'laager' to a battle between Afrikaner and Zulu forces in 1838, during which sixty Boer wagons filled with Voortekkers travelling to the interior of southern Africa formed a defensive circle to successfully repel Zulu spears. Dickson A. Mungazi, *The Last Defenders of the Laager: Ian D. Smith and F. W. de Klerk* (London: Praeger, 1998), pp. 1–2.
[4] Murenga Joseph Chikowero suggests that the 'high-rise fences' which appear in many white Rhodesian memoirs 'are, in a sense, the new version of the 19th-century laager that now serve to keep out the African guerrillas, potential thieves and any other African undesirables'. These fences also simultaneously obscure the extent to which white Rhodesian/Zimbabwean domesticity was reliant on Black labour. Murenga Joseph Chikowero, '"We Were Like Little Kings in Rhodesia": Rhodesian Discourse and Representations of Colonial Violence', in *Kandaya and Don't Let's Go to the Dogs Tonight*' in *Strategies of Representation in Auto/Biography: Reconstructing and Remembering*, ed. Muchativugwa Hove and Kgomotso Masemola (Basingstoke: Palgrave Macmillan, 2014), pp. 116–42 (p. 123).
[5] Gevisser, *Dispatcher*, p. 39.

reimagining Lessing's relationship with the African landscape she called 'my myth country'.[6] If Lessing's first travel memoir illustrates the risks of returning to the colonial past, and remains trapped in a series of insurmountable contradictions, then her second memoir reimagines her childhood homes as microcosms for a failed settler state. Tracking the development of homecoming across these two autobiographical texts, this chapter outlines how an impulse to return to Southern Rhodesia shapes not only the content but also the increasingly fragmented form of Lessing's life writing.[7] When combined with the discussions of *Alfred and Emily* in Chapter 5, this analysis joins recent re-evaluations of Lessing's oeuvre as 'always determined in part by questions of [literary] form', rebuffing the earlier critical consensus summarized by J. M. Coetzee that she 'was never much of a stylist'.[8] Lessing's career-long experiments with autobiographical form underscore the need to question and complicate this assessment.

Born in the ruinous aftermath of the First World War, raised during the final years of the British Empire and emerging as a writer immediately after the Second World War, Lessing was a prolific life writer who returned, many times, to her memories of white settlerdom. As a vocal opponent of the Rhodesian colour bar, she was unable to inhabit the landscape of her childhood, yet returned to her parents' African farm in all of her autobiographies (*Under My Skin*, *Walking in the Shade*), documentary accounts (*In Pursuit of the English*, *The Wind Takes Away Our Words*) and in her speculative life writing (*Alfred and Emily*). All of these texts describe the house and farm as 'like my other skin'.[9] On the one hand, they confirm that Lessing – a lifelong anti-imperialist who declined her CBE on the grounds of there being no empire to command – could not return permanently to the segregated white societies of southern Africa. Yet on the other, they show how her profound connection to this landscape attempted to transcend the tired tropes of ownership and enclosure which define colonial settlement. In the end, this was an unfinished, often frustrated endeavour; Lessing's life narratives depict an autobiographical subject who is always 'going

---

[6] Doris Lessing, *African Laughter: Four Visits to Zimbabwe* (London: Flamingo, 1993), p. 426.
[7] The British settler colony of Southern Rhodesia was merged into the Central African Federation between 1953 and 1965, and following the country's unilateral declaration of independence (UDI) in 1965, it became known as Rhodesia. By 1980, following official independence, it was renamed as Zimbabwe. Although Lessing herself sometimes described her life in 'Rhodesia', this chapter uses the historically correct term of Southern Rhodesia when referring to her childhood in the 1920s and 1930s.
[8] Kevin Brazil, David Sergeant and Tom Sperlinger, 'Introduction', in *Doris Lessing and the Forming of History*, ed. Kevin Brazil, David Sergeant and Tom Sperlinger (Edinburgh: Edinburgh University Press, 2016), pp. 1–9 (p. 6); J. M. Coetzee, 'The Autobiography of Doris Lessing', in *Stranger Shores: Essays 1986–1999* (London: Vintage, 2002), pp. 284–303 (p. 291).
[9] Lessing, *Under My Skin*, p. 195.

home', but never able to arrive at her destination. While critics have previously recognized her interest in 'the spatial and psychological enclosures of a colonial childhood', this chapter delves deeper into the particular, domestic spaces of Lessing's African travel memoirs including the house and farm, her family's encampments in the bush and a muwanga tree which marked the edge of their property.[10] By exploring these in detail, I question what kind of homes her life writing attempts to return to, reading the enclosed sphere of the laager as crucial to Lessing's failed reconciliation with her settler childhood.[11]

Following her criticism of Rhodesia's 'colour bar' during the 1940s, Lessing was banned from re-entering the country in 1956, only returning in 1982, several years after Zimbabwean independence. Despite being positioned at either end of her long exile from southern Africa, bookending her twenty-six-year absence from the country, *Going Home* and *African Laughter* are rarely discussed as companion pieces. This is a perplexing oversight as the latter is clearly a sequel to the former, a fact reflected in their similar, concluding reflections on land distribution and racial discrimination in her homeland. *Going Home*'s final chapter explains how 'the basis of white domination in Southern Rhodesia was the Land Apportionment Act, which took away land from the Africans and gave it to the Europeans'; *African Laughter* ends by suggesting that, because of this legislation, 'most Africans lived in the Native Reserves' and that the legacies of these policies resounded long after empire's end.[12] Lessing was convinced that returning to any habitation in the former settler state meant continuing these colonial histories of land theft and settlement.

Previous discussions of *Going Home* and *African Laughter* have addressed the problems of categorizing either text and the particularities of their respective hybrid forms. For Susan Watkins both are 'autobiographical essays', while Jenny Taylor identifies *Going Home* as a 'loosely defined factual work'.[13] More recently, *Going Home* has been discussed as a record of Lessing's communist politics, the first-hand account of 'a utopian socialist caught up in the impossible polarisation of the Cold War'.[14] In a more specific analysis of autobiographical form, John McAllister describes *African Laughter* as an anti-imperial travel

---

[10] Whitlock, *The Intimate Empire*, p. 200.
[11] *African Laughter*'s glossary defines a laager as 'a camp, a defended place'.
[12] Doris Lessing, *Going Home* (London: Pantha, 1984), p. 240; Lessing, *African Laughter*, p. 441.
[13] Susan Watkins, 'Remembering Home: Nation and Identity in the Recent Writings of Doris Lessing', *Feminist Review*, 85 (2007): 97–115 (p. 99); Jenny Taylor, 'Memory and Desire on *Going Home*': The Deconstruction of a Colonial Radical', in *Doris Lessing*, ed. Eve Bertelsen (Johannesburg: McGraw-Hill, 1985), pp. 55–63 (p. 55).
[14] Henry Stead, '"Comrade Doris": Lessing's Correspondence with the Foreign Commission of the Board of Soviet Writers in the 1950s', *Critical Quarterly*, 63:1 (2021): 35–47 (p. 36).

narrative, a reimagining of colonial travelogues where a 'male outsider moves purposefully through space and time, observing ... from an objective point of view'.[15] Lessing's meandering, circular journeys in the text have subsequently been read as reflecting her 'anti-colonial politics'.[16] Yet by discussing *Going Home* as *African Laughter*'s predecessor, this chapter highlights how Lessing tracked her frustrated attempts to return home across multiple, anti-imperial travel memoirs, written both during and after colonial rule.

The readings throughout this chapter acknowledge that Lessing's life writing is an extensive project which cannot be confined to a single text.[17] This is underscored by *Under My Skin*'s description of those 'shifting perspectives' which mean seeing 'your life differently at different stages, like climbing a mountain while the landscape changes with every turn'.[18] Yet this simile should be read with caution; there is no summit or final ascent from which we might map the terrain of Lessing's life. Instead, her autobiographical experiments are marked by rewritings and occasional contradictions, with each additional memoir subtly complicating her relationship with the colonial past. As Chapter 5 explores in more detail, her final life narrative *Alfred and Emily* has previously been read as a conciliatory conclusion to her life story and especially with her Rhodesian childhood, yet the text's counterfactual lives are imbued with Lessing's real memories. By sending the reader spiralling back into the network of her life writing, this last, autobiographical experiment raises more questions than it answers. The comparative readings in this chapter look to nuance more general assessments of Lessing as an author consumed with 'a yearning for home – not literally but in terms of redefining the self'.[19] Her travel memoirs record journeys which attempt to return, both imaginatively *and*

---

[15] John McAllister, 'Knowing Native: Going Native: Cognitive Borderlines and the Sense of Belonging in Doris Lessing's *African Laughter* and Dan Jacobson's *The Electric Elephant*', in *Zimbabwean Transitions: Essays on Zimbabwean Literature in English, Ndebele and Shona*, ed. Mbongeni Z. Malaba and Geoffrey V. Davis (Amsterdam: Rodopi, 2007), pp. 25–38 (p. 28).

[16] Sarah De Mul, 'Zimbabwe and the Politics of the Everyday in Doris Lessing's *African Laughter*', in *Migratory Settings*, ed. Murat Aydemir and Alex Rotas (Amsterdam: Rodolpi, 2008), pp. 139–55 (p. 140).

[17] If *Going Home* is accepted as Lessing's first life narrative, and *Alfred and Emily* as her final, experimental memoir, then her life writing project extends across a remarkable sixty-year period. Many critics have previously interpreted Lessing's fiction (particularly her Children of Violence series) as life writing. However, the texts Lessing published explicitly as memoirs, autobiographies and travel narratives are discussed here as distinct from her autobiographical fiction. I nevertheless concur with Susan Watkins that whether these are 'classified as novel, essay, memoir or official autobiography', Lessing is consistently 'attracted to autobiographical forms and has [long] been preoccupied with the blurred dividing lines between fact, truth and fiction'. Susan Watkins, *Doris Lessing* (Manchester: Manchester University Press, 2010), p. 29.

[18] Lessing, *Under My Skin*, p. 12.

[19] Dennis Walder, *Postcolonial Nostalgias: Writing, Representation, Memory* (Abingdon: Routledge, 2011), p. 92.

literally, to the personal coordinates of Lessing's myth country (the house, the farm, the muwanga tree). The tight boundaries of the Rhodesian laager are the crucial structure which constrains and constructs these life narratives in equal measure.

Born in 1919 in Persia (modern-day Iran), Doris Tayler's early life was spent in Kermanshah where her English parents, Alfred and Emily Tayler, had moved immediately after the First World War. In 1924, while on a brief visit to England, the Taylers attended the British Empire Exhibition and were intrigued by an advertisement for farming in Southern Rhodesia, filled with false promises of wealth and easy success. According to Lessing, this 'changed my parents' lives and set the course of mine and my brother's'.[20] Rather than returning to Kermanshah as planned, they instead became beneficiaries of a government scheme which encouraged British ex-servicemen (like Alfred) to take up new careers as colonial farmers, obtaining land and equipment at subsidized prices. As Dane Kennedy explains, British families emigrating to 1920s Rhodesia joined a white society that was 'rigidly stratified along racial, ethnic and cultural lines'.[21] A privileged minority of white farmers, who made up less than 5 per cent of the country's population, owned one-third of its farming land.[22] Settler families controlled and owned 'the greater part of the most fertile' soil.[23] Despite this, Alfred's attempts to farm maize quickly failed and Emily was bitterly disappointed that their lives of 'dinner parties, musical evenings, tea parties [and] picnics [in Persia] was gone'.[24] The couple had dreamed of returning to England and becoming landowners after a few, prosperous years. In reality they became trapped by their debts to Rhodesia's Land Bank and unable to return, struggling to stay financially afloat in a small colonial backwater. By 1949, in flight from her settler upbringing, Lessing boarded a ship bound for Britain and settled in London for the rest of the twentieth century.

While rehearsing these biographical facts it is important to be clear: Lessing's relationship with her former home was never one of straightforward critical distance. She acknowledged that 'everything that's made me a writer happened to me growing up in Southern Rhodesia' and although her first memoir likened settler society to 'a mass disease', her family's former farm is the landscape

---

[20] Lessing, *Under My Skin*, p. 46.
[21] Kennedy, *Islands of White*, p. 149.
[22] David McDermott Hughes, *Whiteness in Zimbabwe: Race, Landscape and the Problem of Belonging* (New York: Palgrave Macmillan, 2010), p. 73.
[23] Allison Goebel, *Gender and Land Reform: The Zimbabwe Experience* (London: McGill-Queen's University Press, 2005), p. 7.
[24] Lessing, *Under My Skin*, p. 59.

to which all her life narratives return.²⁵ While her final life narrative was purportedly an 'antidote to what I actually lived in – Rhodesia ... the last throbs of the British Empire', *Alfred and Emily* confirms that there is no remedy to the 'disease' of colonialism in these autobiographical texts.²⁶ Instead they return, over and over, to the 'long, cigar-shaped dwelling' that was built by her parents on a hill overlooking the veld, and describe Lessing as unable to settle anywhere permanently 'since I left that first house on the kopje'.²⁷ Conceptually, that 'first house' is the central, indispensable location of her autobiographical writing. Even its name – Kermanshah Farm – is imbued with nostalgia for her family's lost future in Persia.²⁸

All this is to say that 'going home' to Southern Rhodesia was both practically and ideologically difficult for Lessing. Re-entering the beloved landscape of her childhood meant returning to a colonial past which compromised her anti-imperial politics. Her later relationship with Robert Mugabe's Zimbabwe was no more straightforward.²⁹ Her early opinion that the new regime was a 'success, for all its faults' gave way to later denouncements of 'Mugabe's reign of terror'.³⁰ The assertion that the Tayler's farm was her only true home therefore jostles, uneasily, alongside her understanding that returning to this site meant complicity with 'the paranoia, the adolescent sentimentality, the neurosis' of white settler society.³¹ If Southern Rhodesia was the point to which Lessing's life writing would always return, the journey homewards was a complicated passage.

Lessing's attachment to Kermanshah Farm is as profound as Ballard's connection with Amherst Avenue and Lunghua, or Lively's ur-house of Bulaq

---

[25] Eve Bertelsen, 'Interview with Doris Lessing', in *Doris Lessing*, ed. Eve Bertelsen (Johannesburg: McGraw-Hill, 1985), pp. 93–120 (p. 93); Lessing, *Going Home*, p. 17.

[26] Lessing, *Alfred and Emily*, p. 186.

[27] Lessing, *Alfred and Emily* (London: Fourth Estate, 2008), p. 174; Lessing, *Going Home*, p. 30; The value Lessing attributes to this site causes Lara Feigel, one of several memoirists to pursue Lessing's influence upon her own life, to make a pilgrimage 'to the Highveld and [to attempt to] locate the hill where Lessing's house once stood'. Feigel's journey re-enacts Lessing's own disappointed return trips to this hillside, which she records in both *African Laughter* and *Alfred and Emily*. Lara Feigel, *Free Woman: Life, Liberation and Doris Lessing* (London: Bloomsbury, 2018), p. 38.

[28] Lessing, *Going Home*, pp. 37–8.

[29] Lessing was alert to first Rhodesia's and later Zimbabwe's dramatic, shifting fortunes. In *The Wind Blows Away Our Words*, she explains that, in the early 1950s, critics of Southern Rhodesia (then still a British colony) were 'patronised, put down, laughed at', and debates on the subject would 'empty the House of Commons'. But several decades later it became commonplace 'to criticise the white regimes in South Africa'. This shift in opinion was, she argues, too late to prevent the violent excesses of the apartheid regime in South Africa and Rhodesia's seven-year war of independence (also known as the second Chimurenga). – Doris Lessing, *The Wind Blows Away Our Words* (London: Picador, 1987), pp. 70–1.

[30] Lessing, *African Laughter*, p. 9; Doris Lessing, 'On Not Winning the Nobel Prize', 7 December 2007, https://www.nobelprize.org/prizes/literature/2007/lessing/25434-doris-lessing-nobel-lecture-2007/ (accessed 19 November 2019).

[31] Lessing, *Going Home*, p. 299.

Dakhrur. White Rhodesian and Zimbabwean life writing after Lessing – particularly following Mugabe's infamous land reforms – has become a popular autobiographical subgenre which tends to lament the end 'of a lost white tribe' and obscure the violence of colonial rule.[32] Lessing stands as the unlikely predecessor to such imperial nostalgia, and her life writing rarely confuses an attachment to her 'myth country' with a longing for colonial rule. Rather than attempting to rehabilitate the structures of white settlement, Lessing's autobiographical returns expose the boundaries and hypocrisies of this confined world. Yet her travel memoirs reveal a relationship with empire which became more nuanced over time; *Going Home*'s compromised attachments to the house on the hill eventually extend into *African Laughter*'s complex understanding of individual homes as representative of an embattled settler state. Lessing may have been unable to conclusively escape from the enclosures of white settlement, yet her autobiographical returns document both the limits and continuing legacies of life in the Rhodesian laager.

Going Home: 'The hill where the house used to be'

Lessing's second autobiography records that, after seven years of living as an exile in London, she 'needed to go back' to Southern Rhodesia; by 1956 her childhood 'seemed so distant, so cut off from me, and I was dreaming every night, long sad dreams of frontiers and lost landscapes'.[33] This return trip was the basis for *Going Home*, a travel narrative which scrutinizes a uniformly conservative settler society from an outside, dissident perspective.[34] Throughout her seven-week journey 'home', white Rhodesians would plead with Lessing

---

[32] Douglas Rogers, *The Last Resort: A Memoir of Zimbabwe* (London: Short Books, 2010), p. 139; Lessing, along with her contemporaries Daphne Anderson and Muriel Spark emphasizes that the memoirs of mid-twentieth-century life writers in Rhodesia are far more critical of white minority rule than their later, white Zimbabwean, successors. In her consideration of 'postcolonial nostalgia', Astrid Rasch has already discussed the 'outpouring of memoirs by white Zimbabweans' after 2000, while Rory Pilossof notes that many of these authors – the sons and daughters of Rhodesian white farmers – prefer to imagine that their lands had previously been 'barren, "empty" lands', using this as a defence 'of ownership, place and belonging that has a long tradition in Zimbabwe/Rhodesia'. Astrid Rasch, 'Postcolonial Nostalgia: The Ambiguities of White Memoirs of Zimbabwe', *History & Memory*, 30:2 (2018): 147–80 (p. 151); Rory Pilossof, *The Unbearable Whiteness of Being: Farmers' Voices from Zimbabwe* (Harare: Weaver Press, 2012), p. 164.

[33] Lessing, *Walking in the Shade*, p. 172.

[34] Lessing's vociferous criticism of white rule in Southern Rhodesia was unmatched by her predecessors and contemporaries, with the exception perhaps of Arthur Shearly Cripps (1869–1952), an Anglican priest who agitated for Black rights throughout his fifty years in the country. Lessing's second autobiography pays homage to Cripps as a lonely voice of white dissent in Southern Rhodesia. *Walking in the Shade*, p. 179.

to 'write something nice about us for a change', while her criticism of white minority rule led to physical threats and strangers attempting to pour drinks over her in crowded bars.[35] Yet *Going Home* also articulates an abiding and profound connection to southern Africa. Even before Lessing disembarks from the plane she luxuriates in the return to 'my air, my landscape and, above all, my sun'.[36] Shortly after her arrival Lessing considers returning to her family's farm:

> All the way from Salisbury I was telling myself that now I would be firm, and turn off from Banket up past the police station, and along that red-dust road. ... Yes. I said, turning the car sharply over the glittering hot railway lines, 'now I must certainly go and see how the hill where the house used to be rises empty and bush-covered from the mealie fields.' But I did not go.[37]

Despite Lessing's familiarity with these local geographies – she can *imagine* navigating the railway tracks, roads and fields that might lead to this site – the house is an absence at the centre of this personal, mapped terrain. No longer on the top of the hill, it forms a lacuna at the heart of Lessing's imagined cartography of home, an empty space surrounded by bush. This is the first description of a possible return to the property in Lessing's life writing. It reveals the emotional connection she maintains to her childhood home and acknowledges the impossibility of re-entering a house that had 'returned to the soil, was swallowed by the bush' less than a year after her family abandoned it in the 1940s.[38] *Going Home* is ostensibly a work of reportage; it was written thanks to Lessing's sponsorship by the Soviet news agency Tass, who paid her to document the changing politics of Southern Rhodesia. As Taylor notes, Lessing's authorial position shifts throughout the narrative: at times she is a journalist, vigorously interrogating trade union leaders, and at others she is a life writer, exploring her own contradictory connections to her former homeland.[39] This undoubtedly results in 'a political and cultural crisis' in the text, one that manifests 'not least in its inability to produce either a stable narrative voice or a fixed implied reader'.[40] Yet Lessing's compulsion to see 'the hill where the house used to be' is the first of many attempts to return in her life writing. The oscillating movement between 'I must go' and 'I did not go' should be recognized as the

---

[35] Lessing, *Going Home*, pp. 67, 188, 277.
[36] Ibid., p. 10.
[37] Ibid., p. 208.
[38] Ibid., p. 37.
[39] Taylor, 'Memory and Desire on *Going Home*', p. 56.
[40] Ibid.

beginning of a contradictory impulse which propels all of her later memoirs and autobiographies.

While deferring any actual act of return, *Going Home* instead offers an imaginary trip to the family's farmhouse. An entire chapter is devoted to describing how the Tayler family constructed their home with limited materials and tools, offering a step-by-step guide to building a home on the colonial frontier. Lessing tells her reader how 'you cut trees from the bush' to make the initial foundations and the skeletal frame of the roof, before taking earth from an ant heap which has 'already been blended by the jaws of a myriad workers'.[41] After coating the frame in a mixture of this substance and ox blood, and fitting a thatched grass roof, the house becomes 'a living thing, responsive to every mood of the weather; and during the time I was growing up it had already begun to sink back into' the landscape.[42] Lessing recreates a home which is here closer to a living organism than an inanimate structure. She describes her family's occupation of the property as short-term, as if they are tenants of the bush, with their house barely distinguishable from the surrounding environment. The farmhouse made from mud and thatch is on temporary loan to the Taylers, its building materials prised by human labourers from the jaws of worker ants. Lessing anticipates that eventually these same creatures will reclaim their rightful property; she remembers how the industrious insects would often start their own trek into the interior of the family home, sending 'outriders into the house' and creating 'a red winding gallery, like an artery, on the walls'.[43] The transitory nature of the farmhouse – which was already sinking back into the landscape when the family occupied it – appears at odds with the permanent sense of belonging that Lessing ascribes to it, with her declarations that the 'first house on the kopje' remains her only true home.[44]

The impermanence of the farmhouse is crucial to both this expression of belonging and to the memoir's impulse to 'go home'. According to Lessing there 'are two sorts of habitation in Africa. One is of brick, cement, plaster, tile and tin – the substance of the country processed and shaped; the other sort is made direct of the stuff of soil and grass and tree'.[45] This draws a dubious comparison between her own childhood and the lives of Black Africans because she lived in a dwelling

---

[41] Lessing, *Going Home*, p. 39.
[42] Ibid., p. 41.
[43] Ibid., p. 54.
[44] Ibid., p. 37.
[45] Ibid., p. 38.

Figure 3.1 Photograph of Kermanshah Farm in the 1920s, Doris Lessing's home in Southern Rhodesia. ©Doris Lessing Will Trust, reproduced with permission of Jonathan Clowes Ltd.

that was directly rooted in the soil. The house, she emphasizes, was made from materials that 'most of the natives of the country live in'.[46] This implicit (and entirely unsustainable) claim to Indigeneity through an umbilical connection to the ground attempts to distinguish her family from those white farmers who live in houses of brick and cement, ensconced and removed from the bush.

Prior to *Going Home*, Lessing had already explored the archetypal settler condition of embattled quarantine in *The Grass Is Singing* (1950), where her protagonist Mary suffers a premonition that her rural farmhouse will 'be killed by the bush'.[47] Mary is plagued by hallucinations of vines throttling her verandah and 'geraniums [growing] side by side with blackjacks' in the chaos of her former garden.[48] Her terror of the bush, and the imagined ruin of her farm, suggests how – in Lessing's writing – there are consequences to living in the first kind of house, made from bricks, where 'the substance of the country [has been] processed and shaped'.[49] By inhabiting such structures, the white occupant remains a permanent stranger, staring out at a threatening, unfamiliar

---

[46] Ibid.
[47] Doris Lessing, *The Grass Is Singing* (Oxford: Heinemann, 1973), p. 242.
[48] Ibid.
[49] Lessing, *Going Home*, p. 38.

environment. When it reconstructs her former home as a temporary building and an organic entity, *Going Home* manoeuvres (with limited success) to write beyond the fears of ruin and invasion which define Mary's settler homestead.

In this initial attempt at homecoming, Lessing's first travel memoir is contorted by the legacies of settlement, pursuing an untenable appropriation of African dwellings. The text may attempt to exempt her from 'the neurotic rigidities of white settlerdom', but it reveals how the Tayler family lived and worked on stolen land, even if their house was built with mud and wooden poles.[50] By pushing up against the physical and emotional structures of settlement, Lessing's first re-construction of home demonstrates the risks of her relationship with Southern Rhodesia. On the one hand, this memoir discusses the need for territorial decolonization, stating that 'Africa belongs to the Africans: the sooner they take it back the better'.[51] Yet this is immediately followed by the qualification that 'a country also belongs to those who feel at home in it'.[52] The inconsistencies in her twinned arguments show Lessing's political belief in land restitution being undermined by her powerful emotional connection to that same landscape, as a settler subject who clearly 'feel[s] at home' in the bush.

Eve Tuck and K. Wayne Yang insist that 'relinquishing stolen land' is key to contemporary decolonization movements, articulating an argument which can help unravel the contradictions of Lessing's first memoir.[53] For while she might be willing to relinquish the farm as a territory, her life writing refuses to renounce a psychological, affective relationship with the landscape. On the one hand, Lessing's emphasis on the psychological rather than the territorial is indebted to an intellectual tradition of decolonizing the mind, rather than the spatial and material demands of more recent decolonial debates.[54] But on the other, these successive generations of decolonial thought highlight the irreconcilable contradictions of *Going Home*, where an anti-imperial settler longs to return to her colonial roots. In this sense Lessing's early life writing shuttles between two diametric opposites: To make a claim upon the southern African landscape is an act of appropriation which places her in the company of other white farmers,

---

[50] Ibid., p. 226.
[51] Ibid., p. 11.
[52] Ibid.
[53] E. Tuck and K. W. Yang, 'Decolonisation Is Not a Metaphor', *Decolonisation: Indigeneity, Education & Society*, 1:1 (2012): 1–40 (p. 19).
[54] Earlier articulations of decolonization, made by Ngũgĩ wa Thiong'o and others acknowledged that colonialism 'imposed its control of the social production of wealth' and the seizure of land but nevertheless insisted that 'its most important area of domination was the mental universe of the colonised'. Ngũgĩ wa Thiong'o, *Decolonising the Mind: The Politics of Language in African Literature* (London: Heinemann Educational, 1986), p. 18.

yet she is nevertheless compelled to return to the site of her colonial childhood. While this memoir was written half a century before Robert Mugabe's notorious fast-track land reforms, it anticipates the complexities of Zimbabwe's later territorial decolonization, which saw thousands of white land owners evicted from their former properties. If, as Julie Cairnie suggests, 'the complications of white women's claims to home space in colonial and postcolonial Zimbabwe' largely centre upon their 'claiming or refusing the colonial bequest: a home and a farm in Africa', *Going Home* sees Lessing shuttling between these opposing poles of refusal and reclamation.[55] In broad terms, she was alert to the politics of land ownership in colonial Africa, remaining scathing of memoirists like Karen Blixen who, in *Out of Africa* (1937), 'never saw that her 6000 acres were not hers'.[56] Lessing viewed farmer-settlers like Blixen as little more than squatters, yet *Going Home* is unable to square the territorial *and* epistemological concerns of her anti-imperialism with the repeated claim that Southern Rhodesia was her only true home.

The rough materials, uneven floors and bumpy walls of her family's farmhouse afforded Lessing a particular intimacy with her environment. Recalling the rough surfaces of her bedroom wall she notes how 'I knew the geography of that wall as I knew the lines on my palm' (whether she or the reader can divine the meaning of these creases remains uncertain).[57] Nevertheless, as a familiar extension of her own body, Lessing also recalls how the property was marked with the faint impressions of others who had moved through it, lightly imprinting themselves on its surfaces:

> [In my bedroom] there were areas of light, brisk graining where Tobias the painter had whisked his paint-brush from side to side … there was another patch where he had put his hand flat on the whitewash. Probably there had been something in his bare foot and he had steadied himself with his hand … Then he had taken out whatever was in his foot and lifted his brush and painted out the hand mark. Or thought he had. For at a certain moment of the sunrise, when the sun was four inches over the mountains … that hand came glistening out of the whitewash like a Sign of some kind.[58]

---

[55] Julie Cairnie, 'Women and the Literature of Settlement and Plunder: Toward an Understanding of the Zimbabwean Land Crisis', *ESC: English Studies in Canada*, 33:1–2 (2007): 165–88 (p. 167).

[56] Doris Lessing, 'A Deep Darkness: A Review of *Out of Africa* by Karen Blixen', in *A Small Personal Voice: Essays, Reviews, Interviews*, ed. Paul Schlueter (New York: Alfred A Knopf, 1974), pp. 147–55 (p. 151).

[57] Lessing, *Under My Skin*, pp. 51, 195.

[58] Lessing, *Going Home*, p. 52.

Here the certainty of Tobias's movements and the precise circumstances in which his palm print could be viewed are given in measurements ('when the sun was four inches over the mountains'), but these quickly give way to unfamiliar and unknown possibilities: '*probably* there had been something in his bare foot … he *thought* he had' painted out his own hand (emphasis my own). During its daily re-emergence the mark on the wall appears like the prehistoric palm prints of a cave painting (several of which, in the nearby Ayrshire hills, were familiar to the young Lessing).[59] But the meaning of a hand which is a 'Sign' remains uncertain, despite this imaginative re-enactment of its origins. The authority of Lessing's narrative voice wavers during this recollection, as the question of what 'kind of sign' it is remains unanswered.

This handprint occupies the heart of Lessing's first memoir, its enigmatic description working in opposition to nineteenth- and early twentieth-century colonial travelogues which ordered unfamiliar landscapes for a metropolitan readership. Such travel narratives were, in Bill Ashcroft's estimation, inseparable from 'debate[s] about possession … about who owns the world'.[60] Yet Lessing refuses to imagine the house as the central location in an ordered report of her journey. The meandering, often confusing trajectory of *Going Home* is not one of assured possession, but of tentative failure. As the self-effacing title suggests, Lessing never quite arrives at her intended destination. Similarly, her reconstruction of the farmhouse reveals that there are few fixed or stable coordinates in this account. Similarly to the 'Wanted on Voyage' trunk in *Alfred and Emily* (discussed in Chapter 5), *Going Home* describes the house through a narrative that zooms inwards – from the hill, to the house, to its interior walls, to the handprint – but refuses to offer a conclusive interpretation of its meaning.

If the bedroom wall is an extension of Lessing's body, then the persistently reappearing handprint also leaves its mark on the author. What is remarkable is perhaps not the print's presence, but its distinct position within a property that bears endless impressions upon its surfaces: The construction of the Tayler's farmhouse involved 'great handfuls of mud' being slapped by labourers against wooden poles while any remaining gaps were filled with 'handfuls of grass'.[61] Lessing dubiously claimed many of these building materials were accidentally

---

[59] Lessing, *Alfred and Emily*, p. 211.
[60] Bill Ashcroft, 'Afterword: Travel and Power', in *Travel Writing, Form and Empire: The Poetics and Politics of Mobility*, ed. Julia Kuehn and Paul Smethurst (New York: Routledge, 2008), pp. 229–41 (p. 230).
[61] Lessing, *Going Home*, p. 40.

sourced from a nearby burial site, meaning that 'the walls of our house had in them the flesh and the blood of the people of the country'.[62] This alarming reference (omitted from all her later life narratives) imagines that many bodies, both living and dead, have come into contact with the property's walls. Yet Lessing's intimate relationship with just one of these leads her to a hypothetical origin story. The mark is the originary sign of a creator – it also perhaps implies the signatory act of an illiterate worker – which occupies the heart of Lessing's core natal location. In the end, it reveals only the limits of knowledge in the settler imaginary, its meaning resolutely unclear.

Whitlock identifies the emerging palm print on Lessing's bedroom wall as one of the 'most intimate moments of longing, memory and identification' in *Going Home* which confirms the land's 'prior occupation'.[63] In this reading, Tobias represents those communities who occupied southern Africa before the arrival of white settlers. Yet this mark also indicates the limitations of Lessing's attempts to inhabit her 'myth country'. She might speculatively imagine how Tobias *may* have leaned on the wall and *might* have examined the underside of his foot, but she cannot offer a resolution which secures the meaning of this mark. Instead, we gain a partial view of the many hands which shored up Lessing's childhood home, a farmhouse which had purportedly 'been built with affection'.[64] The lives of labourers like Tobias (who appears only in this scene, and never again in the vast corpus of Lessing's life writing) are largely obscured in her memories of the house on the hill. The house and the act of life writing are, in this moment, irrevocably intertwined, as a single handprint registers an absent labourer on both the surface of the property and the textual surfaces of the memoir. When she claims that the house remained standing through affection, we might ask: whose sentiments, apart from the author's, are supposedly supporting its unstable foundations? What do the impressions of these hands actually reveal of their original creators? Neither the stories of labourers who created it nor the blood and bones of the ancestors mixed into the building materials can be fully narrated in this reconstruction of her home. Lessing has been described as 'an expert in unsettlement', yet even as *Going Home* strains against the colonial imaginary, the physical and psychic boundaries of the farmhouse – which reflect the laager's firm outlines – remain intact.[65]

---

[62] Ibid.
[63] Whitlock, *The Intimate Empire*, p. 197.
[64] Lessing, *Going Home*, p. 40.
[65] Lorna Sage, *Doris Lessing* (London: Methuen, 1983), p. 11.

In this attempt to recover 'every detail of that house' which was 'like my other skin', Lessing's description of many handprints mingling on walls that are her own body could be read as a rebuttal of miscegenation, a clear rejection of a segregated settler society.[66] Living in Southern Rhodesia meant existing 'within a slowly narrowing and suffocating cage' for Lessing, and her first memoir neither escapes nor resolves the difficulties of feeling homesick for this incarceration.[67] It is, therefore, precisely the point that her first account of homecoming is an unfinished process, disconcerted by memories of the colonial frontier. This extends James Arnett's suggestion that 'there was no excusing, or recusing, [Lessing] from [her] entanglement in coloniality ... she was a colonial subject, albeit one who endeavoured to engender anti-colonial politics and society'.[68] The unfinished acts of return in *Going Home* reflect the vexed nature of Lessing's lifelong relationship with empire and her deeply held anti-imperialism.

It is also important to note that remembering the farmhouse as an impermanent structure subverts the processes of imperial monumentalization that Lessing witnessed throughout her seven-week trip in 1956. Throughout the memoir she disparages the creation of many formal markers celebrating white supremacy. Included amongst these are then-prime minister Lord Malvern's approval of the largest man-made lake in the world (Lake Kariba) in the early 1950s, which Lessing viewed as an attempt to match Cecil Rhodes' legacy of a named settler state. If Malvern hoped to create 'a monument big enough to retire on', then the lake aimed to concretize a progressive history of colonial settlement.[69] Paul Hogarth's drawings which accompany *Going Home* depict other imperial statues and memorials, including a statue of Paul Kruger standing high on a plinth in Church Square, Pretoria.[70] Such manifest expressions of white progress are the antithesis of Lessing's childhood home, an emblem of colonial failure which started sinking back into the bush within months of its creation. While apartheid regimes in both Southern Rhodesia and South Africa preferred to depict colonized peoples as the beneficiaries of empire, Lessing's first travel

---

[66] Lessing, *Going Home*, pp. 55, 195.
[67] Ibid., p. 18.
[68] James Arnett, 'Colonizing, Decolonizing: Bad-Faith Liberalism and African Space Colonialism in Doris Lessing's Screenplay *The White Princess*', *Journal of Screenwriting*, 10:1 (2019): 81–95 (p. 82).
[69] Lessing, *Going Home*, p. 218.
[70] This particular statue still stands in Pretoria's Church Square today and, following the 2015 removal of Cecil John Rhodes's statue from the University of Cape Town, has been the subject of an ongoing controversy in South Africa. As of 2023, however, Paul Kruger remains on his plinth overlooking Church Square. – Adrian Blomfield 'Radical South African Party Calls for Statue of Boer Leader Paul Kruger to Be Removed', *The Telegraph*, 20 May 2018, https://www.telegraph.co.uk/news/2018/05/20/radical-south-african-party-calls-statue-boer-leader-paul-kruger/ (accessed 4 February 2022).

memoir rejects these glossed histories of exploitation and dispossession. Her refusal to preserve the farmhouse as a personal monument to her colonial childhood is an extension of this. As this chapter's conclusion notes, this has not prevented some literary critics from making romanticized pilgrimages to the site once known as Kermanshah Farm.[71] But Lessing herself was careful to depict the farm as an essentially inaccessible property to which neither she nor any interested visitor could satisfactorily return.

In conclusion, the long legacies of settlement shape both *Going Home*'s thematic concerns with homecoming *and* the memoir's form. The book's recent editions end with several postscripts written across 1956 and 1957, along with a series of afterwords Lessing added during the 1960s, 1980s and 1990s. These postscripts describe the discovery that she had been made a prohibited immigrant in Rhodesia during 1956, meaning that her travel memoir ends with the logistical impossibility of any immediate return. Several later notes document her shifting political persuasions during her subsequent decades in exile, claiming that these were 'added almost in desperation to try and keep up with events'.[72] While some critics have read these additions as 'the retraction of a confession' because they disavow Lessing's previous communist sympathies, they confirm the memoir's commitment to homecoming as a work in progress, defying the policed borders of the Rhodesian laager.[73] Lessing's flawed attempts to reconstruct and imaginatively return to her family's farm were inseparable from her lifelong commitment to dismantling imperial power. As the final afterword to *Going Home* is dated 1992, the year of *African Laughter*'s publication, Lessing's second travel memoir acts as the sequel to her first. The four journeys described in this second text form a reflective quartet, considering the pitfalls and possibilities of returning to her myth country.

African Laughter: Settler Life in the Postcolonial Present

The most critically neglected of Lessing's life narratives, *African Laughter* chronicles four trips she made to Zimbabwe during the country's first, tumultuous decade of independence: It documents a collective, post-war 'state

---

[71] See chapter nine of Lara Feigel's *Free Woman* (2018).
[72] Doris Lessing, 'Afterword', in *Going Home* (London: Flamingo, 1992), p. 255.
[73] Taylor, 'Memory and Desire on *Going Home*', p. 58.

of shock' in 1982; the cautious optimism 'which transformed the atmosphere' after Zimbabwe's 1988 Unity Accord[74] and the later, devastating impact of the AIDS crisis during her journeys in 1989 and 1992.[75] In the twenty-six years between *African Laughter* and *Going Home*, Lessing repeatedly told herself that she did not wish to return to her former homeland, yet acknowledged that these 'rational considerations did not reach some mysterious region of myself'.[76] In London, she frequently 'dreamed the same dream' of being back in the bush, or walking the streets of Salisbury (now Harare).[77] On her first trip in 1982 little seemed to have changed after independence, as for many white communities life in 'the Southern Rhodesian lager [sic]' continued apace.[78] *African Laughter* records that the isolated houses of white farmers resembled miniature fortresses in the new Zimbabwe and that a collective, embattled mentality continued the toxic legacies of the colour bar.[79]

The book begins with two maps captioned 'Then ... Southern Rhodesia'; and 'Now...Zimbabwe', printed on opposite pages, with one depicting southern Africa during the colonial era and the other after independence.[80] These lead to an opening chapter which briefly outlines the ninety-year history of the settler state, describing how a 'shield shaped country in the middle of the map', was central to Cecil Rhodes' hallucinatory vision of painting the African continent 'red from Cape to Cairo'.[81] This beginning consigns Southern Rhodesia to the past tense, as the symbol of a dismantled empire. The key cartographic difference between the maps of 'then' and 'now' is the striking addition of the man-made Lake Kariba (whose construction Lessing had witnessed in *Going Home*), which was designed to give Rhodesians their own 'inland sea' for boating and angling.[82] In a series of autobiographical asides, Lessing reveals how her own borders were also remade in the spaces between the Rhodesian past and the Zimbabwean

---

[74] Lessing, *African Laughter*, pp. 48, 152.
[75] See Anthony Chennells, 'Doris Lessing's Versions of Zimbabwe from *The Golden Notebook* to *Alfred and Emily*', *English Academy Review*, 32:2 (2015): 53–69; Sarah De Mul, 'Zimbabwe and the Politics of the Everyday in Doris Lessing's *African Laughter*', in *Migratory Settings*, ed. Murat Aydemir and Alex Rotas (Amsterdam: Rodopi, 2008), pp. 139–56; John McAllister, 'Knowing Native, Going Native', pp. 25–38.
[76] Lessing, *African Laughter*, p. 12.
[77] Ibid.
[78] Lessing, *African Laughter*, p. 31.
[79] Alexandra Fuller also records how families who stayed in Rhodesia during the bloody years of the second Chimurenga (during the 1970s) were increasingly forced to shelter in farmhouses 'behind razor-gleaming fences, bristling with their defence'. Alexandra Fuller, *Don't Let's Go to the Dogs Tonight* (London: Picador, 2002), p. 102.
[80] Lessing, *African Laughter*, n.p.
[81] Ibid., p. 3.
[82] McDermott Hughes, *Whiteness in Zimbabwe*, pp. 30, 49.

present. She describes her longing to return to southern Africa as a secret 'lake of tears', which 'slop about, or seep, or leak, secretly making moist what I thought I kept dry'.[83] The fixed and neatly bordered cartographies which begin *African Laughter* are undermined by a liquid longing for home, expressed through the image of an internal reservoir. Kariba and Lessing's 'lake of tears' are twinned bodies of water, one emblematic of the settler state, the other indicating an ongoing, fraught attachment to the colonial past. From the outset, then, her second travel memoir questions the closure of imperial history, embedding a personal life narrative of homecoming in a travel report on the changing state of the post-colonial nation.

While *African Laughter* is concerned with documenting daily life in Zimbabwe, the Rhodesian landscape of Lessing's childhood is clearly visible beneath the text's meandering journeys. Contrary to appearances, the initial, opening maps do not help the reader situate themselves geographically, as this travel narrative follows no discernible route across the landscape. Although the memoir is filled with named places and people – chapter titles are frequently given locations such as 'a trip to Simukai' and 'the garden in Harare' – these disjointed scenes are disorientating.[84] For Sarah De Mul, *African Laughter* 'challenges the traditional travel plot of a singular, chronological journey from departure to arrival'.[85] This reading might be complicated by Lessing's voluntary work 'with the non-governmental organisation (NGO) Book Team' throughout the 1980s, who travelled across Zimbabwe to gather 'the common wisdom of the people on a range of topics such as governance … agriculture and land management'.[86] Collecting this colloquial knowledge was intended to help supplement the scarce number of printed texts in the country. *African Laughter*'s form, which abandons the internal chronology of a cohesive narrative and instead records the voices of ordinary Zimbabweans, reflects Lessing's collective work with Book Team. While the text is undoubtedly an unconventional travel memoir, it develops from her earlier attempts to return to the house on the hill, reflecting on what it means to inhabit the enclosures of the Rhodesian laager.

During her first trip to Zimbabwe in 1982, Lessing once again defers her return to the family farm after her brother, Harry, warns her not to 'go back', describing how his own attempt at homecoming almost 'did me in'.[87] Lessing

---

[83] Lessing, *African Laughter*, p. 13.
[84] Ibid., p. 372.
[85] Sarah De Mul, 'Doris Lessing, Feminism and the Representation of Zimbabwe', *European Journal of Women's Studies*, 16:1 (2009): 33–51 (p. 40).
[86] James Arnett, 'Doris Lessing and the Ethical African Archive', *Tulsa Studies in Women's Literature*, 37:2 (2018): 435–44 (pp. 435–6).
[87] Lessing, *African Laughter*, p. 37.

heeds his advice, and instead returns to a different, temporary homestead from her childhood by driving through the Marondera District (known by white Rhodesians as the Marandellas). During the 1930s, this was the Tayler family's preferred camping ground, a place they viewed as the furthest extension of their property: 'As a child the Marandellas was the other pole to our farm.'[88] Her return to the former campsite in the early 1980s is the first of a series of homecomings in *African Laughter*. Once there, Lessing remembers how her family would set up their quarters for the night:

> The 'boy' cut branches to make an enclosure about twenty feet by twenty, but round, in the spirit of the country. This leafy barrier was to keep out leopards, who were still holding on, though threatened, in their caves in the hills. We could have lain out under the trees without the barricade for any leopard worth its salt could have jumped over it in a moment and carried us off. No, the walls were an expression of something else, not a keeping out, but a keeping together, strangers in a strange land. My parents needed those encircling, branchy arms.[89]

These holidays marked the few occasions when the family would stray beyond the mud walls of their home and into the wilderness beyond. In a description which references *Going Home*'s instructions for building a farmhouse in the bush, Lessing notes how her parents relied on a Black employee to provide an illusory boundary, separating them from their surroundings. The symbolic meaning of this structure develops rhetorically from an 'enclosure' to a 'barrier' to a 'barricade', none of which would protect the Taylers from the possible predations of a leopard. The round, fenced-in area 'in the spirit of the country' refers to a kraal, a traditional circle of African huts surrounded by posts. It also suggests how their campsite imitates the roughly circular outline of landlocked Southern Rhodesia, evoking both the shield-shaped country visualized at the beginning of *African Laughter* and the insularity (the 'laager mentality') of white Rhodesian life. The imagined threat of leopards excuses her family's need for a circular camp which is both a temporary homestead and a microcosm for the settler nation.

Lessing wryly recalls that, on these journeys beyond the farm, her parents would preserve 'their customs as if they were still inside the house', washing in white porcelain bowls and sticking to regular mealtimes.[90] Here she implicitly distinguishes between making a home in southern Africa and being *at home*

---

[88] Ibid., p. 17.
[89] Ibid., pp. 21–2.
[90] Ibid., p. 23.

there. This return to the Marandellas highlights her family's estrangement from their chosen homeland. If her parents viewed the campsite as a tight, intimate embrace, comforted by 'branchy arms', Lessing views this space as representative of the contradictory claims to white belonging in Southern Rhodesia. Even as they purport to stray into the bush, her parents' temporary encampments reflect their fearful incarceration in the domestic structures of settlement.

By contrast, however, Lessing and her brother were raised in this landscape and felt relatively at home there. The children would relish any opportunity to sleep outside:

> We two had a pact ... that we should help each other not to fall off to sleep ... I lay rigid, face absorbing moonlight, starlight, as if I were stretched out to night-bathe. I knew that this lying with no roof between me and the sky was a gift, not to be wasted ... This lying out at night might never happen again. On verandahs – yes, but there always seemed to be mosquito nets and screens between you and the night. And it didn't happen again. I never again slept under the sky in Africa.[91]

If the verandah was the architectural emblem of white colonial life, it was nevertheless, for Lessing and her brother, an impediment to their relationship with the land.[92] This distinctive inside/outside space, perched on the outer reaches of the home but separate from the wilderness beyond, is dismissed by two children who crave a more direct connection with the African sky. Both seek a relationship with their surroundings which is unmediated by the 'mosquito nets and screens', rejecting those features of settler domesticity that might protect their bodies from a hostile climate. By staying awake, staring directly at the stars, Lessing attempts to break out of the material and imaginative laager constructed by her parents. She intends to escape vertically from the confines of their encampment through bodily contact with the sky. Yet, like her descriptions of the farmhouse as her 'other skin', Lessing's attempt to build a habitation which escapes the literal and symbolic boundaries of settlement has only limited success.[93] Even this early act of communion marks the beginning of her exile: 'I

---

[91] Ibid., p. 27.
[92] In his reflections on the colonial bungalow, William J. Glover notes that verandahs had multiple functions for imperial households, not least as a shelter which provided cool air and respite during hot summer months. However, Glover also notes the potentially subversive nature of this liminal space lay in its simultaneous use as a site for white recreation where 'servants [also] often slept at night, and took rest in their shade during the day'. The verandah, in other words, could be a contact zone which challenged the rigid, racially segregated, structures of colonial settlements. William J. Glover, '"A Feeling of Absence From Old England": The Colonial Bungalow', *Home Cultures: The Journal of Architecture, Design, and Domestic Space*, 1:1 (2004): 61–82 (p. 76).
[93] Lessing, *Under My Skin*, p. 195.

never again slept under the sky in Africa'. Neither the kraal, nor the laager, offer a permanent dwelling place in her myth country.

Lessing's journey through the Marandellas and her subsequent reminiscences with her brother about these camping trips are the closest she comes, in 1982, to returning to Kermanshah Farm. On the one hand, these scenes highlight how venturing away from the family homestead allowed both Tayler children alternative forms of habitation, for 'being in the bush was to be with the animals, one of them'.[94] But even as they provisionally affected life inside a green leafy 'boma' or 'kraal', mimicking the habitations of African communities, in actuality their home-away-from-home remains the laager, the archetypal residence of the settler. When the family sleep beneath the sky, kitted out in pyjamas and snug blankets, their supposed connection to the landscape only confirms the tenuous nature of their settlement.

After driving through the Marandellas Lessing realizes that her brother now lives inside a permanent, defensive encampment of his own. His house is built inside 'a fence that reminded me of pictures of internment camps, a good twelve feet high, of close mesh', while within the enclosure 'two large Alsatians bounded and barked'.[95] Once again, the security measures of the white Rhodesian home (where meshed fencing has replaced leafy boughs) locks the inhabitants into their quarantined lives. As Chapter 2 has already explored, the slippage between internment camps and colonial households was all-too familiar to J. G. Ballard, growing up in Shanghai's International Settlement. But Lessing's brother maintains a Rhodesian life inside post-colonial Zimbabwe by being incarcerated in his farmhouse. His high walls are more like a prison than a refuge. Although Lessing anticipates that she will be the exile in their reunion, Harry – like his parents – is also expelled from the landscape, cut off behind the high fortifications of his home. He uneasily tells his sister that 'I often wonder if I've lived my life right ... I should have been in the bush'.[96] Here both siblings are united – one in London, the other in southern Africa – by an inability to escape the physical and psychological boundaries of white rule. In this scene of supposed homecoming, both are separated from the landscape of their childhood, peering out at a distance from behind a meshed wire fence.

African Laughter defers Lessing's return to the house on the hill by detouring to those holidays which were 'the best times of my childhood'.[97] Yet this

---

[94] Lessing, *African Laughter*, p. 24.
[95] Ibid., p. 34.
[96] Ibid., p. 41.
[97] Ibid., p. 40.

manoeuvre also demonstrates that, in Lessing's life writing, white domestic space is inseparable from the Rhodesian nation. This is most explicit in a scene where Harry lapses back into 'the monologue' – the circuitous, racist criticism of Zimbabwe's new government that his sister encounters throughout *African Laughter*. Harry's outrage focuses on the new, African president living inside '*our* Government House' as he rants that President Canaan Banana 'hasn't been in it a week before he has chickens running all over the gardens, *our* gardens, and all his friends and relations camped in the place, like a kraal'.⁹⁸ This horrified description of the official residence of Rhodesia's governor being repurposed and renamed as Zimbabwe's State House, reveals the close relationship between home and the settler state in *African Laughter*. The irony of Harry's objections to camping aside, his dislike of President Banana taking up residence in this house-of-the-nation emphasizes how 'the Rhodesian laager' is always conceived through its racial other: the African kraal.

The early chapters of *African Laughter* are important because it is only *after* Lessing recalls her family trips, and spends time in her brother's fortified home, that the text becomes a meandering, fragmented travel narrative. Indeed, for the majority of '1982'– the memoir's first section – it is possible to plot Lessing's route across the country, from her arrival by plane, trip to the Marandellas, fortnight in her brother's house, before she 'take[s] off' to explore Zimbabwe, causing an abrupt shift in the narrative's form. The previously linear travelogue becomes fractured, the text's internal chronology breaks down, and Lessing's movements are broken into small entries with abstract titles such as 'rain' and 'the assistant'.⁹⁹ There is a temporal confusion created by vague descriptions such as 'one afternoon' or that 'I have spent a day ... two days ... three days in offices in Harare'.¹⁰⁰ Amidst detailed accounts of Zimbabwean life, Lessing's own role as narrator becomes increasingly obscured. But it is crucial that this change in the memoir's form is prompted by her first attempt at homecoming in the Marandellas, and the subsequent realization that she will not be able to immediately return to Kermanshah Farm. In 1982 'the same reluctance that in 1956 [in *Going Home*] made it impossible to turn the car's steering wheel into the track of the farm gripped me still'.¹⁰¹ As structure of *African Laughter* becomes increasingly fragmented, Lessing's second travel memoir is compromised by the now-familiar, conflicting impulses to both escape from and return to the laager

---

⁹⁸ Ibid., p. 42.
⁹⁹ Ibid., p. 130.
¹⁰⁰ Ibid., p. 230.
¹⁰¹ Ibid., p. 139.

of her childhood, working to get back to the house on the hill. Unable to resolve these opposing forces, *African Laughter* embarks on a series of journeys which have neither points of departure, nor a final destination.

The book begins with the initial promise of return, the fulfilment of *Going Home* wherein Lessing will return to the farm and rediscover her myth country. But when the much-delayed scene of her homecoming arrives (occurring in the book's second volume), this moment is an anti-climax. Lessing realizes that it is not the absence of the original farmhouse which caused her brother such pain, nor was it the fact 'that they cut the top off "our" hill'.[102] Rather his distress was caused by 'the bush. It had gone. Where he had spent his childhood were interminable red fields, *his bush* – gone'.[103] Lessing's rejection of the typical settler justification for owning land through productivity is registered through a shift in punctuation and typeface. The hill becomes 'our' hill, the landscape becomes '*his bush*', with these inflections ironizing the claim that it still belongs to the white family – the Taylers – who had inhabited it several decades earlier. Lessing distances herself from this, distinguishing between her own feelings of attachment and her brother's suggestion that he can continue to own the farm and surrounding bush.

By forcing her gaze away from the altered landscape and the spectacular, elevated view from the kopje, Lessing looks towards the more modest environs of the farm:

> Everywhere over the flat place that tops the hill are disused brick buildings, and, half hidden in grass, a brick and concrete line with rusty iron rings which had been pigs, or perhaps cows. A barn was up here too: surely unintelligent. … What I was looking at was not only the scene of our life, that had left no traces, nothing, for the ants and the borers and the termites had demolished it all, but at the remains of another later effort, which had failed. Everything here spoke of failure. … What we were looking at, I was sure, was just such another effort as my parents' – who were always trying a little bit of this and a little bit of that. One might believe that their spirit had infected the people who came after them.[104]

In a deflective move that echoes *Going Home*'s description of a handprint on the bedroom wall, the narrative voice of this passage refuses to interpret what Lessing sees during her charged moment of return. *Perhaps* the rusted iron rings imply pigs, or perhaps cows. The only flash of certainty is her recognition of

---

[102] Ibid., p. 314.
[103] Ibid.
[104] Ibid., p. 316.

mutual failure, as Lessing positions her parents' inability to successfully work the land within a long litany of commercial failures upon the site. While the Tayler's farmhouse is long gone, ageing and depleted bungalows stand in its place. The connections Lessing draws between different generations of inhabitants contradicts the arguments of many white Rhodesians, including her brother, that 'they [Black Zimbabweans] can't run anything'.[105] These fantasies of racial supremacy rewrite Rhodesian history by falsely claiming that white farmers had, prior to independence, enjoyed unmitigated success. By contrast, Lessing insists that her parents failed on this farm, and that this has 'infected' the attempts of their successors who also cannot make the land profitable. In the charged context of land ownership in Southern Rhodesia and Zimbabwe, this line of continuity is a highly subversive manoeuvre. As David McDermott Hughes acknowledges, Rhodesian writers frequently 'crafted a property claim and self-image around an absent native unworthy of his environment'.[106] Lessing's return to Kermanshah Farm dismantles her family's self-aggrandising myths by insisting both that the land does not belong to her (it is never *her* bush) and that they were no different to their successors in failing to make good use of the soil. Her descriptions of rusting equipment transform the farm into a site of imperial ruin, suggesting how colonial legacies continue to impact upon Zimbabwe in the late twentieth century. Her homecoming challenges any claim her family can make to this land, emphasizing that despite their efforts, they had 'left no traces' of their occupation.

Later in 1992, in the book's fourth and final chapter, Lessing plans another 'quick trip to my myth country' wanting to return to 'that hill always steeped in moonlight, starlight, sunlight'.[107] Her fantastical image of a simultaneous day and night is brought to an abrupt halt by a large sign which impedes her progress: 'Trespassers will be Prosecuted'.[108] This transforms Lessing from a former resident to an intruder; the question of how she can be connected to the farm remains unanswered at the close of *African Laughter*. While no longer a prohibited immigrant, she finds herself on the external side of the fence, outside the enclosure of belonging in Zimbabwe. Her aim of returning to, but not claiming possession of, the farm is refused in this final journey, as the perimeter of the former laager is sealed. McAllister suggests that both of Lessing's returns in *African Laughter* are 'the antithesis of the climactic moment that conventional

---

[105] Ibid., p. 42.
[106] McDermott Hughes, *Whiteness in Zimbabwe*, p. 7.
[107] Lessing, *African Laughter*, p. 426.
[108] Ibid.

travel narratives typically make out of reaching their goal'.[109] Yet across *African Laughter*'s fragmented, non-linear narrative, Lessing's conflicted relationship with Kermanshah Farm resurfaces, again and again, in *African Laughter*'s wandering travelogues.

African Laughter is the culmination of Lessing's experiments with the travel memoir form, extending *Going Home*'s efforts to wrestle with the contradiction of a lifelong anti-imperialist attempting to return to Southern Rhodesia. Yet Lessing's journeys provide a nuanced account of settler life as an enclosed encampment. If *Going Home* attempts to reconstruct the domestic epicentre of Lessing's myth country – the house on the hill – *African Laughter* acknowledges, twenty-six years later, that this manoeuvre is untenable. Instead of trying to rebuild, Lessing's actual return is focused on an act of dismantlement, deconstructing the farm as an ideal of white success, or the secure foundation of a settler's laager. It becomes a symbol of entrapment, an enclosure of imperial failure which her parents were not only unable to escape, but which they have passed down to future generations of Zimbabweans. In her final, speculative memoir Lessing continued to experiment with autobiographical forms which might circumvent her earlier travel narratives, trying to both get back and 'get free' from her memories of colonial life. Despite the scope of her long life writing project, the contradictions of these manoeuvres would remain ultimately unresolved.

Conclusion: The Old Muwanga Tree

Many of Lessing's homecomings converge at the site of a distinctive muwanga tree which marked the edge of the cleared land surrounding her family's farmhouse. Although it is curiously absent from *Going Home*, the muwanga is described at length in *African Laughter*, *Under My Skin* and *Alfred and Emily*. Otherwise known as *Pericopsis angolensis*, a plant native to Zimbabwe, this species can reach considerable heights, often growing to over 20 m, and Lessing remembers the tree as the tallest landmark in the area.[110] It appears first in *African Laughter*, when Lessing asks her brother 'what happened to the muwanga tree?' and mourns its absence during her first return to the farm in 1988: 'Gone was

---

[109] McAllister, 'Knowing Native, Going Native', p. 30.
[110] Keith Coates Palgrave, *Trees of Southern Africa* (Cape Town: Penguin Random House, 1997), p. 297.

the big muwanga tree that once dominated all this landscape'.[111] It is described in *Under My Skin* as a vital coordinate of her childhood: 'In front of the house was a big mawonga [sic] tree, its pale trunk scarred by lightning, an old tree full of bees and honey'.[112] By *Alfred and Emily*, she recalled that the tree was 'always full of birds, sporting a conspicuous broken branch which had buckled beneath the weight of a locust swarm'.[113] Reading across these descriptions, the muwanga tree emerges as a border line which distinguished the family farm from the surrounding, uncultivated bush. Inhabited by bees and birds, it initially appears to offer a symbol of home that the Tayler family shared with other creatures. The seasonal returns of migratory birds who roosted in its branches marked the circular passing of the seasons. Lessing frequently remembers the distinctive 'black lightning scar' which marked its trunk, a reminder of the challenging climate that her family contended with throughout their tenure on the farm.[114]

The muwanga occupies a key symbolic function in Lessing's life writing. As the tallest tree for several miles around, it functions as a local landmark, yet it also promises a specific legacy for the Taylers once they are gone. According to *African Laughter*, Lessing's parents would repeatedly declare '"you can bury us under the old muwanga tree", meaning it was certainly not as good as an elm or an ash or an oak, but the next best thing'.[115] They imagined that this grave site might anchor them to a new homeland, providing burial rites in southern Africa. It was prized by Lessing's parents *precisely because* it was not a plant which could thrive in the English countryside, it stood distinct from the imported 'guava trees, plantains [and] marigolds' in Lessing's mother's garden.[116] Similar flowers surrounded settlers' farmhouses in their district, creating a colourful boundary line which 'marked white occupancy'.[117] The muwanga, unlike these imported intruders, belongs to the bush rather than the farm, seeming to promise the Taylers a form of posthumous Indigeneity. In Lessing's life writing this tree is the site which exemplifies her family's desire to be at home in Southern Rhodesia.

Initially the muwanga also seems to establish a particular genealogical certainty, acting as a family tree which records the lives of multiple generations. Lessing and her brother would therefore become its inheritors, as heirs to this farm. By claiming the tree, her parents hoped to commemorate their own lives

---

[111] Lessing, *African Laughter*, p. 313.
[112] Lessing, *Under My Skin*, p. 55.
[113] Lessing, *Alfred and Emily*, p. 231.
[114] Lessing, *African Laughter*, p. 313.
[115] Ibid.
[116] Lessing, *Under My Skin*, p. 52.
[117] Ibid.

and to secure the futurity of their descendants, who would presumably inhabit the land after their deaths. Lessing had her own, personal form of communion with the muwanga; as a teenager seeking sanctuary from a fractious mother, she would 'sink in the shade of [the] tree not a hundred yards from the house' reading and daydreaming of adult freedom.[118] Lara Feigel, who made a pilgrimage to the location of Kermanshah Farm while writing her own memoir, *Free Woman* (2018), imagines how Lessing might have 'read sprawled under the Muwanga tree at the bottom of the hill … the ridges of her spine tessellating with the roots protruding from underneath her'.[119] In a description which rewrites scenes from *Under My Skin*, Feigel pictures the tree as an extension of Lessing's developing body, its roots anchoring her to the southern African soil.

However, to read the muwanga tree as an anchor, a tomb or a clichéd living representation of genealogy – one which shores up the Taylers' claims to being 'at home' in Southern Rhodesia – misreads the vexed forms of homecoming in Lessing's life writing. For rather than grounding her permanently to the Zimbabwean landscape, the muwanga tree reveals only an unstable, tenuous position in her myth country. It does not offer longevity, nor can it provide a secure connection to the land. Its dual, unstable meaning mirrors the fraught renditions of settler family trees, ancestry and genealogy in Frame's autobiographies (discussed next in Chapter 4). This is made explicit in Lessing's final retelling of her return to Kermanshah Farm, in *Alfred and Emily*, which once again describes 'the mawonga [*sic*] tree', and her parents' frequent declaration: 'Well, that old tree will still be here when we are gone'.[120] But *Alfred and Emily* adds that the tree 'lasted not much longer than they did'; it was felled by lightning shortly after her father's deteriorating health drove her parents back into the suburbs of Salisbury.[121] The literal meaning of the tree as grounding or rooting them to the soil is misleading. In actuality, it cannot provide a permanent monument to their lives in Southern Rhodesia. The muwanga is a warning that we should read *across* Lessing's life narratives and remain attentive to the complexities of her multiple returns home, not least because Lessing herself recognized that the tree could not become her permanent residence. When Feigel describes a trunk tessellating with the young author's spine, she imagines it connecting her bones to the soil beneath her feet. Yet in actuality, the tree reveals how the unresolved tensions of Lessing's repeated attempts at homecoming now impact on a new

---

[118] Lessing, *Under My Skin*, p. 160.
[119] Feigel, *Free Woman*, p. 25.
[120] Lessing, *Alfred and Emily*, p. 232.
[121] Ibid.

generation of life writers influenced by her work. Going back to Kermanshah Farm, to life in the 'Rhodesian laager', and even to her beloved muwanga tree, is not only impossible but arguably undesirable in Lessing's life writing.

The muwanga is instead a deliberately dismantled monument to a settler childhood. Lessing undermines and questions its central position in her autobiographical writing because, like the 'cenotaphs and tombs of Unknown Soldiers' that Benedict Anderson describes in *Imagined Communities* (1983), this muwanga tree is 'saturated with ghostly *national* imaginings'.[122] It must not become a tomb for Lessing's parents, or a figurative set of natal roots for the author, as both might ensure the futurity of Southern Rhodesia and Lessing was resolutely, ideologically opposed to preserving the settler state. Her life writing may be compelled to return, over and over, to the site of the muwanga, but this is always to uproot its symbolic functions. Like the farmhouse itself, no monument to her childhood can remain standing. By narrating the muwanga's eventual collapse, Lessing describes how, like the house on the kopje, it quickly became indiscernible from the surrounding bush.

Lessing had already described her 1988 return to Kermanshah Farm in *African Laughter*, yet in *Alfred and Emily* she expands this account to include her mild altercation with a drunk farmworker, when she insists that 'there used to be a big tree here', and he angrily retorts that 'there was never any tree'.[123] He adds that even if there had once been a muwanga tree, Lessing is using 'the wrong name' and she retreats from the property believing that she has just seen 'history being unmade, the past forsworn'.[124] Once more, the tree represents the contested histories of the settler state. As *Alfred and Emily* reimagines her parents' lives in an 'unmade' history, exploring the alternative possibilities of a world without the First World War, Lessing's attachment to the muwanga as a marker of Rhodësian history is doubly complicated in this exchange. Her final, speculative memoir attempts to surpass the legacies of white colonial rule by rewriting history but is ultimately unable to do so. What remains clear in the charged tussle over the memory of the tree is that, in the newly independent Zimbabwe, any record of the family's colonial lives are being extinguished and all physical traces of their tenure are erased. This vital co-ordinate of Lessing's childhood is not just forgotten but categorically denied (there was *never* a tree here). While it should not become a memorial to white settlerdom, neither does

---

[122] Benedict Anderson, *Imagined Communities: Reflections on the Origin and Spread of Nationalism* (London: Verso, 2006), p. 10.
[123] Lessing, *Alfred and Emily*, p. 229.
[124] Ibid.

Lessing want its existence – and by extension her own memories of Southern Rhodesia – to be denied.

The muwanga is both an ironic symbol of permanence in Lessing's life writing and a vital touchstone that exposes the contradictions in her attempts to go home, the near-obsessional attempts to write and re-write her memories of empire. Despite its central position in her autobiographical writing, this tree cannot root Lessing to southern Africa. Like the secure, branching arms which enclosed the Taylers on their camping trips, the muwanga tree offers only the illusion of safe anchorage. By pursuing the distinctions between Lessing's two African travel memoirs, this chapter emphasizes the risks of remembering the colonial past and the difficulties of returning – whether literally or imaginatively – to life in the Rhodesian laager. In the end, Lessing was always 'trying to get free' from the legacies of empire.[125] All of her life narratives are concerned with unfinished business, exposing a series of entanglements with settler colonialism that will not, or cannot, be undone.

---

[125] Lessing, *Alfred and Emily*, p. viii.

4

Possessions, Property and Post-Imperial Melancholia in Janet Frame's Autobiographies

Introduction: Life Lines and Autobiographical Space

The obituaries that followed Janet Frame's death in 2004 reflected on the life of 'New Zealand's best known but least public author', whose extraordinary biography was more familiar to many readers than her accomplished, experimental prose.[1] As the daughter of a railway worker, Frame was born and raised in relative poverty on the South Island and began writing from an early age. Yet after she first moved away to college in the early 1940s, and submitted an essay which confessed to a recent suicide attempt, Frame's tutor recommended her committal to Seacliff Lunatic Asylum.[2] Her six weeks in Seacliff were a 'concentrated course in the horrors of insanity and the dwelling-place of those judged insane, separating me forever from the former acceptable realities and assurances of everyday life'.[3] Frame went on to be admitted to numerous institutions over the following decade. She was misdiagnosed with schizophrenia, and subject to hundreds of electroconvulsive therapy (ECT), with each 'the equivalent, in degree of fear, to an execution'.[4] It was only after she was scheduled for a prefrontal lobotomy in 1951 that her first book, *The Lagoon and Other Stories*, won a major literary prize, prompting the hospital's superintendent to cancel the planned procedure.[5] While it's possible to suggest

---

[1] Michael King, 'Janet Frame', *The Guardian*, 30 January 2004, https://www.theguardian.com/news/2004/jan/30/guardianobituaries.booksobituaries (accessed 29 September 2022).

[2] Frame's second autobiography records how her psychology tutor suggested that his students write 'a condensed autobiography' as part of their course. When Frame's submission divulged that she had recently swallowed a large quantity of aspirin he swiftly recommended her for psychiatric 'treatment' in Seacliff. Janet Frame, *An Angel at My Table*, in *The Complete Autobiography* (London: Women's Press, 1990), p. 189.

[3] Ibid., p. 193.

[4] Ibid., p. 224.

[5] Michael King, *Wrestling with the Angel: The Life of Janet Frame* (London: Picador, 2001), p. 112.

that life writing (the university assignment) landed her in the asylum in the first place, Frame always insisted that writing 'actually saved my life'.[6] Her three autobiographies, and Jane Campion's subsequent biopic *An Angel at My Table* (1990), furthered the growing public interest in Frame's life and work.[7] Yet as Thora Pattern – a narrator in her semi-autobiographical novel *The Edge of the Alphabet* (1962) – reminds us, life writing is a complex and potentially violent business for Frame. Thora blends 'the life lines' of various named and unnamed characters in the novel, before reciting a litany: 'life line, umbilical cord, fishing line, trip wire, strangling rope'.[8] By recreating a lifespan from birth to death, this sequence describes how genealogies can sustain like an umbilical cord, ensnare like an angler's line or cause both accidents and intentional destruction. As Frame's readers, we have been warned.

Like all of the life writers discussed in this book, Frame's autobiographies remember a childhood imbued with the legacies of British colonial rule. Her formal education praised 'the Empire, the King, the Governor-General, the Anzacs at Gallipoli, [and] Robert Falcon Scott at the South Pole'.[9] Moving in ever-widening concentric circles, her early understanding of imperial masculinity here spans the globe, expanding out from Britain's monarch to polar exploration in the extremes of the southern hemisphere. After travelling to London in 1956 – where she lived for the majority of the next seven years – Frame shared the dismay of many former colonial subjects who moved from so-called peripheries to the metropole. Her first impressions were of a depressed, post-war city where 'bombed sites [were] not yet rebuilt, overgrown with grass and weeds and scattered with rubble'.[10] Perhaps unsurprisingly, previous postcolonial readings of Frame have focused on this archetypal 'journey in', depicted in both her third autobiography, *The Envoy from Mirror City*, and revised in fictional works like *The Edge of the Alphabet*. In contrast, this chapter demonstrates that a preoccupation with imperialism is threaded *throughout* Frame's three autobiographies. The first two volumes – *To the Is-Land* and *An Angel at My Table* – offer startling accounts of how the colonial past shapes daily life in Aotearoa/New Zealand, detailing the

---

[6] Frame, *An Angel at My Table*, p. 221.
[7] Claire Bazin details how, by the time Frame's autobiographies were published during the 1980s, her earlier novels were largely out of print. Bazin concludes that, had it not been for these three life narratives, which were immediately popular in both Aotearoa/New Zealand and Europe, Frame's 'novels, poetry and even short stories might have been forgotten'. Claire Bazin, *Janet Frame* (Tavistock: Northcote House, 2011), p. 4.
[8] Janet Frame, *To The Edge of the Alphabet* (New York: George Braziller, 1962), p. 214.
[9] Frame, *To the Is-Land*, p. 34.
[10] Frame, *The Envoy from Mirror City*, p. 309.

ways in which 'colonisation and its legacies continue to stand at the heart' of the modern nation.[11]

Frame's autobiographies record an itinerant upbringing, from her early years in a family of 'railway people' (who sometimes inhabited wooden sheds beside the tracks), to her later experiences of rented rooms, boarding houses, huts and short-term accommodations. What these texts describe as a profound 'homelessness of the self' has been previously read in the sealed context of Frame's notorious asylum years and as the result of her extended incarceration.[12] However, this chapter demonstrates that her acute sense of homelessness and displacement responds to broader social and political contexts, including the inheritances of European imperialism in the South Pacific. All of Frame's autobiographies question her fixed relationship with Aotearoa/New Zealand's landscapes, Pākehā communities and even her own family history. Frame's life narratives are preoccupied with seeking alternative, often fluid, forms of habitation and belonging in the aftermath of empire. As these autobiographies launch their unconventional search for a home, they interrogate the legacies of colonialism and land seizure in a post-settler society.

These readings view Frame's interest in temporary accommodations as the rejection of a particular kind of property ownership, one which was instrumental to British imperialism. This contextualizes her life writing in a post-Enlightenment intellectual tradition whereby land across the former British Empire was transformed into private property, becoming a commodity available for purchase and sale. In Aotearoa/New Zealand, the development of a British-controlled land market was crucial to the country's colonization during the nineteenth century.[13] As Anne Salmond highlights, this ensured that Māori 'ancestral land [was separated] from its inhabitants and was transformed into a series of bounded, abstracted, static identities' by colonists.[14] The 'complex networks of whakapapa and [land] use rights' developed by Māori communities for five centuries before the arrival of European settlers were now systematically

---

[11] Ballantyne, *Webs of Empire*, p. 13.
[12] Frame, *To the Is-Land*, p. 110.
[13] Between 1800 and 1911, Māori communities in Aotearoa/New Zealand lost almost 90 per cent of their land holdings, partly due to legislation including the 1865 Native Lands Act, which allowed British authorities to restructure the land market while quashing widespread Māori resistance to sales. As Stuart Banner documents, 'in 1800, the Maori had owned over 60 million acres of land; by 1911, they owned only 7 million, much of which was not well suited for farming'. – Stuart Banner, 'Conquest by Contract: Wealth Transfer and Land Market Structure in Colonial New Zealand', *Law & Society Review*, 34:1 (2000): 47–96 (p. 48).
[14] Anne Salmond, *Tears of Rangi: Experiments Across Worlds* (Auckland: Auckland University Press, 2017), p. 330.

repressed (although never wholly replaced) by colonial understandings of sovereignty, property and ownership.[15]

Frame's own ancestors arrived in Aotearoa/New Zealand as part of a nineteenth-century chain migration prompted by the Scottish enclosures (itself an internal act of British colonialism), when thousands fled to colonies in the South Pacific, hoping to escape destitution. When Frame's life writing problematizes home as a fixed possession, she advances an understanding of private property which 'emerges with and through colonial modes of appropriation', engaging with complex histories of seizure and settlement.[16] Moreover, as owning land was 'central to the formation of the proper legal subject in the political sphere', then Frame – as both an impoverished tenant's daughter and a former asylum inmate – would have been, at various points in her life, excluded from this narrow category of the rights-bearing human.[17] Her critical response to home as an owned property is resistant to the possessive politics of individualism that would strip both her, and many Māori communities (albeit in markedly different ways) of legal recognition.[18]

In short then, when Frame refuses to imagine home as an owned or fixed location in her life writing, she transforms an experience of dispossession into anti-imperial critique at the end of empire. Her autobiographies consistently seek a more provisional and fluid form of tenancy which offers refuge from the strictures of post-settler (Aotearoa/New Zealand) and post-imperial (Britain) societies. A resistance to property and possession is manifest in the everyday details of her life narratives, from household goods and family histories in *To the Is-Land*, to figurative and literal dwelling places in *An Angel at My Table*, through to temporary jobs and accommodations in *The Envoy from Mirror City*.[19] In the broader context of this book, Frame is the sole author to have

---

[15] Ibid., p. 326.
[16] Brenna Bhandar, *Colonial Lives of Property: Land, Law, and Racial Regimes of Ownership* (London: Duke University Press, 2018), p. 3.
[17] Bhandar, *Colonial Lives of Property*, p. 4.
[18] It is important to state that Frame's relationship with Māori communities and histories developed significantly over the course of her long career. In an early biographical essay, Frame claimed that 'my step-great-grandmother was a full-blooded Māori', but was later scathing of Pākehā who tried 'to falsify genealogical tables so that they might be able to trace an obscure relative who was a Maori'. As Frame herself seems to have later realized, 'settler nativism', the practice wherein a non-Indigenous person 'locate[s] or invent[s] a long-lost [Indigenous] ancestor' is often used 'to mark [settlers] as blameless in the eradications of Indigenous peoples'. Janet Frame, 'Beginnings', in *Beginnings: New Zealand Writers Tell How They Began Writing*, ed. Robin Dudding (Wellington: Oxford University Press, 1980), pp. 25–33 (p. 27); Janet Frame, *A State of Siege* (London: W. H. Allen, 1967), p. 120; Tuck and Yang, 'Decolonisation Is Not a Metaphor', p. 10.
[19] While I remain cognizant of Michelle Keown's warning that 'the question of whether Janet Frame can be considered a "postcolonial" writer is a vexed one', this chapter follows Bill Ashcroft, Gareth Griffiths and Helen Tiffin (2002), Rod Edmond (1995) and John McLeod (2004) in suggesting that her writing can be productively read through postcolonial scholarship. Michelle Keown, *Pacific Islands Writing: The Postcolonial Literatures of Aotearoa/New Zealand and Oceania* (Oxford: Oxford University

permanently returned to the country of her birth after travelling to London; in 1963 she moved back to the southern hemisphere, to life 'on the edge of the farthest circle'.[20] Her return coincided with a period of land-rights protest and social reform in her home country, culminating in the Māori-led Land March of 1975, and significant occupations at both Raglan golf course (1978) and Bastion Point (1977). These events challenged a settler model of possessive individualism, championing Indigenous epistemologies in which 'the whenua (land), its waterways, forests and people (tangata whenua) are inextricably linked'.[21] While they are rarely read in relation to these events and cultural shifts, Frame's autobiographies – which were written throughout the 1980s – observe the unsettling legacies of colonialism through this wider context.

It is necessary to acknowledge, from the outset of this chapter, that there are considerable difficulties to defining any texts as Frame's life writing. While *To the Is-Land*, *An Angel at My Table* and *The Envoy from Mirror City* are discussed here as distinct autobiographies, this focus comes with a caveat; the boundaries between fiction and life writing are permeable in Frame's oeuvre and it is challenging – even foolhardy – to discuss one without reference to the other.[22] As Roger Robinson notes, 'plots, preoccupations and metaphor[s] recur and merge' across her novels, short stories and autobiographies.[23] For example, her early memories of Tommy Miles's death – a railway ganger who was run over by 'the express train on the railway line outside our place' – are recorded in *To the Is-Land* and retold in the posthumously published autobiographical novel *Towards Another Summer* (2007).[24] In the later iteration of this scene, Grace Cleave, a writer who resembles Frame, recounts her father speaking of Tommy

---

Press, 2007), p. 66; Bill Ashcroft, Gareth Griffiths and Helen Tiffin, *The Empire Writes Back: Theory and Practice in Post-Colonial Literatures*, 2nd edn (New York: Routledge, 2002), pp. 102–7; Rod Edmond, '"In Search of the Lost Tribe": Janet Frame's England', in *Other Britain: Other British: Contemporary Multicultural Fiction*, ed. A. Robert Lee (London: Pluto Press, 1995), pp. 161–74; John McLeod, *Postcolonial London: Rewriting the Metropolis* (Abingdon: Routledge, 2004), pp. 59–92.

[20] Frame, *To the Is-Land*, p. 94.

[21] Salmond, *Tears of Rangi*, p. 350.

[22] As each of Frame's autobiographical volumes were published separately during the 1980s, this chapter discusses them as discreet and separate entities. Yet this is complicated by readings, such as Andrew Dean's 'parallel' interpretation of two Frame novels, which emphasize how objects and events move across the boundaries of her texts. Dean notes how 'the bus ticket that floats over Grace Cleave's wall and into her garden in *Towards Another Summer* seems to have been thrown from [Frame's earlier novel] *The Adaptable Man*, where Unity Foreman, a writer, watches a "bus ticket drifting over the garden wall"'. This chapter therefore acknowledges that Frame's oeuvre is an interconnected network where individual texts link to their predecessors and even anticipate their successors. Andrew Dean, *Metafiction and the Postwar Novel: Foes, Ghosts, and Faces in the Water* (Oxford: Oxford University Press, 2021), p. 89.

[23] Roger Robinson, 'New Zealand', in *The Commonwealth Novel Since 1960*, ed. Bruce King (Basingstoke: Macmillan, 1991), pp. 105–20 (p. 107).

[24] Frame, *To the Is-Land*, p. 22.

Lyles with 'a terrible doom in his voice', before revealing that 'you see, it was my father who drove the train that killed him'.[25] As the two accounts of Tommy Miles's//Lyles's death suggest, repetitions in Frame's oeuvre conceal and reveal in equal measure. Even if the 'real story' most likely lies between the two accounts, any objective or final rendition is dispersed throughout numerous retellings. Frame's readers are left to locate meaning in the interactions *between* these texts. Therefore, while this chapter distinguishes between Frame's autobiographies and fictions in the interests of clarity, it also acknowledges the blurred lines between such categories.

Critics have traditionally interpreted Frame's autobiographies as 'an analeptic or hermeneutic tool – a precious key – with which to reread the novels'.[26] This assessment relies on a tired and reductive trope that Frame's life might somehow 'unlock' the secrets of her fiction *and* curtails any discussion of the autobiographies as literary texts in their own right.[27] In an attempt to remedy these oversights, this chapter draws on Frame's fiction to generate new readings of her life writing, operating under the assumption that all of her work inhabits an autobiographical space.[28] Following Philippe Lejeune, this allows autobiographies and novels by a single author to be understood '*in relation* to the other', contesting any competitive distinction between life writing and fiction.[29] This chapter pursues Frame's critical engagements with empire, rather than being mired in descriptions of how the autobiographies cross-reference her wider oeuvre. Including her in a cohort of post-imperial life writers builds on previous comparative studies of Frame, whether as a metafictional author (Dean), or as

---

[25] Janet Frame, *Towards Another Summer* (London: Virago Press, 2008), p. 75.
[26] Bazin, *Janet Frame*, p. 4.
[27] I refer here to Patrick Evans's argument that 'there are no greater secrets to [Frame's] writing than the depth of its autobiographical bases and, distinctively, the author's need to write her life in a way that asserted control of it'. – Patrick Evans, 'Dr Clutha's Book of the World: Janet Paterson Frame, 1924–2004', *Journal of New Zealand Literature*, 22 (2004): 15–30 (p. 22).
[28] I am, by no means, the first to suggest that Frame's oeuvre inhabits an autobiographical space. According to Dean, Frame's metafictional strategies 'became so concerned with her autobiographical space that she wrote against [her] readers' and her recourse to metafiction 'close[s] down interpretative possibilities rather than open[s] them up'. Numerous critics have noted that Frame's texts encourage a form of frustrated reading, where a multitude of possible interpretations are curtailed by a prescriptive authorial presence. For Alexis Brown, Frame's interest in authorial control and the reception of her writing highlights the often 'adversarial and controlling relationship Frame has with her readers'. – Dean, *Metafiction and the Postwar Novel*, p. 106; Alexis Brown, 'An Angel at My Table (1990): Janet Frame, Jane Campion, and Authorial Control in the Auto/Biopic', *Journal of New Zealand Literature*, 34:1 (2016): 103–22 (p. 105); Boileau, Nicolas Pierre, 'Places of Being: Janet Frame's Autobiographical Space', *a/b: Auto/Biography Studies*, 22:2 (2007): 217–29.
[29] According to Lejeune, this competitive distinction can be summarized in André Gide's belief that 'perhaps we come closer to truth in the novel' than in autobiography. Lejeune, *On Autobiography*, p. 27; André Gide, *If It Die…An Autobiography*, trans. Dorothy Bussy (New York: Vintage Books, 2001), p. 187.

a postcolonial arrivant in London (McLeod).³⁰ Contrary to previous dismissals of Frame's autobiographies as her 'least troubling works', these texts are complex and experimental forms of self-representation which offer new perspectives of life writing at the end of empire.³¹

Frame engages with imperialism through the minutiae of her life, from the everyday objects which furnish her childhood home (discussed further in Chapter 5), to the temporary accommodations she lived in both during and after her university years. Like Lively, Ballard and Lessing, she asked what it meant to inhabit a former frontier of white settlement, and this chapter highlights how life writing at the end of empire includes authors who lived *after* direct colonial rule. Yet unlike the other memoirists discussed here, Frame's life narratives are less concerned with returning to a particular location (like a colonial mansion, an internment camp, or a settlers' laager) and more preoccupied with *dismantling the idea of home and secured belonging altogether*. Addressing each of Frame's autobiographies in turn, this chapter begins with a discussion of confused settler genealogies and unruly objects in *To the Is-Land*. By then turning to *An Angel at My Table*, it discusses alternatives to enclosure and property ownership in Pākehā society. This rejection of belonging-via-possession then informs the reflections on white colonial identity and Britain's post-imperial melancholia in *The Envoy from Mirror City*. By responding to territorial and cultural decolonization during the late twentieth century, Frame's autobiographies search for – but do not necessarily locate – a home which challenges the legacies of colonialism in both the South Pacific and Britain.

Ancestral Myths and Uncertain Origins in *To the Is-Land*

To the Is-Land ostensibly narrates Frame's 1930s childhood in different railway towns across the South Island. During this time her brother Bruddie began

---

[30] Perhaps because of her oeuvre's internal references, Frame has largely been discussed in detailed single-author studies (Cronin 2011, Delrez 2002, Oettli-van Delden 2003). While accomplished, these isolate her from literary contemporaries whose work might inform her own preoccupations as a writer. By situating Frame in a cohort of post-imperial white life writers, this chapter argues that her relationship with the British Empire must be extended beyond the biographical reading that she was permanently 'in the wrong place because, as a Pākehā [white] New Zealander, she [was] at home neither in New Zealand nor in Britain'. Carmen Luz Fuentes-Vásquez, *Dangerous Writing: The Autobiographies of Willa Muir, Margaret Laurence and Janet Frame* (Amsterdam: Rodopi, 2013), p. 170. See also Dean, *Metafiction and the Postwar Novel* and McLeod, *Postcolonial London*.

[31] Gina Mercer, 'A Simple Everyday Glass: The Autobiographies of Janet Frame', *Journal of New Zealand Literature*, 11 (1993): 41–8 (p. 44).

suffering violent epileptic fits, the family's debts escalated (partly due to Bruddie's medical bills) and her elder sister died in the local swimming pool, leaving behind 'a blankness, a Myrtle-missing part' in family life.[32] Almost ten years later, in 'a double lightning strike' Frame's younger sister, Isabel, also drowned in Picton Harbour. Amidst these personal tragedies, the narrative describes the family's numerous homes in Otago's remote 'landscape of wild spaces', where the sky shimmered with 'Antarctic ice'.[33] Having eventually settled in the coastal town of Oamaru, 'halfway between the equator and the South Pole', Frame's school teachers constantly 'reminded [us] of the distance of New Zealand from the rest of the world'.[34] On the surface, then, this southern childhood was marked by personal tragedies, but largely removed from global events. Yet in actuality, Frame's 'remote' Otago upbringing was embedded in the networks of empire. The young Janet would listen as her relatives sent gossip and news 'along invisible wires, words full of meaning and importance describing the Great Dunedin and South Seas Exhibition [1925–6] and the visit of the Duke of York' (the future King George VI visited the region in 1927).[35] Exhibitions for overseas trade and memories of royal visits connected her family's modest lives in the South Pacific to imperial Britain. Frame's imaginary 'invisible wires' sketch distinctly colonial cartographies, evoking the undersea telegraph cables of the 'all-red line' which connected territories across the British Empire (see Figure 4.1). Much later, after listening to her history teacher's rantings about 'the purity of race' and the 'inferior' outcomes of miscegenation ('citing the intermarriage of the Maoris and the Chinese'), Frame realized that eugenicist ideas were transmitted to her community via the networks of a global empire. Her experiences of white supremacy were subtler than Lessing's confrontations with the Rhodesian colour bar, but like Ballard and Lively, she would later confront an education which asserted the supposed superiority of European and settler cultures. In *To the Is-land* Frame's South Island childhood is positioned within a global web of communications, imperial trade and spurious racial hierarchies.

This understanding of a networked empire is reflected in Frame's descriptions of her Scottish grandparents, who travelled to Aotearoa/New Zealand in the mid-nineteenth century. She describes how her childhood was interwoven with the stories of these mythical predecessors, as the tales of who 'did this, was this, lived and died there and there', were part of daily family life.[36] These

[32] Frame, *To the Is-Land*, p. 88.
[33] Ibid., p. 29.
[34] Ibid., p. 110.
[35] Ibid., p. 13.
[36] Ibid., p. 10.

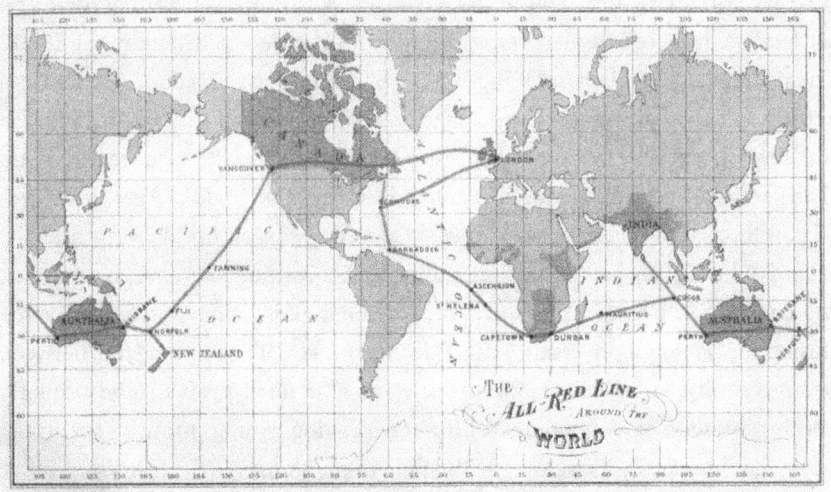

Figure 4.1 The all-red line of electrical telegraphs linking large swathes of the British Empire from 1902 onwards.

ancestral beginnings formed a series of shifting myths, anticipating Frame's later contention that 'there is no such thing as a "pure" autobiography' or a fixed life story.³⁷ While her first autobiography promises to differentiate between 'the myth and the reality'³⁸ of family history, such distinctions are quickly blurred:

> As a child I used to boast that the Frames 'came over [to Britain] with William of Orange'. I have since learned that this may have been so, for Frame is a version of Fleming, Flamand, from the Flemish weavers who settled in the lowlands of Scotland in the fourteenth century. I strengthen the reality or the myth of those ancestors each time I recall that Grandma Frame began working in a Paisley cotton mill when she was eight years old.³⁹

Frame's vague etymology implies that there 'may have been' connections between the fourteenth-century Flemish weaver-immigrants and Grandma Frame's early life in a Paisley cotton mill. Her paternal grandparents were indeed part of the mass exodus of Scots who escaped poverty by emigrating to Aotearoa/New Zealand during the nineteenth century.⁴⁰ But the Flemish

---

³⁷ Ibid., p. 131.
³⁸ Ibid., p. 7.
³⁹ Ibid.
⁴⁰ The Scottish weaving town of Paisley, Grandma Frame's birthplace, faced widespread poverty in the early nineteenth century and by 1842 a quarter of the town's population, 'some 12,000 people, had been kept from actual starvation by the means of soup kitchens'. After pleading with the British government for assisted passage, a large number of residents emigrated to Aotearoa/New Zealand, beginning a chain migration route used by Mary Paterson (later Frame) in 1874. Jock Phillips and

weavers potentially link Frame to much earlier histories of immigration and settlement, as these textile workers moved from Flanders to Britain in the 1300s. The reference to William of Orange – who became King of England, Ireland and Scotland in 1689 – confuses the passage's genealogies even further. King William was several centuries too late to bear responsibility for the Flemish weavers 'who [had] settled in the lowlands of Scotland' during the Middle Ages. The lines of continuity Frame appears to draw in this description are dubious and the record of her family history becomes unstable. According to Frame's biographer, the connection between her surname, Fleming, and Flamand was discovered through a passing conversation at a dinner party.[41] The relationship between her private life and these public histories of settlement proves to be similarly contingent, with the etymology of 'Frame' proving as inaccurate as the initial boast that her family 'came over with William of Orange'.

Such discrepancies, combined with Frame's telling description of 'reality *or* myth' suggests that the two are broadly interchangeable in her life writing. Indeed, the Frame family legends were 'slightly different' in each retelling.[42] While the opening of *To the Is-Land* might appear to braid together the threads of her personal history, tracing a line of inheritance from Aotearoa/New Zealand, to Scotland, to Flanders (modern Belgium), these autobiographical beginnings really suggest that all origins are invented. This destabilizes the repeated comparisons between authors and weavers in Frame's autobiographies, and the metaphors of enmeshing and weaving which recur throughout her wider oeuvre.[43] By mythologizing her ancestors, Frame not only complicates the woven genealogies of her fiction but also seeks to avoid the trappings of settler family history. This manoeuvre attempts to decouple her from the known coordinates of a family tree, acknowledging that she was the immediate descendant of Scottish migrants, yet still rending her provenance as deliberately uncertain.

For Anne McClintock 'the crisis of origins' is one of 'the stalwart themes of colonial discourse', in large part because colonial acts of ' "discovery" [were] always

---

Terry Hearn, *Settlers: New Zealand Immigrants from England, Ireland and Scotland, 1800–1945* (Auckland: Auckland University Press, 2008), p. 1; Michael King, *The Penguin History of New Zealand* (London: Penguin, 2003), p. 170.

[41] King describes how Frame came across her possible Flemish ancestry at a dinner party, in 1969, where she happened to meet 'a singer named Robert who, like her, had a grandmother named Paterson who came from Paisley'. He informed her 'that the Frames were descended from Flemish weavers who had crossed to the Scottish Lowlands in the fourteenth century, and that her name was originally Flamand'. – King, *Wrestling with the Angel*, p. 341.

[42] Frame, *To the Is-Land*, p. 10.

[43] In *The Carpathians* (1989), for example, weaving is depicted as a particular 'kind of knowing', drawing on traditional Māori connections between flax-work and genealogy. Janet Frame, *The Carpathians* (New York: George Braziller, 1988), p. 86.

late … the inaugural scene is never in fact inaugural or originary: something has always gone before'.[44] McClintock highlights that extravagant acts of colonial arrival and settlement were contingent on the tenuous *invention* of origins, often marked visibly through flags, place names, maps and monuments. Frame's own uncertain family tree – and the shaky, mythologized account of her beginnings – exposes the artificiality of origin myths, refusing to anchor her autobiographies to a moment of colonial arrival. *To the Is-Land* opens with an anti-genealogy that rejects linear narratives of imperial progress. Rather than becoming the successor of settlement in Aotearoa/New Zealand, Frame prefers to dismantle her own ancestral origins.[45] Yet as we will next see, *To the Is-Land* also focuses on 'ordinary everyday objects that might in the end become extraordinary', lingering 'in places not glanced at by others'.[46] The legacies of empire emerge not through grand narratives of discovery, but in the minute details and everyday detritus of her childhood.

The connections between objects, origins and empire in *To the Is-Land* are first evident in an early description of Frame's childhood home in Dunedin. Here she traces the history of the property's furnishings, explaining that these were bought by her parents 'when Dad returned from the war':

> He and Mother set up house in Richardson Street, St Kilda, Dunedin, helped by a rehabilitation loan of twenty-five pounds, with which they bought one wooden kerb, one hearth rug, two Morris dining chairs, one duchesse, one oval dining table, one iron bedstead and flock mattress, one kitchen mat, these items being listed on the document of loan with a chilling reminder that while the loan remained unpaid, the King's representative (the agreement was between "His Majesty the King and George Samuel Frame") had the right to enter the Frame household to inspect and report on the condition of the "said furniture and fittings".[47]

---

[44] McClintock, *Imperial Leather*, p. 28; p. 30.
[45] This manoeuvre is complicated by Frame's need to reject intrusive critical arguments that the origins of her life might explain the complexities of her fiction. Patrick Evans's infamous suggestion that Frame's writing conceals some 'kind of uncomfortable aboriginal truth, some skeleton in the oedipal closet', being the most obvious example of many. Frame's problematization of truth in her autobiographies and her articulation of origins as myth undoubtedly anticipates such reductive readings and reflects her uncomfortable relationship with her own critical reception. Subsequent generations of Frame scholars have cautioned against what Jan Cronin describes as the 'prescriptiveness and elusiveness' in Frame's writing which might encourage readers to look 'for answers and solutions' in her work. – Patrick Evans, 'The Case of the Disappearing Author', *Journal of New Zealand Literature*, 11 (1993): 11–20 (p. 17); Jan Cronin, *The Frame Function: An Inside-Out Guide to the Novels of Janet Frame* (Auckland: Auckland University Press, 2011), p. 16.
[46] Frame, *To the Is-Land*, pp. 117, 115.
[47] Ibid., p. 10.

Frame's father George 'responded to the call of King and Empire' in 1916, serving on the Western Front before returning home, somewhat reluctantly, in 1919.[48] By this time Aotearoa/New Zealand was a British dominion and Frame describes her family's first house as furnished by the modest rewards for her father's military service. But the document of loan also emphasizes that these goods are purchased via the finances of the Empire. Through this catalogue of objects, Frame personifies imperial authority as an intruder inside the house, creeping through individual rooms to comment on and inspect her family's furnishings. If the agent is a representative of the king, then Frame's childhood home is subjugated to a colonial taxonomy; the goods and furnishings are ordered through the king's loan. But she also describes her family as mortgaged to an imperial power through the twinned figures of the royal representative and the sovereign. As David Cannadine notes, the royal presence was commonplace even across territories which were no longer official colonies; 'the imperial monarchy intruded itself into the individual lives and collective consciousness of imperial subjects in numerous ways', most obviously through coins and stamps which bore the royal image.[49] The sovereign was undoubtedly imprinted onto the lives of the Frame family; as a child, Frame's sense of time was ordered by the royal presence, as her 'earliest recollections' were of when 'the Prince of Wales had visited Dunedin'.[50] The family's later years in Oamaru became the time 'after the King's furniture had been paid for'.[51] Frame's recollections of this snooping – even feared – official with his document of loan reveals how, long after the debt was paid, the private interiors of her family home were configured, furnished and experienced through a prism of imperial power. The possibility of 'the King's representative coming to inspect the iron bed' became another component in the origin myths that her family shared.[52]

In her short story 'Between My Father and the King', Frame reworks this episode from her parents' early marriage, describing once more how her father returned from the war with

> a very important document which gave details of my father's debt to the King, and his promise before witnesses to repay the King the fifty pounds borrowed to buy furniture: a bed to sleep in with his new wife, a dining table to dine at,

---

[48] King, *Wrestling with the Angel*, p. 16.
[49] David Cannadine, *Ornamentalism: How the British Saw Their Empire* (London: Penguin, 2001), p. 103.
[50] Frame, *To the Is-Land*, p. 11.
[51] Ibid., p. 125.
[52] Ibid., p. 126.

linoleum and a hearthrug to lay on the floor, two fireside chairs for man and wife to sit in when he wasn't working and she wasn't polishing the King's linoleum and shaking the King's hearthrug free of dust.[53]

In this version (which doubles the real twenty-five pounds owed by George Frame), the agreement between king and subject is explicitly one of subjugation. Not only is the narrator's father indebted to the monarch, but her mother is condemned to the perpetual upkeep of these items. Her household labour is playfully imagined not as matrimonial servitude, but as patriotic duty to the imperial sovereign. Yet just as Frame's autobiographies consistently highlight how heirlooms will eventually transform into junk, this short story catalogues the items in order to track their ruin.[54] The narrator goes on to note: 'in our conscienceless childhood days we ripped the backs from the kitchen chairs ... pencilled and crayoned the dining table, scuffed the linoleum, bounced on the bed'.[55] The fictionalized Frame children stage a juvenile rebellion against imperial authority by destroying the king's possessions. The consequences of their actions register when the monarch's representative appears at the front door, announcing that 'I happened to be passing through Richardson Street, Dunedin, and I thought I'd inspect your bed and mattress and chairs and linoleum and hearthrug and wooden fireside kerb', leading her parents to conduct 'a tour of the far-flung colonial furniture'.[56] The wry humour in this exchange evokes a view of Aotearoa/New Zealand as, to use Michelle Keown's phrase, 'a constellation of tiny "islands in a far sea", remote from European colonial centres of power'.[57] While representatives of the British Crown were unlikely to ever be in the vicinity of Richardson Street, Dunedin, the story imagines that the furnished property, bought on loan, is itself a colony. The family's living room is transformed into another territory to be owned and occasionally toured by the monarch. Beneath the story's sharp humour, the king's possessions raise an omnipotent and potentially sinister imperial power, one which enters and alters the domestic arrangements of homes across the former Empire.

---

[53] Janet Frame, 'Between My Father and the King', in *Between My Father and the King: New and Uncollected Stories* (Berkeley, CA: Counterpoint, 2013), pp. 10–12 (p. 10).
[54] In *The Envoy from Mirror City*, Frame returns to her late father's house and sorts through 'the family "treasures"' noting that 'each object was alive with its yesterdays'. But the conviction that these items might serve as heirlooms quickly dissipates when the objects become 'a heap of apparent rubbish'. This abrupt shift suggests how our perception of objects – and their meaning in Frame's own family – is subject to change. – Frame, *The Envoy from Mirror City*, pp. 432–3.
[55] Frame, 'Between My Father and the King', p. 11.
[56] Ibid.
[57] Keown, *Pacific Islands Writing*, p. 4.

Unlike the numerous accounts of the king's representative in *To the Is-Land*, 'Between My Father and the King' gives an inventory of these furnishings before offering an alternative list of goods and payment. Here the father figure creates his own catalogue of debt, outlining the injuries he sustained during active service in the First World War: 'back, shrapnel in; lungs, remains of gas in; nights, nightmares in; days, memories in'.[58] The damage that his children cause to the furniture therefore becomes a re-enactment of the violence inflicted on his body and mind by the British state. In a letter to the sovereign, he explains that 'the corresponding dents and stains and wear and tear in my life surely atone for the wear and tear of your precious kerb and hearthrug'.[59] The result is a counter-document of loan, a rewritten litany of settlement and debt. At the story's close he reconfigures his relationship with the monarch's authority through a small act of resistance to this colonial power.

Although there are many exchanges between Frame's fiction and her life writing, this short story echoes the practice of cataloguing and documenting objects in the autobiographies. The inventories of personal items in *To the Is-Land* are steeped in the legacies of empire, from the king's furniture to the heirlooms and documents hoarded inside the family's duchesse dresser (discussed further in Chapter 5). While these everyday goods are often broken and frayed beyond their intended use, they reveal how colonial histories lodge in the minutiae of daily life, lingering in often-unexpected locations. As *To the Is-Land* recalls how Frame and her siblings 'ripped the backs from the King's dining room chairs and used them as sleds', resistance to the powerful, ordering structures of imperialism takes place in the domestic, intimate spaces of her life writing.[60]

Neither the stories of ancestors nor the battered, totemic objects in Frame's first autobiography offer a stable point of origin in her autobiographies. All of Frame's writing maintains a fascination with the relationship between possessions and their owners; one of her earlier novels describes how 'the layers of life' can peel from the body and, 'like discarded skins still stay attached to the furniture' long after death.[61] Yet the record of family history in *To the Is-Land* is notably tethered to those objects which resulted from the Frames' 'passion for making things'.[62] Like the stories of the ancestors, these offer tantalizing but ultimately frustrating glimpses into their shared beginnings. For example, if

---

[58] Frame, 'Between My Father and the King', p. 12.
[59] Ibid.
[60] Frame, *To the Is-Land*, p. 56.
[61] Janet Frame, *Scented Gardens for the Blind* (London: Women's Press, 1998), p. 19.
[62] Frame, *To the Is-Land*, p. 7.

Grandad Frame 'survives as a presence' in 'the wooden spurtle' (a traditional Scottish spoon) he made as a young man, what does this item actually reveal of his life or the family's Scottish origins? The carefully described physicality of objects in *To the Is-Land* – the wooden spurtle, or George Frame's handmade leather workbag – obscures their fragile meanings. Their materiality reveals only the absence of material history. While Frame's interest in 'objects of use, things produced by the family labour' has previously been interpreted as evidence of her family's 'genealogies, geographies of place, origins, myths and memories', these objects actually trouble origin myths, revealing the shifting insubstantiality of family history.[63] Frame's ancestors may have been 'given as mythical possessions', but in her first autobiography these disperse, rather than secure, the record of her life amongst the networks of empire.[64]

Tenancy and 'claiming the feature of the land' in *An Angel at My Table*

An Angel at My Table opens in 1943 with Frame's arrival in Dunedin and closes in 1956, when she departs Aotearoa/New Zealand aboard the *Ruahine*, bound for Southampton, England. Throughout this period Frame's troubled relationship with place and belonging culminated in her catastrophic incarcerations in psychiatric institutions. This prompted an ongoing cycle of displacement, instigating 'a dreadful feeling of nothingness' and the sense that 'there was no place on earth for me'.[65] Although she was released from hospital several years after winning the Hubert Church memorial award for her writing, Frame remained fearful that she might be re-admitted by New Zealand's health authorities. She left – or perhaps fled – her home country to spend seven years in Europe, living largely in London, with sojourns in Ibiza, Andorra and rural England (a period covered in *The Envoy from Mirror City*).

Frame's second autobiography belongs to what J. M. Coetzee terms the 'literature of unsettled settlers'.[66] Her fraught depictions of dispossession respond not only to her years of incarceration but also to the legacies of Pākehā

---

[63] Lydia Wevers, 'Self Possession: "Things" and Janet Frame's Autobiography', in *Frameworks: Contemporary Criticism on Janet Frame*, ed. Jan Cronin and Simone Drichel (Amsterdam: Rodopi, 2009), pp. 51–67 (p. 59).
[64] Frame, *To the Is-Land*, p. 10.
[65] Ibid., pp. 212–13.
[66] J. M. Coetzee, *White Writing: On the Culture of Letters in South Africa* (London: Yale University Press, 1988), p. 4.

settlement. *An Angel at My Table* addresses a historical context which stretches back to the Treaty of Waitangi (1840), which promised to grant Māori people 'the undisturbed possession of their lands and estates', but then allowed the British government to encourage European settlement through artificially low land prices throughout the following century.[67] As Chadwick Allen notes, the question 'of indigenous land and cultural rights' remains the subject of fierce debate in Aotearoa/New Zealand.[68] Frame's reluctance to tether herself to specific geographical sites or locales in her second autobiography responds to these still-unfolding legacies of empire. By rejecting previous models of colonial settlement, it pursues a provisional existence for Frame as a temporary tenant rather than an established owner of property or land. By describing her life in attic rooms, rented bedrooms and even garden sheds, it documents a transitory existence which does not attempt to possess territory. On the one hand, temporary dwellings could be debilitating – a fact underscored by Frame's long years in psychiatric institutions. Yet, on the other hand, short-term accommodation might also offer a politically-charged form of tenancy, offering alternatives to the structures of enclosure, settlement and ownership in mid-twentieth-century Pākehā society.

Numerous critics have noted that Frame's writing is characterized by 'the search for a "my place"'.[69] This extends from Toby Withers's lament that 'there is no place for me 'in *Owls Do Cry* (1957), to *The Carpathians*'s (1988) scathing descriptions of homeowners who cling to their bungalows as a 'place of being', fearing the homeless who 'may not ally their being to a house or gate or an item of furniture'.[70] Although *An Angel at My Table* is structured by chapter titles such as 'Garden Terrace, Dunedin', 'Willowglen' and the 'Grand Hotel', these addresses provide neither literal nor metaphoric accommodation, confirming only Frame's fundamental 'homelessness of [the] self' (Figure 4.2).[71] As electric shock treatment left her marooned in a 'territory of loneliness' like 'that place where the dying spend their time before death', we should heed Jan Cronin's warning that '"place" in Frame's work is not necessarily about "place" in

---

[67] 'Article the Second', *Treaty of Waitangi*, 1840, https://nzhistory.govt.nz/politics/treaty/read-the-treaty/english-text (accessed 29 September 2022).
[68] Chadwick Allen, *Blood Narrative: Indigenous Identity in American Indian and Maori Literary and Activist Texts* (Durham: Duke University Press, 2002), p. 108.
[69] Isabel Michell, '"Turning the Stone of Being": Janet Frame's Migrant Poetic', in *Frameworks: Contemporary Criticism on Janet Frame*, ed. Jan Cronin and Simone Drichel (Amsterdam: Rodopi, 2009), 107–35 (p. 112).
[70] Janet Frame, *Owls Do Cry* (London: Virago Press, 2014), p. 98; Frame, *The Carpathians*, p. 16.
[71] Frame, *To the Is-Land*, p. 110.

Figure 4.2 'Fifty-six Eden Street, Oamaru', the former Frame family home, listed as a chapter title in her autobiographies and now a small, working museum.

socio-political ways'.[72] Yet her troubled descriptions of home, settlement and belonging *do* respond to the legacies of land theft in Aotearoa/New Zealand.[73] While place may be frequently 'deployed as a hypothetical site' in Frame's writing, her troubled attempts to locate alternative forms of dwelling are nevertheless situated in the specific geographical locale of her home country's settler past.[74] By focusing on the autobiography's descriptions of uninhabitable homes, these readings reveal how Frame explores alternative, provisional forms of settlement after empire's end.

After her move away from the family home in Oamaru, Frame describes her first months living with relatives in Dunedin:

> My knowledge of Aunty Issy and Uncle George was limited. I looked on them as I looked on most adults and relatives as 'formidable', living in a completely

---

[72] Frame, *An Angel at My Table*, p. 213; Jan Cronin, '"Encircling Tubes of Being": New Zealand as a Hypothetical Site in Janet Frame's *A State of Siege* (1966)', *Journal of New Zealand Literature*, 23:2 (2005): 79–91 (p. 79).

[73] Alex Calder emphasizes how, in Aotearoa/New Zealand, this crime could take place through different means, including 'through purchase or swindling, invasion or treaty.' – Alex Calder, *The Settler's Plot: How Stories Take Place in New Zealand* (Auckland: Auckland University Press, 2011), p. 109.

[74] Cronin, 'Encircling Tubes of Being', p. 80.

> separate world where I could not imagine myself as belonging – the world of constant recitation of comings and goings of countless relatives and friends, of names of places, all spoken with the certainty of possession, of knowledge that each person was in a destined right place.[75]

Frame's relatives establish themselves 'in the right place' through kinship, the recited connections which cement their claim to being at home. However, because Frame does not have 'the certainty of possession', she is therefore excluded from being 'in [the] destined right place'. Her isolation highlights, to use Alex Calder's phrase, how 'settlement requires not only access to land, but also rituals of belonging'.[76] The possession of land in colonial societies was affirmed both through the acquisition of territory, and via repeated social exchanges. Frame's relatives secure their home through the re-enactment of such rituals, including her mother's rehearsals of the family tree in *To the Is-Land*. Yet in *An Angel at My Table*, Frame is excluded from the processes by which place becomes property and must discover other, alternative dwellings. Her childhood experiences of poverty means that home ownership is a fearful, rather than a liberating proposition; 'all the worries of the world' were contained in her parent's 'payments to the Starr-Bowkett Building society', as a missed cheque would mean 'we'd be turned out of our house again'.[77] Place as an owned and mortgaged possession was a fearful burden, and a predicament Frame seeks to avoid.

Instead of spending evenings with her aunt and uncle, Frame prefers to occupy the margins of Dunedin, making 'detours along the bush-covered Town Belt' and aligning herself with a community of other, unseen young women whose 'lives were frail, full of agonies of embarrassment'.[78] Frame inhabits the literal and social fringes of the city, skirting around its 'bush-covered' boundaries, and later living in temporary lodgings bereft of basic amenities. For her, the city's epicentre is 'the Southern Cemetery', which offered respite from long hours spent 'with Aunt Isy in the small dining room by the fire'.[79] This

---

[75] Frame, *An Angel at My Table*, p. 151.
[76] Calder, *The Settler's Plot*, p. 121.
[77] Frame, *An Angel at My Table*, p. 191. Frame's fearful descriptions of her family's payments to the Starr-Bowkett society seem contrary to the co-operative's principles of mutual self-help, as this unusual financial network allowed members to pool their resources and become home-owners. The foreboding nature of the Starr-Bowkett book implies that it may be the act of owning and being mortgaged to a property, rather than the institution itself, which is the feared process for Frame. For the Starr-Bowkett's history, see G. R. Hawke's *The Making of New Zealand: An Economic History* (Cambridge: Cambridge University Press, 1985) and Maxine Darnell's 'Attaining the Australian Dream: The Starr-Bowkett Way', *Labour History*, 91 (2006): 13–30.
[78] Frame, *An Angel at My Table*, p. 158.
[79] Ibid.

unkempt plot was largely unnoticed by other city-dwellers but was, for Frame, more welcoming than the tightly confined suburbs of the living. While working in a series of temporary jobs, she noticed other communities who were tolerated only on the fringes of Dunedin society, empathizing with the 'misfits who drift without much sympathy or help from hotel to hostel and boarding house'.[80] She understood how such liminal places might act as shelters for the vulnerable.

Frame's interest in temporary forms of tenancy highlights who is excluded from her family's foundational belief of being settled 'in the right place'.[81] This is most explicit in her descriptions of the silent, lobotomized patients who she saw 'being "retrained" to "fit in" to the everyday world'.[82] By recording the forgotten lives of those who cannot establish home as a permanent possession, *An Angel at My Table* scrutinizes Pākehā society and searches for a means of dwelling where to inhabit is not necessarily to possess. While there are clear differences between psychiatric hospitals and the post-settler state, Frame draws our attention to who is excluded from both institutions. This focus emphasizes that as empire is primarily concerned with 'the actual geographical possession of land', property ownership is crucial to being recognized as a rights-bearing subject.[83] As Brenna Bhandar reflects, European colonialism 'ushered in a relationship between ownership and subjectivity, wherein the latter was defined through and on the basis of one's capacity to dominate'.[84] Responding to this close relationship, Frame rejects a model of personhood contingent on property ownership and 'being in a destined right place'.[85]

An Angel at My Table's subtle critique of land ownership, settlement and possession is extended in *The Envoy from Mirror City*, when Frame returns to Auckland in 1963 and witnesses 'much talk of "reclaimed" land, "desirable" property … seeing a new kind of greed for whatever could be touched, measured, seen and priced'.[86] She is particularly scathing of those who 'hoped and prayed for and paid for a *view*' before adding, with alacrity, that 'no one was saying what or whom the land belonged to before the famous reclamation'.[87] For Frame, this development boom was a form of neo-colonization, one which attempted to deny her country's imperial past and to erase the presence of Māori

---

[80] Ibid., p. 232.
[81] Ibid., p. 151.
[82] Ibid., p. 223.
[83] Said, *Culture and Imperialism*, p. 93.
[84] Bhandar, *Colonial Lives of Property*, p. 4.
[85] Frame, *An Angel at My Table*, p. 151.
[86] Frame, *The Envoy from Mirror City*, p. 423.
[87] Ibid.

communities.[88] But while the slippage between 'paid' and 'prayed' excoriates the suggestion that white home ownership results from divine intervention, Frame's emphasis on 'a view' also parodies a colonial set piece called the 'monarch-of-all-I-survey scene'.[89] Popular in nineteenth- and early twentieth-century literature, Mary Louise Pratt outlines how this scene entails a (usually male) European explorer discovering a previously 'unknown' site and surveying the landscape, thus fusing 'aesthetics and ideology'.[90] In Frame's satirical reworking, suburban home owners in Auckland re-stage their own scene of colonial discovery when they 'paid for *a view*'.[91] The efforts to cultivate alternative forms of tenancy in *An Angel at My Table* therefore anticipate the explicit criticism of real estate in *The Envoy from Mirror City*. Frame's focus is always upon *who* is excluded from these cycles of settlement and possession, from impoverished Pākehā (such as live-in hotel staff or asylum patients), to Māori communities whose land rights remained largely unrecognized in government legislation.

During her first lonely year as a student in Dunedin, Frame travelled to Central Otago, where the landscape – particularly 'a turbulent green churned-white river, known ... downstream as the Clutha' – had an immediate impact on her.[92] She explains how:

> From my first sight of the river I felt it to be a part of my life (how greedily I was claiming the features of the land as 'part of my life') ... snow-green, mud-brown and borrowing rainbows from light ... a being that persisted through all the pressures of rock, stone, earth and sun, living as an element of freedom but not isolated, linked to heaven and light by the slender rainbow that shimmered above its waters. I felt the river was an ally, that it would speak for me.[93]

This description might initially be read as Frame – finally – emulating the proprietorial desires of her relatives and staking a claim to the landscape, an impulse she acknowledges as 'greedy' in parenthesis. Here she denounces the need for ownership, only to then claim 'the features of the land' as part of her autobiography. Several years after this encounter, Frame took the name of the river as her own, unusually choosing to publish with her birth name and live

---

[88] As Claudia Orange outlines in *The Treaty of Waitangi* (1987), the increase in Māori protests throughout the 1950s and 1960s responded to government legislation which ignored Māori land rights, 'disregarded Māori values and aimed at economic rationalisation and use'. Claudia Orange, *The Treaty of Waitangi* (Wellington: Bridget Williams Books, 1987), p. 242.

[89] Mary Louise Pratt, *Imperial Eyes: Travel Writing and Transculturation*, 2nd edn. (New York: Routledge, 2008), p. 200.

[90] Pratt, *Imperial Eyes*, p. 201.

[91] Frame, *The Envoy from Mirror City*, p. 423.

[92] Frame, *An Angel at My Table*, p. 166.

[93] Ibid.

under the pseudonym Janet Clutha.[94] The Clutha in Central Otago is named after the River Clyde in Scotland which passes the town of Paisley, offering a further, tantalizing connection to Frame's Scottish grandparents. Frame's renaming therefore both evokes her ancestors *and* gestures towards the complex forms of whakapapa (the networks of Māori genealogy) which view the 'associations between people and waterways [as] deep and intimate'.[95] As the Whanganui River in Aotearoa/New Zealand was the first in the world to gain legal recognition as a living being, Frame's encounter with the Clutha is inseparable from the broader cultural significance of waterways in her homeland.

Yet in this first meeting with the Clutha, Frame's focus is not on a terrestrial communion with the soil in which she 'claims the features of the land', nor does she anchor herself to a fixed set of coordinates through an act of settlement. Instead she strongly identifies with a location that is dispersed amidst the fast-flowing waters. Her descriptions of the immoveable 'rock, stone [and] earth' are potentially misleading as her actual moment of charged self-identification is with a shimmering mirage – the rainbow – which hovers above the water. Even as she appears to pursue a grounding moment of self-identification, rooted in the topographical features of Central Otago, this evaporates into an optical illusion conjured by a combination of water and sunlight. Far from 'claiming the features of the land', Frame fixates on a temporary, fragile prism of light, hanging between the celestial and the terrestrial.[96] What emerges from this passage is not a form of belonging predicated on the proper noun (wherein Frame identifies with the Clutha and is later officially renamed as 'Nene Janet Paterson Clutha'). This meeting with the river eschews a grounded form of habitation based on ownership and possession in favour of a more figurative dwelling. In short, Frame directs the most powerful expression of self-identification in her autobiographies towards an ephemeral display of refracted light.[97]

The insistence that the river will speak for her reverses a tradition of colonial travel writing in Aotearoa/New Zealand in which 'the land was not felt to be

---

[94] The new full name that Frame took on by deed poll in 1958 was Nene Janet Paterson Clutha. Her biographer writes that Nene was 'because of her admiration for the Maori chief Tamati Waka Nene, and the fact she had been called 'Nini' as a child'. Paterson was her Scottish grandmother's surname. – King, *Wrestling with the Angel*, pp. 191–2.
[95] Salmond, *Tears of Rangi*, p. 300.
[96] Frame, *An Angel at My Table*, p. 166.
[97] Frame's biographer confirms that this encounter with the Clutha was a formative one: 'So strongly did this powerful current fascinate and attract her that her companions came upon her one night, prone on the edge of the river in what they described as a "trance-like" state'. – King, *Wrestling with the Angel*, p. 56.

fully a European possession until it had been travelled through and catalogued'.[98] When she describes the immaterial features of Central Otago, Frame refuses such models of acquisition and ownership, reversing a logic of abstraction used for 'maintaining settler possession over indigenous territory'.[99] The proposition that a river can own *her* implicitly critiques a literary tradition wherein 'writing in and about New Zealand' became part of 'the processes of colonisation, [and was used] in the implementation of imperial power'.[100] Rather than locating where her place in the world might be marked on a map or treaty, Frame turns towards other epistemologies, looking for a permanently unsettled and fluid form of belonging.

There is a notable contrast between the formal structure and the aesthetic concerns of *An Angel at My Table*. Ostensibly, the chapter titles announce a linear, progressive narrative focused on named addresses, from Garden Terrace, Dunedin, to Frame's now-famous stay in Frank Sargeson's army hut at Takapuna.[101] Yet these are misleading, as Frame is neither at home nor definitively located at any of these locations. If, as Cheryl Harris suggests, European colonies were built on 'particular forms of possession' then Frame's second autobiography searches for kinds of Pākehā belonging beyond the settler model of ownership.[102] In one sense, Frame's refusal to live with her birth name or to offer a fixed address as her home might be seen as anticipating her later retreat to the hallucinatory realm of 'Mirror City' in *The Envoy from Mirror City*. It would be easy to view this removal as the result of Frame's years of hospitalization, or an attempt to escape biographical readings of her work.[103] Yet more generatively these autobiographical manoeuvres can be read as anti-imperial critique, placing Frame in conversation with other white life writers from across the former empire. Just as Lessing repeatedly attempted to escape her confined life in the Rhodesian laager, Frame too looks for an existence outside the enclosures of the colonial past. As the final section of this chapter will discuss, these interests

---

[98] Peter Gibbons, 'Non-Fiction', in *The Oxford History of New Zealand Literature in English*, ed. Terry Sturm, 2nd edn (Oxford: Oxford University Press, 1998), pp. 31–119 (p. 52).

[99] Bhandar, *Colonial Lives of Property*, p. 183.

[100] Gibbons, 'Non-Fiction', p. 32.

[101] After almost eight years in psychiatric institutions, Frame was introduced to the Takapuna-based author Frank Sargeson in 1955. She went to live in an army hut in Sargeson's garden, where she completed her first novel *Owls Do Cry* (1957). Although Frame's hut was destroyed in the early 1960s, Sargeson's preserved home is now a museum on the outskirts of Auckland, where handwritten postcards from Frame are still pinned to the corkboard walls.

[102] Cheryl Harris, 'Whiteness as Property', *Harvard Law Review*, 106:8 (1993): 1707–91 (p. 1722).

[103] As Alexis Brown notes, Frame's concern with the reception of her work focused on 'replacing one narrative with another – especially in relation to the public perception of her diagnosis of mental illness'. – Brown, 'Authorial Control in the Auto/Biopic', p. 105.

were complicated by her years in London. By recording her time as a white New Zealander abroad, Frame extends the anti-colonial concerns of her previous autobiographies, reaching for new forms of life writing at the end of empire.

London and the End of Empire in *The Envoy from Mirror City*

The Envoy from Mirror City depicts Frame's seven years of exile in Europe – living primarily in London's basements, boarding houses and bedsits – before she returned, permanently, to Aotearoa/New Zealand in 1963 after the death of her father. Frame lived in temporary accommodations across the city and was gripped by what she called 'place names', but which are specifically the final destinations of bus routes: 'Tooting Bdy, Hatfield North, Crystal Palace, High Barnet'.[104] Her third autobiography rarely mentions the cultural landmarks in the city's centre, instead focusing on the suburban peripheries (much like her earlier explorations of the bush-filled belt that surrounded Dunedin). While living amongst an international community from colonies, dominions and former colonies of the British Empire, she felt acutely lonely in overcrowded houses where lodgers were often confined to individual rooms.[105] On the one hand, Frame was a white immigrant from a Commonwealth country and was 'favoured in having my ancestors placed among the good, the strong, the brave ... the patronising disposers'.[106] Yet on the other, she struggled against the New Zealander's awkward reputation of being 'more English than the English' which obscured the inevitable differences between this new, strange city and the country of her birth.[107]

For many, *The Envoy from Mirror City* cements Frame's position in a wider cohort of 'writer-travellers of the 1950s and 1960s' who witnessed the 'rolling back of empire'.[108] Yet her journey to the metropole overshadows the imperial concerns threaded *throughout* her autobiographies. As this study has already demonstrated, Frame's arrival at Southampton Docks does not mark the moment when her life writing becomes concerned with the legacies of colonialism. The remainder of this chapter therefore discusses two vital, and hitherto overlooked elements of *The Envoy from Mirror City*. First, that Frame's representation of

---

[104] Frame, *The Envoy from Mirror City*, p. 368.
[105] Similar depictions of lonely neighbours, fearful landlords and cramped lodgings, can be found in many memoirs of post-war migrants in Britain, including Buchi Emecheta's *Head Above Water* and Beryl Gilroy's *Black Teacher* (1976).
[106] Frame, *The Envoy from Mirror City*, p. 312.
[107] Ibid., p. 308.
[108] Edmond, 'In Search of the Lost Tribe', p. 162.

racial hierarchies in London critiques the formations of whiteness which were so integral to British colonialism. Second, that her conversations with traumatized Londoners repeating their experiences of the Blitz documents the early development of what Paul Gilroy calls post-imperial melancholia. Frame witnessed a period in British history when the 'intertwining of decolonisation and metropolitan life was especially intense'.[109] The violence of the Partition of India, the after-effects of the Suez Crisis and an increase in race riots at home combined during this era to create a 'psychological watershed which exposed the Commonwealth's frailties'.[110] Despite post-war efforts to secure Britain's central position in the newly-established Commonwealth, widening cracks in the nation's imperial project were becoming visible. By exploring these gaps and inconsistencies, *The Envoy from Mirror City* probes Britain's still-unfolding relationship with its colonial past.

Throughout her time in London, Frame encountered people from across the British Empire, from the Singaporean roommate who searched with her for the 'real circus' at Piccadilly, to Nigel from West Africa who took her on several dates and fellow lodger Patrick O'Reilly, who assumed that, 'as a colonial', Frame 'would understand what the English had done to Ireland'.[111] Although Frame viewed these meetings as a chance to learn about 'the people who until now had been only statistics, stereotypes', these relationships are notably marked by awkward failure or, in O'Reilly's case, a complete breakdown.[112] Although Frame saw herself as a 'colonial New Zealander abroad without any real identity', she found only fleeting moments of connection with other colonial subjects.[113] While the 1948 British Nationality Act created many 'Citizens of the United Kingdom and its Colonies', Frame suggests that colonial arrivals in London were regarded – and viewed each other – as strangers in a strange land. Her perspective on post-war Britain was also, undoubtedly, inseparable from her status as a 'desirable' immigrant. As an arrival from a white settler dominion, Frame noticed that she received preferential treatment compared to the West Indian staff who worked beside her in various temporary jobs.[114]

---

[109] Bailkin, *The Afterlife of Empire*, p. 5.
[110] Ibid., pp. 4–5.
[111] Frame, *The Envoy from Mirror City*, pp. 301, 311, 304.
[112] Ibid., p. 311.
[113] Ibid., p. 308.
[114] As Kathleen Paul explains, Britain viewed its relationship with white dominions as so important during the post-war period that – despite urgently needing a labour force at home – official government policy encouraged roughly 125,000 people to emigrate each year to Aotearoa/New Zealand, South Africa and Canada. Kathleen Paul, *Whitewashing Britain: Race and Citizenship in the Post-War Era* (Ithaca, NY: Cornell University Press, 1997), p. 25.

The Envoy from Mirror City subsequently records how whiteness was constructed and bestowed upon certain communities in London. When Patrick O'Reilly presumes 'there was a bond between' himself and Frame because neither are English, underlying this statement is the assumption that he and Frame are united as white subjects from colonial peripheries.[115] O'Reilly's overt racism towards those he claims are 'stealing all the work' indicates, however, that his colonial solidarity has strict limitations.[116] While Patrick implies that *he* cannot be viewed as an immigrant who 'steals' jobs, as an Irishman he would have been subject to casually prohibitive forms of racism in 1950s London. As Richard Dyer explains, the Irish diaspora were only temporarily 'assimilated into the category of whiteness' and were often provisionally included as a social buffer against Black, Asian and other ethnic minority communities.[117] Whatever he might claim, Patrick's own position as a racial subject in post-war Britain is far from straightforward.[118] By contrast, Frame's status as a white New Zealander meant that she was unlikely to be included in the notorious vacancy advertisements announcing 'no children, pets, coloured, or Irish'.[119]

Despite this advantage, however, Frame goes to great lengths to hide both her medical history and her reliance on National Assistance from her employers and landlords in London. She and Patrick inhabit distinct but equally precarious positions in the city, barely classified as 'acceptable' white tenants and employees, while never permitted to progress beyond this initial, conditional inclusion. After all, Patrick has to keep reminding himself that 'he was a successful bus driver who had refused promotion to inspector ... because he preferred to be active, up there driving the bus'.[120] Frame notes that despite these repeated declarations and his formidable work ethic, he cannot dispel the lingering suspicion that an Irishman would never be promoted to the role of inspector. If Patrick prefers to see himself and Frame as approved-of immigrants, she knows that this label could be removed as quickly as it was bestowed. Frame quietly insists that he,

---

[115] Frame, *The Envoy from Mirror City*, p. 304.
[116] Ibid., p. 305.
[117] Richard Dyer, *White: Essays on Race and Culture*, 2nd edn (New York: Routledge, 2017), p. 19.
[118] Noel Ignatiev's *How the Irish Became White* (1995) outlines how Irish immigrant communities in the United States had 'to enter the white race' as a 'strategy to secure an advantage in a competitive society'. However, as Ignatiev emphasizes, 'while white skin made the Irish eligible for membership in the white race it did not guarantee their admission'. Ignatiev's comments suggest how and why Patrick's position in London is so tenuous. Rather than enjoying and benefitting from solidarity with other new arrivals in London, Patrick's partial acceptance as an employee and tenant is contingent on his recognition as a white subject, which in turn demands that he distinguish himself from other immigrant communities. Noel Ignatiev, *How the Irish Became White* (New York: Routledge, 1995), pp. 3, 59.
[119] Frame, *The Envoy from Mirror City*, p. 386.
[120] Ibid., p. 319.

and the other tenants in their lodgings, are 'reject[s] of a demanding world', placing herself in this community of outcasts.[121]

It is not only through her conversations with Patrick that *The Envoy from Mirror City* registers contradictory attitudes to race and whiteness in 1950s Britain. The post-war nation needed workers from across the Commonwealth, yet Frame sees how this labour force are subjected to humiliating forms of racism by their employers and customers. She notes that immigrant communities endured abuse, fuelled by endless newspaper stories of sexual exploitation where '[white] women were prostitutes, the black men pimps, the white men unfortunate victims'.[122] Frame reflects on the hypocrisies of such confected lies, not least when she realizes that Britain's newly established National Health Service is heavily reliant on immigrant workers from 'Africa, Ireland, the West Indies and [even] one or two [nurses] from New Zealand'.[123] Her realization that Britain's Black communities are the unacknowledged foundation for rebuilding the post-war nation leads her to reflect again on Māori land theft in Aotearoa/New Zealand. Witnessing racism in London leaves Frame able to imagine new solidarities between different colonized peoples, questioning her schoolteachers' arguments that 'Maori and Pakeha had equal opportunities' and that Māori men 'just happened to be better at operating heavy machinery.[124] Exploring the subtle instabilities of her own whiteness therefore allows her to unpack the contradictions of racialized hierarchies in both Aotearoa/New Zealand and Britain.

As Frame's years abroad are often characterized by loneliness, her early encounters with the group of workers she calls 'the storytellers of Battersea' are a rare and important exception.[125] While briefly working as a housemaid at the Battersea Technical College Hospital, a number of fellow cleaners would permit Frame to hover on the edges of their conversations. She observes how, over the meal of 'morning tea' served at 11.00 am:

> I found myself unexpectedly living as if during the days of the Second World War ... The discussion of the television programmes was clearly seen as an introduction to the major topic, and perhaps as a reassurance that the events to be vividly recounted were now also in a shadow world of the past. Yet day after day the women talked of the war, reliving horrors they had never mentioned and

[121] Ibid., p. 319.
[122] Ibid., p. 312.
[123] Ibid., p. 373.
[124] Ibid., p. 296.
[125] Ibid., p. 306.

could only now describe, while I, with a shuddering eerie sense of the overturning of time that one is often persuaded may flow so neatly from past to present to future, sat silently listening, feeling a growing respect for the relentlessness of experience ... Perhaps if the war had not been a shared experience the memories might not have had the combined force that enabled them temporarily to abolish the present.[126]

Over a decade after the end of the Second World War, Frame is surprised to see her colleagues collectively transform their traumatic memories – that 'shadow world of the past' – into a perpetual present. She registers the delay between the women's experiences and their ability to discuss these, as the group can only share their recollections years after the war. Moreover, when the participants in this daily conversation look back to their former lives, they 'temporarily abolish' their current, post-war existence. *The Envoy from Mirror City* records 1950s London as teeming with new arrivals from former colonies, yet Frame sees the British as locked into a different historical narrative. Although the end of empire and the Second World War are closely intertwined, Frame's colleagues are unable to address or discuss the decline in Britain's imperial power. Rather than witnessing the effects of formal decolonization – which are evident in the changing city all around them – the storytellers remain trapped inside in the recitals of their war-time experiences.

The storytellers could be engaging in a collective, therapeutic exchange, but Frame views this daily routine as destructive rather than restorative. Conjuring the wartime past erases their current selves and banishes any sense of the future, leaving the storytellers 'reliving horrors' which see them trapped in time.[127] During these conversations Frame felt able to 'relive the war as the Londoners had known it', yet she had already seen how 'the relics' of the Blitz were still visible in 1956, as the 'bombed sites' across the city were 'not yet rebuilt'.[128] Like Lively, Ballard and Lessing, Frame's early impressions of Britain were of a decimated post-war landscape. Yet she alone suggested that the remaining bomb sites were becoming monuments, or even reliquaries for sacred memories. In their conversions during tea breaks, Frame's fellow cleaners in Battersea are engaged in a collective act of worship, venerating Britain's war years.

The Envoy from Mirror City witnesses the reconstruction of a devastated country, and Frame benefits from new public services including the NHS and

---

[126] Ibid., p. 309.
[127] Ibid.
[128] Ibid.

National Assistance. The post-war era was, as David Edgerton notes, a time when 'a British developmental state focused on changing the nation, on building a new national future'.[129] However, Frame's third autobiography also depicts a nation turning inwards, beginning to create myths that avoid or preclude scrutiny of any relationship with its former colonies. There is a clear distinction between the storytellers of Battersea – who witnessed the war first hand – and contemporary evocations of the need for 'Blitz spirit' in the aftermath of Brexit, or during the early months of the Covid-19 pandemic.[130] Yet Frame witnesses a new, national narrative focused on Britain's wartime history, glimpsing a phenomenon that would be, decades later, identified as post-imperial melancholia.[131] For Gilroy, this involves an 'overarching figuration of Britain at war against the Nazis' evacuating other, postcolonial histories from the public consciousness.[132] If the Second World War is 'the favoured means to find and to restore an ebbing sense of national identity', then this leaves modern Britain as marked by 'an inability even to face, never mind actually mourn, the profound change in circumstances and moods that followed the end of Empire and consequent loss of imperial prestige'.[133] There are implicit connections between the conversations Frame observes in Battersea, and the casual racism aimed at many of her fellow migrants. Her third autobiography charts the contradictions of an increasingly insular nation whose largest metropolis is no longer the centre of a global empire.

Throughout her early years in London, Frame was struck by a story of 'the former Underground station with its hundreds of entombed Londoners caught in an air raid'.[134] The image of the buried victims (which presumably recalls the real, mass fatalities in Balham station during a 1940 air raid) is highly suggestive: the city's inhabitants are trapped under the weight of its symbolically charged rubble. The iconic sign of metropolitan mobility (the tube station) has been transformed into a symbol of stasis and permanent internment. Like the storytellers of Battersea, or Frame's fellow lodger Tilly who believes that, 'if I'd had my post-war credits … life would have been very different for me', these

---

[129] David Edgerton, *The Rise and Fall of the British Nation* (London: Penguin, 2019), p. 281.
[130] Alastair Macdonald, 'May Evoked Blitz Spirit to Show EU Brexit Progress', *Reuters*, 11 April 2019, https://www.reuters.com/article/uk-britain-eu-blitz-idUKKCN1RN26Z (accessed 29 September 2022).
[131] Reflecting on the evocations of the Second World War during the Covid-19 pandemic in Britain, Peter Mitchell writes that imperial nostalgia collapses 'the historical distance between the Second World War and the pandemic', therefore erasing the 'meaningful ways that the world of Covid-19 was made by the world of the Second World War'. –Mitchell, *Imperial Nostalgia*, p. 27.
[132] Gilroy, *After Empire*, p. 97.
[133] Ibid., pp. 96, 98.
[134] Frame, *The Envoy from Mirror City*, p. 309.

Londoners are trapped beneath the weight of recent history, unable to emerge from the debris of their recent past.[135] Living as lodgers, or earning paltry wages as cleaning staff, they remain closed within 'shelters' that are actually living tombs, cut off from the rapidly changing metropolis and locked into a recent history that is being repurposed as national myth. Frame asserts that these repeated stories of war covertly lock 'everyone in place', sustaining the iniquities of an English class system that she viewed as 'medieval'.[136] Frame's meetings in Battersea, and her later conversations with Tilly, reveal how a fixation with remembering this conflict prevents Londoners from imagining – let alone agitating for – alternative and more egalitarian futures. These repeated stories create, in Frame's words, an air of stultifying calm that 'not even the prospect of a storm [could] dislodge and rearrange'.[137] Anticipating later arguments on the repressed memories of empire in post-war Britain, Frame's third autobiography reveals how these repeated, suffocating stories obscure any potential 'image of the nation that can accommodate its colonial dimensions'.[138]

Conclusion: Homecoming and 'the words of London'

Throughout her travels across London, Frame pieces together 'items and images absorbed in early history lessons', as she blearily recalls 'the Angles. The Saxons. The Picts and the Scots. The Romans'.[139] Despite her best efforts, she cannot arrange these shadowy figures into a clear historical timeline; Frame's recitations of British tribes never make it past the fifth century. Unlike Lively, who in *Oleander, Jacaranda* orients herself by the Roman ruins beneath St Paul's Cathedral, these half-remembered histories disorientate Frame as she travels by bus across the city. She instead focuses on what she calls 'the words of London', contained in 'stacks of newspapers and magazines, sheets of advertisements in the windows ... the illuminated advertising signs, the menus chalked on

---

[135] Ibid., p. 386; Frame had already explored this image of buried bodies in her novel, *Yellow Flowers in the Antipodean Room/The Rainbirds* (1969), which describes the 'dead in Balham Tube Station' whose bones are later discovered 'by County Council workmen digging drains'. This memory of civilian fatalities is returned to several times by Godfrey Rainbird, a protagonist who has himself recently awakened from the dead. The bodies beneath Balham tube station haunt him as he adjusts to his new (after)life. Janet Frame, *Yellow Flowers in the Antipodean Room* (New York: George Braziller, 1969), p. 39.
[136] Frame, *The Envoy from Mirror City*, p. 310.
[137] Ibid.
[138] Gilroy, *After Empire*, p. 115.
[139] Frame, *The Envoy from Mirror City*, p. 306.

blackboards … the graffiti in the public lavatories'.[140] Delighted by these writings both in and on the city, Frame hungrily consumes signs with darker meanings, including the placards of the homeless which read: 'War Wounded. Stumps for Legs. Blind From Birth'.[141] But in this kaleidoscope of urban life, the disjunctive parts of temporary texts and half-remembered history lessons will not form a comprehensive whole. The 'words of London' are inscribed on dissolving, rain-soaked cardboard, onto blackboards wiped clean of their chalky menus, and in bathroom graffiti quickly overwritten with new obscenities.

In a post-war era defined by new ethnic myths, as Britain attempted to ignore or denigrate the influx of arrivals which marked the end of its Empire, Frame is busily engaged with an alternative storytelling project. It is here, in the gap between the ephemeral 'words of London' and her fellow Londoners' retreat into their memories of war, that we might locate one of her many valuable contributions to life writing at the end of empire. While others have read *The Envoy from Mirror City* as part of a post-war literature where 'new narratives are written and new communities emerge', Frame actually depicts an environment where historical narratives cannot or will not stick to the page.[142] Honing in on the ephemeral and ignored words of the city, she abandons rewriting in order to reverse the writing process itself. No narratives, new or otherwise, will emerge here. Frame remains determined to dismantle the stability of the written record and her attempts at disassembly view fragmentary stories of the city as an alternative to new, totalizing national histories. In a similar way, all of Frame's autobiographies work to dismantle master narratives, pulling apart the seemingly secure connections between inherited objects and familial origins, or the use of place names to indicate a stable sense of home and belonging.

O'Reilly's racism towards Black immigrants, his and Frame's ambivalent sense of their own whiteness, the repetitive collective memories of the Second World War and the dissolving 'words of London' are all connected. As Frame departs for Aotearoa/New Zealand in 1963, she notes that her time in the city bore witness to 'the Suez crisis' and the arrival of 'the West Indian novelists', yet these events are barely registered in her actual interactions with Londoners.[143] When Frame travels to the country her relatives still insist on calling 'home', she sees the waning of imperial power from inside the metropole and watches the British look away from the collapse of their imperial power. If *The Envoy*

---

[140] Ibid.
[141] Ibid., p. 371.
[142] McLeod, *Postcolonial London*, p. 185.
[143] Frame, *The Envoy from Mirror City*, p. 417.

from Mirror City represents Frame's final attempt to establish a home in her life writing, her journey in, and eventual return out, confirms the impossibility of a permanent habitation for this unhoused colonial subject at the end of empire.

The Envoy from Mirror City depicts an imperial centre where the former grand narratives of colonial power are being both challenged and reconsolidated. Yet, as this chapter has demonstrated, Frame's final life narrative is part of her wider autobiographical interest in empire and its aftermath. Her autobiographies repeatedly declare that she intended to be 'alone, creator and preserver of my world', free to interpret her life 'as I wished'.[144] They have been subsequently read as defensive, the work of an author who is attempting to wrest meaning from her readers.[145] Frame hoped that her official life narratives might set the record straight, particularly on the subject of her schizophrenia misdiagnosis.[146] It is important to recognize that, for this author, autobiographical writing could easily become an act of incarceration: official documents were used to imprison Frame for many years in psychiatric institutions and it was a 'condensed autobiography' that disastrously brought her to the attention of the New Zealand health authorities.[147] The image of the author as the sole creator of meaning arguably finds fruition in her retreat to Mirror City, an imaginative realm where reality is abstracted into a series of capricious, watery reflections. If the final image in Frame's life writing is of a removal from the world, then her autobiographies conclude with their author living in a depopulated city of the mind where she is impervious to criticism and external authorities.

But, to paraphrase Jan Cronin, there is a difference between what Frame's life writing says and what it does.[148] While *The Envoy from Mirror City* states that the author is staging a retreat to the inviolate, empty streets of Mirror City, in actuality her third autobiography is, like all of her life writing, deeply concerned with material histories and their continuing legacies. The 'words of London' and the storytellers of Battersea develop directly out of her earlier problematizing of ancestral origins and her rejection of property as a guarantor of personhood in post-settler societies. Her autobiographies locate the afterlives of colonial rule in unexpected and often unlikely locations, whether in the furnishings of a family home, or in the circuitous conversations of tiresome relatives. As we have already seen, the other authors in this study are marked by their efforts to

---

[144] Frame, *The Envoy from Mirror City*, p. 353.
[145] See Dean, *Metafiction and the Postwar Novel* (2021), Brown 'Janet Frame, Jane Campion, and Authorial Control' (2016).
[146] King, *Wrestling with the Angel*, p. 449.
[147] Frame, *An Angel at My Table*, p. 189.
[148] Cronin, *The Frame Function*, p. 13.

recover or return to particular home on the fringes of empire (Lively's mansion, Ballard's camp and Lessing's laager). Frame's place in this cohort is both secured and complicated by her concern with dismantling the idea of home altogether. Her focus is on the future after empire, and her autobiographies explore – inconclusively – how transient dwelling places might be decoupled from the settler past. These autobiographies, when read in concert, track how Frame ultimately refuses to live inside the confines of established genealogies, in the colonial logic of possessing property or in a lost ancestral homeland wracked by post-imperial melancholia. Rather than being defined by an authorial retreat to an immaterial realm, these life narratives offer a particular, unsettling retort to the histories of British colonialism and to the enduring legacies of empire in everyday life.

5

The Lives of Objects: On Suitcases, Trunks, Tallboys and Dressers

On a sunny afternoon in 2019, I found myself in my mother's home office, a room at the cosy centre of her modern, red-brick house. I absentmindedly opened a desk drawer, looking for a pen. My own desk in London contains a tangle of broken chargers, old greetings cards and the fuzzy cigarette filters that regularly turn up, years after I quit smoking. Casting an eye over mum's neatly arranged stationary, I stopped at a single brown pencil, reduced to a stub by decades of sharpening, and decorated with faint orange patterns. I opened the drawer wider, staring through time. I am five, clutching the long pencil in my chubby hand, the brightly painted wood pressing awkwardly into my palm. Mum is in her mid-twenties, and in a low, patient voice she is teaching me how to trace letters using a series of dots on a page. I carefully fill in the constellations. It is the 1990s, and we are in the slow time of the school holidays, laboriously recording that day's diary entry. This is the first act of life writing that I can remember and it feels *hard*. As I sat at mum's desk decades later, trying to finish a doctoral thesis on literary autobiography, I was tempted to regard the pencil as a relic, the remains of another, earlier life. Its presence seemed remarkable because we moved house, on average, every two years throughout my childhood. I often enjoyed these relocations, barely stopping to question my dad's restless mobility as we painted each new set of bedroom walls. By my teenage years, mum and I were alone in the red-brick house, and there weren't many objects left from our early lives together; with each move we had shed our surplus possessions, leaving behind furniture, boxes of books, caches of childish diary entries. This stubby implement had surely survived by chance; perhaps it was useful for labelling cardboard boxes, or lay forgotten in the dark recesses of a shoulder bag. I might have been entirely mistaken in my memory, staring at another old pencil. Later that evening, on the phone to my partner, I struggled to explain why I didn't want to touch this particular object. Instead it had been a relief to close the drawer, shut the portal and turn away from the forgotten life it had briefly brought back into view.

Gaston Bachelard suggests that discoveries in desk drawers can reveal 'images of intimacy': 'drawers and chests' are 'hiding-places in which human beings, great dreamers of locks, keep or hide their secrets'.[1] For Bachelard, storing things in dark recesses preserves 'the things that are *unforgettable*', both for us and for 'those whom we are going to give our treasures'.[2] Drawers filled with objects are therefore sites of memory and containment, depositories for hidden truths which we give or leave for others. In his own autobiographical writing, Roland Barthes describes the desk drawer as a place to keep 'fragment[s] of myself'.[3] The drawers of his Paris apartment contained school report cards, old keys and a portion of his own rib, removed during an operation in 1945. And yet, in contradiction to Bachelard's romantic view of intimate 'hiding-places', Barthes concluded that the drawer's principle function was in fact 'to ease, to acclimate the death of objects'.[4] At most, they are only 'a dusty chapel where, in the guise of keeping [objects] alive, we allow them a decent interval of dim agony'.[5] The drawer then becomes a liminal site which precludes inevitable oblivion. Depending on whose argument we follow, drawers might either ensure 'the death of objects' (Barthes) or offer a romantic form of bequeathment (Bachelard), securing possessions and memories for the future. The drawers in my own flat are certainly where objects go to die, a ritual stopping point between the bookshelves and the bin. Yet, sitting at my mum's desk, I saw how they might become containers for the memories that we pass on — whether intentionally or not — to others. Inside are the objects which comprise our personal archives, preserved for future discovery and use.

It is almost a truism to state that life writers often use encounters with a particular possession or object as a starting point from which to narrate their family histories. Inherited items are what drives Edmund de Waal's pursuit of netsukes in *The Hare with Amber Eyes* (2010), and prompt Frances Stonor Saunder's exploration of her family's history in *The Suitcase* (2021).[6] Found or

---

[1] Bachelard, *The Poetics of Space*, p. 74.
[2] Ibid., p. 84.
[3] Roland Barthes, *Roland Barthes*, trans. Richard Howard (New York: Noonday Press, 1977), p. 61.
[4] Ibid.
[5] Ibid.
[6] Excerpts from Frances Stonor Saunders's memoir were initially serialized as 'The Suitcase' in the *London Review of Books* between July and September 2020. Her description of this object and its contents as 'my awkward inheritances' and 'the remains of the confusions and scatterings of a life lived in dispersal' shaped the beginnings of this chapter. My thanks to both Stuart Murray and Marina MacKay for discussing this article, and the importance of objects in life writing, with me later that year. A full memoir, *The Suitcase: Six Attempts to Cross a Border,* was published as a book

reclaimed objects can help mind the gaps of collective memory, revealing stories concealed in the dense fogs of memory loss, or hidden inside the thickets which shield our most painful recollections. Marcel Proust might have insisted that sensory memories, such as those conjured by his famous madeleine, endure long after personal possessions and 'things are broken and scattered', yet he too was arrested by the capacity of objects to release memories 'hidden somewhere … beyond the reach of the intellect'.[7] The idea that these might prompt involuntary recollections complicates the assumption that inherited possessions always *connect* different generations. Clearly, the memories unleashed by an object also have the power to disrupt established familial narratives, offering new pathways into lost and deliberately forgotten worlds.

For de Waal and Stonor Saunders, the diminutive size of a netsuke, or a tightly packed suitcase has obvious, practical uses for reconstructing transnational family histories. Small objects – which could be carried by hand, or slipped into pockets – are helpful when tracing the routes of forced migration. On a more conceptual level, miniature objects allow many contemporary life writers to confront what Lyndsey Stonebridge calls the 'brute history of modern displacement', narrating the calamitous effects of mass statelessness and exile in the twentieth century.[8] Any material items which testify to these experiences, or survive such terrifying journeys, matter by becoming more than matter.[9]

It is important to be clear: my own relocations as a child were nothing like the fraught homecomings discussed in this book. My temporary homes were internal to Britain, as my family shifted across the landscapes of north-west England, the Midlands and eventually into the university towns of the south-east. On the one hand, spending an afternoon staring at a pencil is an example of extreme procrastination, a depressing and recognizable phenomenon for anyone who has slogged through doctoral study. Yet on the other, this mundane encounter offered a chance to ask how emblematic objects retell the stories of

---

in 2021. Frances Stonor Saunders, 'The Suitcase', *London Review of Books*, 42:15 (2020), https://www.lrb.co.uk/the-paper/v42/n15/frances-stonor-saunders/the-suitcase (accessed 12 December 2022).

[7] Marcel Proust, *Remembrance of Things Past: 1*, trans. C. K. Scott Moncrieff and Terence Kilmartin (Harmondsworth: Penguin, 1983), pp. 50, 48.

[8] Lyndsey Stonebridge, *Placeless People: Writing, Rights, and Refugees* (Oxford: Oxford University Press, 2018), p. 10.

[9] For contemporary memoirists, personal possessions lost in the chaos of forced displacement can become emblems of exile, a condition described by Edward Said as 'the unhealable rift forced between a human being and a native place'. In this discontinuous state, small objects or heirlooms are microcosms for the losses of homes, cultural traditions and family ties. For one of many possible examples, see the Palestinian memoirist Mourid Barghouti's description of his mother's scattered tea set in *I Saw Ramallah* (2005). Edward Said, 'Reflections on Exile', in *Reflections on Exile and Other Essays* (Cambridge, MA: Harvard University Press, 2000), pp. 173–87 (p. 173); Mourid Barghouti, *I Saw Ramallah*, trans. Ahdaf Soueif (New York: American University in Cairo Press, 2000), pp. 46–7.

our own, and our family's, lives. It prompted me to question why academic discussions of 'things' in literary fiction, which explore 'the slippage between having (possessing a particular object) and being (the identification of one's self with that object)' rarely consider autobiographical narrative.[10] While life writing scholars have long been interested in objects as a 'means of accessing memory', auto/biographical studies has more recently been side-tracked by practical – even cynical – conversations as to how 'object biography can be profitably used by creative writers'.[11] A more nuanced form of literary analysis is needed to understand how objects shape and are shaped by the subjects of life writing. For this to happen, life writing must be reinstated at the heart of discussions of autotopography, Jennifer Gonzalez's coinage for those personal belongings like photographs and heirlooms which 'take the form of autobiographical objects' and become 'a spatial representation of identity'.[12]

This concluding chapter therefore offers a discussion of objects belonging to each of the post-imperial life writers discussed in this book. It contends that four material items, each of which contain or store smaller goods, move between the seemingly oppositional views of drawers as a place where objects and memories are stored (Bachelard), versus being a location where they go (in Barthes's words) to die. It is through this potential contradiction that we can trace how everyday objects locate the legacies of empire in interior, domestic settings. These material possessions illuminate further connections between a cohort of life writers who question the inheritances of white settlement; in their overlapping descriptions of particular objects they ask how and where the memories of colonial life might be stored after empire's end.

These readings begin with two items of luggage belonging to J. G. Ballard and Doris Lessing. For Ballard this is a small box, described in *Empire of the Sun*, which contains 'Jim's' possessions at Lunghua. Jim preserves the box and its contents throughout his years in the camp, only to abandon them in a river at the end of the war. For Lessing it is the traveller's trunk which stood at the heart of her family's Rhodesian farmhouse and which seemed to contain her parents' failed dreams of colonial prosperity. The famous, and much-mythologized account of Lessing disembarking at Southampton docks carrying only her third child, a

---

[10] Bill Brown, *A Sense of Things: The Object Matter of American Literature* (Chicago: University of Chicago Press, 2003), p. 13.
[11] Smith and Watson, *Reading Autobiography*, p. 245; Donna Lee Brien, 'Object Biography and Its Potential in Creative Writing', *New Writing: The International Journal for the Practice and Theory of Creative Writing*, 17:4 (2020): 377–390 (p. 385).
[12] Jennifer A. Gonzalez, 'Autotopographies', in *Prosthetic Territories: Politics and Hypertechnologies*, ed. Gabriel Brahm Jr and Mark Driscoll (Oxford: Westview Press, 1995), pp. 133–47 (p. 134).

small suitcase and the manuscript of *The Grass Is Singing* pictures the female writer travelling light, arriving relatively unencumbered from her decades in southern Africa.[13] By encouraging and retelling this account of arrival, Lessing refused to inherit either the heavy trunk or its contents. Both the trunk and the box are ironic symbols of immobility, underscoring how the colonial past cannot be easily transported into a post-imperial future. Sara Ahmed's understanding of imperial whiteness as constituting 'the kinds of orientations we have towards objects and others' offers an important lens through which to view these possessions.[14] Both Ballard and Lessing might eventually surrender their containers of memory, but this only emphasizes the complexity of their later autobiographical attempts to 'go home'.

Discussing the literal and symbolic baggage of colonial life then leads to a consideration of Penelope Lively's and Janet Frame's shared fascination with heavy items of Victorian furniture which stood at the heart of their respective childhood homes. Despite the obvious differences in their socio-economic circumstances, the tallboy (Lively's) and the duchesse dresser (Frame's) were repositories for family archives, containing legal documents of births and deaths, photograph albums and other precious heirlooms evoking their settler ancestry. The latter half of this chapter demonstrates how both furnishings were used and arranged to establish the permanence of the white settler household. Yet as we shall see, neither object is ultimately able to fulfil this intended function. Reading Frame and Lively in tandem offers an opportunity to differentiate between, as well as compare, their responses to the end of empire. While Lively scrutinizes the 'double vision' of her colonial childhood through the changing function of the tallboy, the duchesse becomes indicative of Frame's autobiographical attempts to dismantle home and permanent settlement altogether.

If the trunk, box, tallboy and dresser are all containers of memory, they fulfil Bill Brown's definition of 'significant objects' which are not only 'named and noticed [but] affectionately singled out and lingered over'.[15] As such objects can 'evoke the history of their possession, and thus to transform artefact into history', this chapter shows how life writing transforms artefacts into autobiography.[16] The stability of these solid objects is always in question. With the possible

---

[13] Jenny Diski summarizes this famous arrival with her description of 'a woman of thirty, a small boy, and a typed manuscript' disembarking onto English soil, although she mistakenly imagines that Lessing travelled to England by plane in 1949. Diski, *In Gratitude*, p. 186.
[14] Sara Ahmed, *Queer Phenomenology: Orientations, Objects, Others* (Durham: Duke University Press, 2006), p. 126.
[15] Brown, *A Sense of Things*, p. 87.
[16] Ibid., p. 104.

exception of Lively's tallboy, the lines of imperial and familial continuity are fractured – even broken – by these inherited possessions. These four items indicate the fundamentally unsettled nature of white colonial life, highlighting nuanced, even minute, connections between this cohort of post-imperial life writers.

Imperial historians have long viewed objects, possessions and even 'furnishing schemes' as crucial to 'the maintenance of national and cultural identity' in Britain's colonies.[17] Objects were part of 'the material practices of imperial homemaking [that] reproduced and reinscribed imaginative geographies of nation and empire as home'.[18] Yet life writing demonstrates that 'national and cultural identity' could also be *challenged* by material possessions. The changing meaning of objects might unravel the order of the colonial homestead, rather than simply affirming its imaginative geographies. By extending this book's overarching concern with homes and homecoming, these final, comparative discussions insist that any colonial 'acts of domestication are not private' and were always situated in the public, networked histories of empire.[19] In the readings that follow, the relationship between subjects and objects in life writing emerges as more complex than has been previously assumed. Indeed, objects are not just a means of 'accessing memory' but offer opportunities to overturn and even reverse established autobiographical narratives.[20] It would be easy to dismiss these items as containers which conceal the *real* items of interest inside, reducing them to storage for more important goods and heirlooms. But as we shall see, the tallboy, the dresser, the box and the trunk allow their (former) owners to convey the capricious, unsettled nature of white colonial subjectivity. In the end, they question the security of the homes in which they are kept, enclosing items which disrupt their owners' imperial inheritances.

Dealing with Colonial Baggage: Jim Graham's Box, Doris Lessing's Trunk

After several years of internment, Ballard's alter ego Jim Graham departs from the sealed and 'secure world of the camp' in *Empire of the Sun* with only

---

[17] Jones, *Interiors of Empire*, p. 73.
[18] Blunt and Downing, *Home*, p. 194.
[19] Ahmed, *Queer Phenomenology*, p. 117.
[20] Smith and Watson, *Reading Autobiography*, p. 245.

a 'wooden case containing his possessions'.[21] The handmade box which stores Jim's worldly goods contains a Latin primer, his school blazer and a photograph ripped from *Life* magazine. While the Cathedral School uniform is 'a carefully folded memory of his younger self' in Shanghai, Kennedy's *Latin Primer* is the basis of Jim's formal education in Lunghua.[22] The photograph, which depicts an unknown man and woman arm-in-arm outside Buckingham Palace, has been pinned to the wall of Jim's makeshift sleeping cubicle in an effort to make the couple 'his surrogate parents in the camp'.[23] In order to make his temporary quarters more homely, Jim conjures both a replacement family *and* the image of the British monarch's London residence. If the couple are a proxy for his parents, then Buckingham Palace provides an idealized home-of-the-nation at a time when Jim's national identity is particularly imperilled (he dislikes many of his fellow British prisoners in Lunghua).[24] By combining the institutions of the state with the kinship ties of family, the house and the couple offer replacement attachments for the unaccompanied boy. Yet the palace's famous 775 rooms come in stark contrast with Jim's own cramped quarters, which he shares with a family of three. As he owns no personal photographs, he hopes that the print will 'keep alive the memory of his mother and father, … to sustain his confidence in the future'.[25] In this image, both Jim's future as a young man without family ties and the future of post-imperial Britain seem equally uncertain.

The three objects inside Jim's box are a triptych, an arrangement of three devotional pictures which are designed to be viewed in combination.[26] When read sequentially, these items narrate the story of Jim's past colonial life in Shanghai (the blazer), his present in the camp (the primer) and his anxieties about an unknown future after the war (the photograph).[27] These objects are a

---

[21] Ballard, *Empire of the Sun*, pp. 164, 242.
[22] Ibid., p. 176.
[23] Ibid.
[24] Jim views his fellow expatriates in Lunghua as wasting time in myopic nostalgia and his years in the camp do not give him a high opinion of the British. He dislikes how British prisoners label Lunghua's thoroughfares as 'Petticoat Lane' and 'Knightsbridge'. To his mind, 'naming the sewage-stained paths between rotting huts after a vaguely remembered London allows too many of the British prisoners to shut out the reality of the camp, another excuse to sit back when they should have been helping'. Jim is drawn instead to the militaristic discipline of their Japanese captors, and the allure of popular culture which surrounds the American seamen in E Block. After the fall of Singapore, his view of the camp – and his admiration for other nationalities – confirms his rejection of a post-imperial British identity. Ballard, *Empire of the Sun*, pp. 167–8.
[25] Ibid., p. 210.
[26] Triptychs became popular in Europe during the Middle Ages as the means to exhibit three devotional paintings connected with a hinge, often as part of an altarpiece.
[27] When he is still living at Lunghua, the box shelters several more objects than the blazer, primer and photograph. It contains 'a Japanese cap badge given to him by Private Kimura; three steel-bossed fighting tops; [and] a chess set'. Notably, when it is time to leave Lunghua Jim chooses not to salvage

visual and tactile autobiography, a developmental narrative running alongside the collapse of British imperial power in Shanghai. Unlike the other internees at Lunghua – who arrive with cases of their possessions – Jim arrives in the camp empty-handed, having left the International Settlement without his family.[28] He is unprotected by relatives and has no luxuries to trade. By using his own labour to secure favours from adults, Jim accumulates a small number of personal objects through the camp's bartering and trade system, constructing the box which holds these items with 'Dr Ransome [who] had helped him to nail it together'.[29] Inside he stores the jacket, which is a relic of Jim's colonial childhood, the primer which serves as trophy of his survival in the camp and a talismanic photograph which might (but ultimately will not) secure his future. When viewed together these items are autotopographical, narrating the three key stages of his development in the novel. He keeps them not because of any financial value or trading potential but because they preserve his life narrative in an otherwise volatile environment.

According to Gonzalez, autotopographical objects remain largely 'outside the domain of systematic collection and economic values of objects determined by the marketplace'.[30] The objects inside Jim's memory box are distinct from the other commodities he gathers in Lunghua, which are primarily food rations, and 'the ancient copies of *Life* and *Collier's* that [he] needed as much as the extra sweet potatoes'.[31] This limited interest in worldly goods contrasts with the practices of other adult internees – primarily the American conman Basie – who gain status and power by hoarding commodities in their sleeping quarters.[32] While Jim stores a box of boyish possessions beneath his bunk, Basie keeps a 'rusty biscuit tin' full of old prophylactics under his.[33] These 'grubby rubbers formed Lunghua Camp's main unit of currency' because, unlike cigarettes, the

---

these toys, but chooses three objects which are emblematic of his colonial past, imprisoned present and post-war future. Ibid., p. 170.

[28] While the relationship between Ballard's actual autobiography and his autobiographical novels is discussed in Chapter 2, *Miracles of Life* records Ballard's real memories of being transported to the camp alongside a group of British and European captives bearing suitcases and fur coats. Ballard remembers that some 'had strapped tennis rackets, cricket bats, and fishing rods' to their bags, in the misguided hope that their colonial life of easy recreation could continue inside Lunghua. Ballard, *Miracles of Life*, p. 59.

[29] Ballard, *Empire of the Sun*, p. 175.

[30] Gonzalez, 'Autotopographies', p. 146.

[31] Ballard, *Empire of the Sun*, p. 225.

[32] MacKay's *Ian Watt: The Novel and the Wartime Critic* confirms that ruthless entrepreneurial practices were indeed rife among some Japanese-run prison camps during the Second World War. MacKay subsequently reads Basie's relationship with Jim as a set-piece of prison-camp writing 'when the naïve protagonist's first arrival at the camp supplies predatory older hands with new opportunities for gain'. MacKay, *Ian Watt*, p. 73.

[33] Ballard, *Empire of the Sun*, p. 220.

'number in circulation had barely fallen in three years'.[34] These items suggest the near-total lack of reproductive drive, or interest in sex for pleasure, amongst the depressed and hungry internees. This starving community trade in emblems of frustrated pleasure which provide them with no actual physical sustenance. Jim's box lends an alternative, autotopographical meaning to the 'few possessions that he had assembled with such effort'.[35] Like the prophylactics, these have no practical use inside or outside the camp, yet they allow Jim to preserve his life story and his memories of a colonial childhood during his internment.

Once ordered by the Japanese guards to leave Lunghua, Jim packs the blazer, primer and photograph into his box and joins the column of internees who are all, he assumes, being marched towards a killing-ground. Each are permitted to bring a single item of luggage, and Jim watches as many are overwhelmed by their own suitcases. He suspects that their physical exhaustion is only hastening 'an end that has been implicit ever since … the British had surrendered at Singapore without a fight'.[36] Containing tennis rackets, fancy-dress costumes and golf clubs, the bags are of little use to the prisoners who quickly begin to collapse from starvation and exhaustion. Jim believes that the internees are dying because, like the British garrisons at Singapore, they have failed to maintain their colonial authority. His and the other internees' belongings are vital to this realization of imperial decline. When Mrs Phillips, a former missionary, struggles to keep up with the column, Jim notes that her wicker suitcase 'is all that survived of the decades she had spent in the Chinese hinterland'.[37] The suitcase is more than a souvenir or a memento, as it gestures towards the lost narratives of Mrs Phillips's former life (she dies shortly after her conversation with Jim). Despite the patent absurdity of tennis rackets being carried by those who have barely enough energy to walk, objects like the wicker suitcase are charged with pathos. Colonial life in the International Settlement will be irretrievable, Jim realizes, after the war. These possessions and their owners are already relics from a bygone era.

As the march continues, Jim is 'startled to see that hundreds of suitcases lay on the empty road … the prisoners had abandoned them [and] … vanished into the sky'.[38] He creates an indicative death count from the bags, which serve as proxies for the 'vanished' bodies.[39] Still holding his box, Jim

---

[34] Ibid.
[35] Ibid., p. 255.
[36] Ibid., p. 247.
[37] Ibid.
[38] Ibid., p. 251.
[39] An ambiguity remains in this scene as to whether Jim unconsciously overlooks the corpses which lie by the side of the road, or whether the owners of these luggage items have, like Mrs Phillips, concealed themselves in the long grass.

approaches the bombed remains of Nantao, where a river is littered with corpses and slicked with oil. Standing on the bank just hours before Japan's surrender to allied forces, Jim occupies a liminal position, between land and water, boyhood and adulthood, war and peace. He decides to 'rid himself of Lunghua' and pushes the box into the water, 'watching as it floated away, like the coffin of a Chinese child, [and] the circles of oil raced to embrace it and sent tremors of light across the river'.[40] In one sense, the box joins a wider set of currents; the novel's principle framing device is its opening and closing images of wooden coffins floating on the Yangtze River. These caskets are driven back to shore on strong tides, leading numerous critics to interpret their movements through a Freudian lens, 'as a compulsive repetition of long-buried trauma' (indeed, Jim is hardly free of Lunghua after placing the box in the water).[41] Yet, as Chapter 2 has already demonstrated, all of Ballard's life writing extends a Freudian idea of the uncanny into first a colonial – and later a post-imperial – unheimlich which unsettles his understanding of home. In Nantao, by disposing of the box which resembles a flimsy coffin, Jim gives up the timeline of his life so far, along with the image which anticipates *his projected life after the war and the end of empire*. While the other internees are unable to lug their literal and symbolic baggage any further, Jim's coffin box stages the death of the colonial boy.

This significant object is an ironic symbol of mobility. Like Lessing's trunk – which we will turn to next – it is both a container for Jim's memories of empire and a form of baggage which he cannot transport into the future. In *Queer Phenomenology* (2006) Ahmed suggests that a white, imperial world can be inherited as a dwelling, and that colonialism 'affect[s] not simply how maps are drawn, but the kinds of orientations we have towards objects'.[42] If colonial whiteness is an inheritance, this operates on the microscale of small possessions, as well as on a macro level of official maps and colonial territories, underlining the connections Ballard and Lessing draw between possessions and the end of empire. When Jim surrenders his precious box to the flow of a tidal river, this act intimates that the objects which previously grounded his identity and fulfilled his need for self-representation in the camp *now disorientate him*. White colonial life has come to an end as the objects which once secured the enclave of the International Settlement now symbolize only its ruin. As we shall see, both

---

[40] Ballard, *Empire of the Sun*, p. 255
[41] Samuel Francis, *The Psychological Fictions of J. G. Ballard* (London: Bloomsbury, 2011), p. 128.
[42] Ahmed, *Queer Phenomenology*, p. 126.

the traveller's trunk and Ballard's box are containers of memory conveying the immobility of colonial whiteness at the end of empire.

Like Ballard, Lessing stored her memories of white settlerdom in a single item of luggage. While the contents of Jim's box reflect his own life, the objects in Lessing's trunk belonged to her parents, narrating the early years of their marriage. One of Lessing's earliest pieces of juvenilia was 'a little [written] piece called "The Treasure Trunk"', which explored 'the contents of a [real] old cabin trunk' stored in her family's Rhodesian farmhouse.[43] When the family first relocated to southern Africa, whenever 'my father said [something] about England', Lessing would go to the trunk which was initially 'out of bounds, not to be touched' and sift through the objects inside.[44] Her parents had refused to unpack its contents, hoping that their lives on the frontier would only be temporary, but once they 'understood how unlikely it was the trunk would ever be opened in a real house', and that the objects inside 'would never find their right place', their daughter was allowed to unpack the items stored between layers of crisp, white tissue paper.[45] Lessing's access to this object represented her parents' inability to prosper on the farm (they would never make enough money to build 'a real house' in Rhodesia, constructed of tile and brick, where they could display their personal treasures).[46] Alfred and Emily Tayler transported various possessions to Southern Rhodesia as props to support their new lives and to cement their improved social status. The preservation and eventual decay of these items reveals how the couple became ensnared by the myths of empire; these objects commemorate both a lost future where they would return – wealthy and triumphant to England – and an unrealized, prosperous present in the settler colony.

Lessing's first autobiography uncovers the trunk's contents in stages, almost like an archaeological dig. The upper sections contained fine baby clothes, followed by 'my mother's evening and afternoon dresses in scented tissue paper', and her father's dinner jackets and officer's uniforms.[47] All were cut in a post-war

---

[43] Lessing, *Under My Skin*, p. 104.
[44] Ibid.
[45] Ibid.
[46] As Chapter 3 explores in more detail, Lessing's memoirs distinguished between Rhodesian farmhouses made 'of brick, cement, plaster, tile, and tin [where] the substance of the country [is] processed and shaped' and her own home which was 'made direct of the stuff of soil and grass and tree'. While the latter was the basis for Lessing's relationship with her 'myth country', her parents were horrified to be stuck in this temporary dwelling and hoped to build a grander home in Southern Rhodesia once their financial situation improved. They never did acquire the necessary funds to build a farmhouse of brick and plaster. Lessing, *Going Home*, p. 30.
[47] Lessing, *Under My Skin*, p. 105.

style that was soon to go out of fashion (there was no use for outdated evening wear in the heat and dust of the veld) and Emily's 'wonderful dresses were used for games' by the children.[48] Lessing lamented the unborn siblings who would have worn the children's clothes. Ominously her parents did not, or could not, conceive again after moving to Southern Rhodesia (even in fictions like 'The Second Hut' or *The Grass Is Singing*, Lessing does not permit colonial settlers to successfully nurture new generations). Beneath the trunk's layers of melancholic, unrealised futures, were 'brocade shoes … evening bags … a fox stole with black beady eyes … my father's war medals' and 'packets of old photographs, wrapped in oiled paper against fish moths'.[49] The moths reduced these photographs to the consistency of lace, becoming part of the barrage of 'insects that in the end brought the old house to its knees'.[50]

There is a difference between those objects which commemorate her parents' past lives in Britain (the photographs and medals) and those which anticipate colonial prosperity in Southern Rhodesia (the evening gowns and children's clothes). Yet eventually the photographs are destroyed, the outfits repurposed and cut up, while the house – as Lessing recalled in her other memoirs – sank 'back into the forms of the bush'.[51] All of her family's prized possessions were depleted in the southern African climate and, like Pandora's box, once the trunk is opened it cannot be closed again. A prosperous colonial identity was always beyond the reach of Lessing's family and like the mawonga tree (discussed at the end of Chapter 3) the memory-trunk and its contents reveal the absence of any secure, colonial inheritance in her life writing.

Lessing's final memoir, *Alfred and Emily*, returns to the trunk by exploring the lives her parents had hoped to live in Southern Rhodesia. As an emblematic example of 'speculative life writing' (see Chapter 1 for a discussion of Lively's speculative memoir *Making It Up*), *Alfred and Emily* is a hybrid life narrative; the counterfactual lives of Lessing's parents described in part one are inseparable from the real, autobiographical vignettes in part two.[52] As the book opens in an alternative reality where the First World War never takes place, her parents neither marry nor move to Southern Rhodesia. The second half – structured

---

[48] Ibid.
[49] Ibid.
[50] Ibid.
[51] Lessing, *Going Home*, p. 33.
[52] For further discussions and definitions of speculative life writing, see Chapter 1 and Emma Parker, 'Doris Lessing's *Alfred and Emily*: Speculation in the Aftermath of Empire', *Critical Quarterly*, 63:1 (2021): 110–20; Emma Parker, 'Penelope Lively's Speculative Life Writing', *Moving Worlds: A Journal of Transcultural Writing*, 18:1 (2018): 63–78.

like a more traditional memoir – describes the real objects that filled Lessing's childhood home, including the 'trunks crammed full of plenty from Liberty's and Harrods' and the Persian rugs that were 'wor[n] down to their elemental threads'.[53] Her father's luggage contained 'clothes for cricket' and riding gear, both of which were useless to a physically disabled veteran living on land unsuitable for horse riding – and miles from the nearest cricket pavilion.[54] Alfred dreamt of a genteel colonial life which would allow him to later buy 'a farm in Essex or Suffolk' and become an English land owner.[55] Yet, like the baby clothes in *Under My Skin*, these are costumes for an imagined future. Alfred was trapped by his imperial ambitions, unable to profitably cultivate his land and later dying in Southern Rhodesia.

Emily's possessions in *Alfred and Emily* reveal her aspirations for a middle-class settler existence, as she transported not only dresses and fine clothes to southern Africa but also a 'dozen or so dark-red leather volumes of music scores [in] a trunk, "Wanted on Voyage"'.[56] She had hoped to enjoy tea parties and musical evenings like those she had hosted in Persia, packing modest luxuries alongside practical items such as nursing equipment, 'crayons, chalks, and books'.[57] Whether as an English farmer or as a successful educator and society hostess, Lessing uses her parents' luggage to imply that both were fatally motivated by their idealized, colonial futures. Like Lively's *Making It Up*, *Alfred and Emily* is a speculative life narrative that reimagines Lessing's previous autobiographies and memoirs. As it purports to resolve the author's imperial entanglements, the book was interpreted by critics as a conclusive 'process of filial reconciliation' in which Lessing 'imagine[s] and fashion[s] more satisfying lives for her parents', freeing them from the literal and metaphoric baggage of empire.[58] Yet ultimately the text will not or cannot fully surrender her memories of settler life; in her speculative life writing, Lessing is still opening the trunk and poring over its symbolic contents.[59] In short, *Alfred and Emily* is unable to sustain

---

[53] Lessing, *Alfred and Emily*, p. 220.
[54] Ibid., p. 164.
[55] Ibid., p. 174.
[56] Ibid., p. 164.
[57] Ibid.
[58] Roberta Rubenstein, *Literary Half-Lives: Doris Lessing, Clancy Sigal and Roman á Clef* (New York: Palgrave, 2014), pp. 193, 199.
[59] Even *Alfred and Emily*'s counterfactual first half is underwritten by Lessing's real memories of the veld and the bush. This is emphasized by a description of the alternative, unmarried Emily in part one being disrupted by the memory of Lessing's actual mother addressing a daughter 'who was usually out in the bush somewhere, dusty bare legs in *veldschoen*'. In this disorientating moment, Lessing's actual memories of Rhodesia break into a counterfactual narrative (part one), where the author should have ceased to exist. *Alfred and Emily*, p. 28.

any consolatory vision of reconciliation.⁶⁰ Instead, at the end of her long, life writing project, Lessing remains in pursuit of the colonial past, rearranging the fragments of her settler life. The trunk confirms how persistently she returned to the confines of the laager, experimenting with new autobiographical forms to consider the old inheritances of settlement. If this object symbolizes her family's inability to return to Britain, it also serves as a reminder that Lessing is never quite able 'to get free', to escape from the farm, to put her memories of empire to rest.⁶¹

After Jim floats his box into the river at Nantao, he hopes that 'part of his mind' will remain forever in Shanghai, yet he departs from the camp, the city and his colonial childhood, having explicitly disposed of all physical baggage.⁶² For Lessing, too, the point of the 'wanted on voyage' trunk is that it never leaves the family's farmhouse. The fine, unused clothes in the trunk or the picture of an anonymous, surrogate family inside Ballard's box, all emphasize the disorientating effects of decolonization. For life writers who witness empire's end, the objects which should stabilize white colonial identity quickly become unsettling to their owners. If 'the biographies of things … can make salient what might otherwise remain obscure', these items underscore the tenuous, fragile nature of white colonial life.⁶³ Unlike Lively's tallboy – which we will turn to next – Lessing cannot repurpose her family's trunk, and Jim is unwilling to keep either the box or its autotopographical contents. In a practical, material sense, these possessions are comparable to Barthes's desk drawers; they are indeed where colonial memories and 'objects go to die'. The trunk and the box have no future after empire's end, being left in the colony, rather than transported home to Britain. Whether in their memories of Shanghai or Southern Rhodesia, these life writers find themselves with no secure storage space (or even resting place) for their recollections of the colonial past.

Solid Objects: Frame's Family Duchesse, Lively's Tallboy

In *Interiors of Empire* (2007), Robin D. Jones recounts how furniture in Victorian Britain was often 'purchased to mark particular family events' and was intended

---

⁶⁰ Parker, 'Doris Lessing's *Alfred and Emily* (2008): Speculation in the Aftermath of Empire'.
⁶¹ Lessing, *Alfred and Emily*, p. viii.
⁶² Ballard, *Empire of the Sun*, p. 351.
⁶³ Igor Kopytoff, 'The Cultural Biography of Things: Commoditization as Process', in *The Social Life of Things*, ed. Arjun Appadurai (Cambridge: Cambridge University Press, 1986), pp. 64–91 (p. 67).

to be 'passed to the next generation'.[64] In addition to being functional, possessions therefore 'served individual and family memory'.[65] When this commemorative domestic ritual was exported and translated in Britain's colonies (Jones draws on a series of case studies from Anglo-Indian households), furnishings and material objects 'expressed and constituted the personhood' of white families. These items played 'a significant role in daily negotiations of cultural and national identity', allowing entire households to make themselves 'at home' in unfamiliar environs.[66] Beyond its practical use, furniture in colonial homes had both practical and symbolic functions, becoming a status symbol, an heirloom for future generations and a marker of white imperial identity.[67]

This historical context partially explains Lively's and Frame's shared fascination with particular, heavy items of furniture that were displayed in their respective childhood homes. While these two writers were raised over sixteen thousand kilometres apart, their autobiographical writing suggests that furnishings were accumulated, used and displayed in similar ways by colonial families across the British Empire. In Lively's household, an imposing tallboy (a large, Victorian set of drawers) stood proudly in the main hall of Bulaq Dakhrur and would twice 'navigate the Mediterranean Sea' during her childhood.[68] For Frame, a particular duchesse dresser – which was also transported across the family's successive homes across the South Island – featured a set of drawers that were their 'most hallowed keeping place'.[69] The broader interest in possessions that runs throughout Frame's autobiographies results from both her family's poverty (they had little money to purchase new possessions) and her mother's Christadelphian faith which imbued 'any commonplace object' with holy portents.[70]

Yet before pursuing the connections between the Lively's tallboy and Frame's dresser, it is important to acknowledge the socio-economic and cultural differences between their owners; Frame fondly remembered 'the shining silver kerosene tin which was my only toy' and shared a bed with three siblings throughout her childhood, while Lively was the only child of a wealthy couple

---

[64] Jones, *Interiors of Empire*, p. 85.
[65] Ibid.
[66] Ibid., p. 91.
[67] John Plotz warns us, however, that while such colonial objects might suggest that 'portability is the mechanism ensuring that British culture survives unaltered overseas…the process can also go into reverse, sending from the edges of empire to its core artifacts still freighted with foreign meaning'. John Plotz, *Portable Property: Victorian Culture on the Move* (Woodstock: Princeton University Press, 2008), p. 22.
[68] Lively, *Oleander, Jacaranda*, p. 32.
[69] Frame, *To the Is-Land*, p. 10.
[70] Ibid., p. 9.

who employed a permanent, live-in nanny.[71] The tallboy and the dresser are similar as two ordinary domestic items that became extraordinary containers of memory, yet they offer points of comparison between very different childhoods. On the one hand, they give form to each family's settler genealogies, storing their collective memories for future generations. Furniture in British colonies was, after all, supposed to be a form of memory-work, offering one means of orienting white, imperial identity. But on the other, these solid items reveal the tenuous nature of white colonial life. Like Lessing's trunk, or Ballard's box, the duchesse and the tallboy are objects of significance because they reveal the insecurities of the settler households to which they belong.

Initially the tallboy and the dresser seem to fulfil Bachelard's argument that furnishings can offer 'a center of order that protects the entire house against uncurbed disorder'.[72] Yet these objects both ultimately become imperial centres which cannot hold. They may seem to be a Bachelardian 'dwelling-place', but the tallboy and the dresser are actually closer to the 'dusty chapel' of Barthes's desk drawers.[73] Neither can stabilize their respective properties against the shifting forces of decolonization. Rather than being permanent storehouses of imperial memory, the tallboy and dresser are containers which struggle to continue 'the guise of keeping [objects] alive'.[74] As we will see, both Frame and Lively take solid, respectable furnishings which are intended to signify lasting, white genealogies of empire and trace their gradual decline, before eventually stripping them of any authority (Lively) or emotional and financial value (Frame). Rather than being 'a centre of order', these objects invite a disorder which imperils white colonial identity at the end of empire.

Lively's childhood home at Bulaq Dakhrur was marked by a series of internal and external dividing lines; the lives of children and adults, or of white family members and Egyptian servants, were carefully segregated through a combination of architectural design and strict social rituals. These domestic divisions took place within an enclosed compound which separated the English household from the Egyptian landscape and 'cultivation' beyond. While Chapter 1 has already outlined how the English-styled garden was crucial to maintaining this island of whiteness, the furnishings *inside* Bulaq Dakhrur were also part of this construction. Lively explains that her parents 'shipped [their] furniture out to Egypt', remembering how:

---

[71] Ibid., p. 12.
[72] Bachelard, *The Poetics of Space*, p. 79.
[73] Ibid., p. 86; Barthes, *Roland Barthes*, p. 61.
[74] Barthes, *Roland Barthes*, p. 61.

The front door opened on to a large hall dominated at one end by a fireplace in which a fire was lit at Christmas, for ceremonial purposes. There was a Knole settee [sofa] from which I was banned because I might bounce on it or dirty the cover: I cannot set eyes on a Knole settee, to this day, which a feeling of truculence, the submerged resentment of the *hoi polloi*.[75]

The settee is a disciplinary possession, arranged as part of a staged scene just inside the front door. Above the fireplace was 'a crusader sword' which supplied several family legends (supposedly it had once been used to decapitate 'a cobra found sunning itself on the front doorstep').[76] The entrance hall is an exhibition of upper-class colonial life and identity. Rather than being a living space, the furnishings there were not designed for everyday use, and the decorative fireplace was largely unnecessary in the Egyptian climate. The sword, with its connotations of a medieval, militarized Christianity, is another antiquated symbol used to buttress English colonial identity but which in reality was only used as a conversation starter. If 'groups are formed through their shared orientation towards an object', then the collective identity of Lively's family (whose lives rarely overlapped in the spatially divided household) is secured through possessions like the English furniture in their hallway.[77] The arrangement, display and use of these objects were designed to secure the property as a colonial habitation.

Positioned at the centre of this miniature display is a Victorian tallboy which stored 'objects of importance: my father's papers, photograph albums'.[78] Lively remembers that 'I was forbidden, equally, to open these drawers' and that it had a 'definite aura [which] signified official, adult concerns'.[79] As Lively's father was a colonial administrator, the tallboy's 'official, adult concerns' are connected, indelibly, to the interests of imperial Britain. This container for the private memories of one family is inseparable from the broader, public concerns of empire. The tallboy's outward-facing position in the entrance hall illustrates the ways in which furnishings might stabilize 'a fragmented, unstable, and culturally porous' colonial identity.[80] Yet in *Oleander, Jacaranda*, the boundaries of Lively's colonial childhood are fragile and subject to incursion. Neither the tallboy nor prominent objects like the crusader's sword can shield her family from the unsettling realities of colonial life.

---

[75] Lively, *Oleander, Jacaranda*, p. 32.
[76] Ibid., p. 33.
[77] Ahmed, *Queer Phenomenology*, p. 73.
[78] Lively, *Oleander, Jacaranda*, p. 32.
[79] Ibid.
[80] Jones, *Interiors of Empire*, p. 21.

Unlike the other three objects discussed in this chapter, the tallboy was brought back to London after the Second World War. Lively later inherited this object, which continues to stand in a corner of her north London home. Once signifying the world of colonial administration and 'adult' concerns from which she was excluded, *Oleander, Jacaranda* reports that the tallboy had got 'its comeuppance' and became a store for 'surplus Christmas wrapping paper and discarded spectacles'.[81] Like her memories of empire, this item is accommodated in Lively's present life in Britain; it is a vital coordinate of her colonial childhood, but it also suggests 'an impenetrable past going back at least a hundred years before I first knew it'.[82] She concludes that the tallboy is 'set to outlast me, for sure'.[83] This particular object speaks to the continuities and ambivalence which characterizes Lively's relationship with the end of empire. The tallboy bears little resemblance to the disruptive forces which plague Lessing's life writing, which left her always 'trying to get free' from her colonial memories.[84] Nor is it surrendered like Jim's coffin-box in *Empire of Sun*, when he abandons the objects that might narrate his life during and after decolonization. Lively does not allow the tallboy's original authority, as an emblem of colonial rule, to remain intact. She playfully undoes its intended function by repurposing it, ensuring that the tallboy is no longer on public display. Yet she also maintains 'a respect' for its history.[85] In the end, this object retains a Bachelardian ideal of an 'intimate life', one that existed before Lively's birth, organized her family's years in Egypt and returned to England after the collapse of British imperial power. While Lessing's trunk and Ballard's box seem designed for portability, Lively's tallboy is the only object which is moved (however impractically) from the colonial past into her life after empire.

A decade before Lively's birth in Cairo, and sixteen thousand kilometres away in Richardson Street, Dunedin, newlyweds George and Mary Frame purchased a duchesse dresser which would occupy all of their future homes. The dresser was part of a household 'set up ... by a rehabilitation loan of twenty-five pounds' that George received from the British Crown for his wartime service.[86] Frame recalls that her parents secured a 'document of discharge' from this loan, proving the debt was paid and releasing the family from the possibility of the King's

---

[81] Lively, *Oleander, Jacaranda*, p. 32.
[82] Ibid.
[83] Ibid.
[84] Lessing, *Alfred and Emily*, p. viii.
[85] Lively, *Oleander, Jacaranda*, p. 32.
[86] Frame, *To the Is-land*, p. 9.

representative coming to 'report on the condition of the "said furniture and fittings"'.[87] Frame then records where the document was carefully stored:

> [it was] kept by my parents in their most hallowed keeping place – the top right-hand drawer of the King's duchesse – where were also kept my sister Isabel's caul, Mother's wedding ring, which did not fit, her upper false teeth, which also did not fit, Myrtle's twenty-two-carot gold locket engraved with her name, and Dad's foreign coins, mostly Egyptian, brought home from the war.[88]

The king's duchesse, as it was always known, became the place 'where the family "treasures" were kept'.[89] On first glance, possessions like the document of loan might appear reassuring; seeming to prove the family's independence from the imperial monarch and narrate the main events of their lives (births, marriages, wartime service). Yet while these material items are imbued with personal myths, none are able to fulfil their original intended function and their meaning is not as certain as it might first appear. The first three are – upon closer inspection – useless appendages to bodies: the caul was preserved in the mistaken belief that Isabel 'would never drown', but she later died while swimming in Picton Harbour.[90] The wedding ring and the false teeth no longer fit (or perhaps never properly fitted) onto Frame's mother's body. When a young Frame attempts to spend the Egyptian coins in her local shop, she discovers that they are useless as legal tender, while Myrtle's precious gold locket is stored after her own, tragic death in water. There are narratives and counter-narratives offered by these disconcerting objects, where commemorations of birth (the caul, the birthday locket) become portents of death, or where proof of financial solvency (the document of discharge) underline the resolute poverty of their owners. While the duchesse's description as a 'hallowed place' implies that treasured relics are secured inside, the meaning of solid objects is, in Frame's life writing, never as certain as it first appears.

Several decades later, after emerging from her years in psychiatric hospitals, Frame returns to her family home in Oamaru and decides to have her photograph taken in a professional studio. This process 'was urgent, a kind of reinstating of myself as a person, a proof that I did exist'.[91] As her first book was published without an author's photograph (there were no images of Frame during her

---

[87] Ibid., pp. 9–10.
[88] Ibid., p. 10.
[89] Frame, *An Angel at My Table*, p. 240.
[90] Ibid.
[91] Ibid.

hospitalization), this act is a kind of authoritative signature, 'help[ing] to stake a claim' on her life and work.[92] Professional photographs were, Frame knew, a way to document 'the complete cycle' of life events, yet she wryly noted that there were no images of resurrections like her own. To prepare for this portrait, 'I looked in the top duchesse drawer where the family "treasures" were kept for the amber beads that Grandma gave me, but they were gone, as if I had died'.[93] Inside the drawer are instead 'Dad's medal from the war … his identity disc and his soldier's paybook, and Isabel's tissue-thin *caul*'.[94] The amber beads are a direct inheritance from Frame's settler ancestors, stored inside an object (the duchesse) which maintained her family's connection to the British imperial crown. When she searches for the beads which are supposed to be proof of life, she finds only an absence, a gap 'as if I had died'.[95] These lost or misplaced objects position Frame's dresser closer to Barthes's desk drawers than to Bachelard's romantic notion of the intimate chest or wardrobe. The dresser is only a temporary container for items which either go missing (the beads) or for possessions which will not fulfil their intended function. Family history, settler memory and personal identity are all destabilized, rather than preserved, inside this container of memories.

Imagining whiteness as an inherited property, even as a bequeathed object like the king's duchesse, extends the discussions in Chapter 4 as to why Frame was unwilling to establish herself in a settler society through home ownership.[96] Nor – after her arrival in London – was she comfortable inhabiting her own perceived whiteness, finding a lack in her identity as 'a colonial New Zealander abroad'.[97] Whether she was living as an independent woman helped by national assistance cheques or incarcerated in psychiatric hospitals, Frame's life writing regards her personhood as precarious, and connects this specifically to Aotearoa/New Zealand's post-settler culture. The duchesse, with both its missing and its preserved contents, underscores Frame's refusal to inherit her own genealogy or to inhabit the dwelling places of white colonial life. Yet, while the duchesse and the tallboy are both receptacles for family memory, these objects also accentuate the key differences between Lively's and Frame's response to the colonial past. For Lively, the tallboy is a material manifestation of the 'double vision' which defines her memories of empire.[98] The bulky old item of furniture which stores

---

[92] Ibid.
[93] Ibid.
[94] Ibid.
[95] Ibid.
[96] For discussions of whiteness as property, see both Ahmed's *Queer Phenomenology* and Cheryl Harris's 'Whiteness as Property'.
[97] Frame, *The Envoy from Mirror City*, p. 308.
[98] Lively, *Oleander, Jacaranda*, p. 38.

wrapping paper in her London home is also, simultaneously, the 'portentous, inanimate object' which once greeted visitors to her family's colonial mansion in Egypt.[99] Its authority may be playfully undermined by this repositioning, but it is never firmly or conclusively undone.

These four seemingly inconsequential items, as containers for heirlooms, documents and photographs, emphasize that the legacies of empire emerge in unexpected places in post-imperial life writing. These objects highlight how colonial rule might have been secured and 'put on display' in domestic spaces across the British Empire – from Shanghai to the South Island – but also that interior worlds were where imperial authority was challenged, reimagined and eventually undone. While some of these (like the tallboy) are preserved, others exist only through repeated autobiographical descriptions (like Lessing's erstwhile trunk). Yet all of these items, and the homes to which they originally belong, move between the seemingly oppositional Barthesian and Bachelardian view of drawers, trunks and wardrobes. They follow Bachelard's understanding of intimate spaces of memory, and yet their function is complicated by their role in facilitating – to use Barthes's phrase – 'the death of objects'.[100] These possessions are, after all, locations where the personal inheritances of empire are lost (Frame's beads), ruined (Lessing's dresses and photographs) or even cast aside (Jim's personal effects).

Conclusion: Arrivals and Departures

There is an obvious risk that, by beginning this book with moments of arrival in post-war Britain, these autobiographical journeys might be read as a definitive end to each writer's colonial connections, perhaps even suggesting a firm conclusion to empire itself. Robert Gildea urges us to be sceptical of this latter point, emphasizing that while 'decolonisation was firmly on the agenda' for Britain after 1945, the state worked to recuperate its imperial power throughout the second half of the twentieth century.[101] The life writers in this study may have arrived in Britain during an eleven-year period (1945–56) of formal decolonization, but continuing forms of neo-colonialism allowed Britain to 'let its settlers in Kenya and Rhodesia go' over the following decades, while

---

[99] Ibid., p. 32.
[100] Barthes, *Roland Barthes,* p. 61.
[101] Gildea, *Empires of the Mind,* p. 257.

continuing to 'pursue its economic and strategic interests' in other former territories.[102] Events in the late twentieth century, including the 1980s Falklands war and Zimbabwean independence, continued to reflect 'Britain's self-image as an imperial power'.[103] This is the historical context in which Lively, Ballard, Lessing and Frame began the long process of writing and rewriting their life stories. They returned to examine their memories of empire during an era of imperial decline and simultaneous neo-colonial consolidation. Their personal lives were intertwined with these public – and still ongoing – reckonings with Britain's imperial past.

The four authors at the heart of this book are clearly connected by the facts of their early lives, from their births in colonial territories to their arrivals in the UK. But they are more intimately linked by the ways that they recount these experiences through a multiplicity of narrative forms, from the more traditional routes of autobiography, memoir and autobiographical fiction to new or experimental forays into travel memoirs and speculative life writing. As they witnessed a late twentieth-century era of formal decolonization marked by rising neo-colonialism, these white writers returned, over and over, to probe their personal ties with Britain's imperial past, restlessly exploring new approaches to self-representation. Indeed – for Lively, Ballard and Lessing – these autobiographical experiments continued well into the twenty-first century.

There are several conclusions we should draw from reading these life writers in conjunction, beginning with the first – and perhaps most obvious – statement that their memories of colonialism and white settlement could not be contained in a single volume. This suggests that each viewed empire and its aftermath as a process. As they wrote multiple accounts of their own life stories, each acknowledges that their entanglements with the colonial past could not be drawn to a definitive end. But at the same time, these authors depict the seismic shifts of the post-war period as an important threshold. Once they each stepped off the boat in Britain, there would be no going back to their former colonial or settler lives (Frame alone was able to physically return, but her view of Aotearoa/New Zealand was permanently altered by her years in London). Clair Wills reminds us that all 'immigrants who arrived between 1945 and the mid-1960s' encountered 'a still largely ethnically homogenous' British society.[104] Immigrant communities from the Caribbean, the Indian subcontinent and

---

[102] Ibid.
[103] Ibid.
[104] Wills, *Lovers and Strangers*, p. 65.

other former colonial territories transformed not only their own lives but also those 'of the British people around them' as they settled into new homes.[105] Once the four white life writers in this book arrived in the metropole, they saw how the end of empire had a particular impact on the economic, social and cultural landscape of the modern nation. As Robbie Shilliam notes, 'Britain's postwar economic recovery required labour to be sourced from the colonies', and these authors watched as other colonial arrivals (many of whom were citizens thanks to the 1948 British Nationality Act) contributed the necessary skills to build a burgeoning welfare state.[106] While the life writers discussed here therefore undoubtedly interrogate their memories of settler or colonial life, they also bore witness to an irreversible sea change in the former imperial centre. These changes left each of them unable to go home to their former lives. The majority of their returns would have to be imaginative, and their subsequent, processual accounts of white colonial identity could not be neatly finished in a single life narrative.

This leads to a second, conclusion: that for white settlers and their descendants the inheritances of British colonialism were complex, mutable and always close to home. From the colonial unheimlich which pervades Ballard's autobiographical writing, to the enclaved Rhodesian laager of Lessing's travel memoirs, the familiar spaces of childhood are transformed into ambiguous, even threatening spheres, in life writing at the end of empire. The possessions and furnishings inside these properties may initially appear to be solid objects, but they too are defined by shifting, uncertain meanings. When these life writers explore domestic, interior realms they reveal the instability of whiteness as a social construct, and the precarious (so-called) racial logic which underpinned their segregated childhoods. As 'whiteness was reanimated as a political force' during formal decolonization, tracking the instabilities of colonial identity in the post-war era was a subversive manoeuvre.[107] These writers locate their memories of empire and the vulnerabilities of settler life in the everyday, troubling the boundaries which might otherwise seem to separate public and private spheres, or colonial frontiers and the metropole.

This chapter's third conclusion is to underline the connections between an unlikely cohort of authors (one might be forgiven for first assuming that Lively's

---

[105] Ibid.
[106] Robbie Shilliam, *Race and the Undeserving Poor: From Abolition to Brexit* (Newcastle: Agenda Publishing, 2018), p. 82.
[107] Bill Schwarz, 'Wild Power: The Aftershocks of Decolonisation and Black Power', in *Global White Nationalism: From Apartheid to Trump*, ed. Daniel Geary Camilla Schofield and Jennifer Sutton (Manchester: Manchester University Press, 2020), pp. 71–105 (p. 76).

subtle reflections on the fallibility of memory offer few points of comparison with Ballard's dystopic prose). Yet the readings throughout this book have demonstrated that four life writers with very different public reputations share key, if broadly unrecognized, roles as the ambivalent chroniclers of both empire's end and post-imperial Britain. These authors are drawn into conversation by the ways that their life narratives offer unsettling accounts of imperial homes and stage deliberately inconclusive attempts at homecoming. It is possible that these intersecting concerns have been previously overshadowed by each writer's distinct form of literary celebrity. There remains a certain notoriety attached to each of these individuals, whether as the de facto prophet of a mass-media age (Ballard), the chronicler of female insanity (Frame), 'a woman concerned with small-scale domestic life' (Lively) or as an absent mother and former Communist Party member (Lessing).[108] Remaining too attentive to these particular infamies risks overlooking their overlapping, critical engagements with the legacies of imperialism. Examining how and why each felt compelled to return to their settler childhoods pursues the close ties that extend between their autobiographical narratives. When we view this otherwise unlikely group in combination, a wider landscape of experimental life writing at the end of empire begins to emerge into view.

The life narratives discussed throughout this book are still typically used to verify the details of each author's fiction; critics continue to approach Frame's autobiographies as a means to confirm the asylum scenes in her 1961 novel *Faces in the Water* or ask how accurately *Empire of the Sun* depicts the real childhood Ballard described in *Miracles of Life*. These life narratives not only stand up to close critical scrutiny as literary texts in their own right, but also offer future readers, students and researchers rich possibilities for future inquiry and debate. The presumption that these authors should be celebrated solely as writers of fiction, or that their autobiographical narratives exist in a subservient relationship to their novels, is demonstrably short-sighted. In their life writing each scrutinizes the colonial past, documents their changing roles in post-war Britain and considers the possibilities of a post-imperial future. The prosaic, even banal, domestic settings of these texts might not immediately seem indicative of colonial violence, racial segregation and imperial power, but they are umbilically connected to the contradictions of a nation still wracked by 'the

---

[108] Penelope Lively and Lucy Scholes, 'The Art of Fiction No. 241', *The Paris Review*, 226 (2018), https://www.theparisreview.org/interviews/7209/the-art-of-fiction-no-241-penelope-lively (accessed 10 January 2023).

anguish of losing an empire and the fantasy of rediscovering it'.[109] Life writing offers a chance to puncture some of these inflated, and pervasive, national myths. At the same time, critically reading white autobiographical narrative insists that engaging with colonialism's legacies should be neither the sole responsibility nor the exclusive concern of formerly colonized communities and their descendants.

This book has maintained a focus on the literary qualities and formal innovations of life writing, celebrating what Patrick Hayes has described as the genre's 'inventiveness and imaginative power'.[110] Life writing at the end of empire reflects these possibilities by expanding the horizons of traditional autobiography, experimenting with old-age narratives, autofictional alter egos and replotting the established routes of travel writing. Lively, Ballard, Lessing and Frame each turned, repeatedly, to autobiographical narrative as a means to articulate their critique of and complicity with white settlement. The tense exchanges between these opposing poles may often appear contradictory, but they are nevertheless steadfastly productive, offering opportunities to consider and reconsider each author's fraught relationship with their former homes. As first-hand memories of British colonial rule in the twentieth century become increasingly depleted, autobiographical narrative can offer us new perspectives of the frailties and fracture lines which defined white settlements across the former British Empire. These texts pose difficult questions regarding the role of imperial memory in modern Britain, the continuing importance of colonialism to white subjectivity, and the ways in which these unsettling forces lurk barely beneath the surface of modern and contemporary literature. We have only begun to address how life writing allows us to comprehend both the end of colonial rule and the ongoing afterlives of empire.

---

[109] Gildea, *Empires of the Mind*, p. 260.
[110] Patrick Hayes, *The Oxford History of Life-Writing, Volume 7, Postwar to Contemporary 1945–2020* (Oxford: Oxford University Press, 2022), p. 10.

Bibliography

Adorno, Theodor, 'On Late Style in Beethoven (1937)', in *Essays on Music*, ed. Richard Leppert, trans. Susan H. Gillespie. Berkeley: University of California Press, 2002, pp. 564–8.
Adams, Timothy Dow, *Light Writing & Life Writing: Photography in Autobiography*. Chapel Hill: University of North Carolina Press, 1999.
Ahmed, Sara, 'A Phenomenology of Whiteness', *Feminist Theory*, 8:2 (2007): 149–68.
Ahmed, Sara, *The Cultural Politics of Emotion*, 2nd edn. New York: Routledge, 2014.
Ahmed, Sara, *Queer Phenomenology: Orientations, Objects, Others*. Durham: Duke University Press, 2006.
Allen, Chadwick, *Blood Narrative: Indigenous Identity in American Indian and Maori Literary and Activist Texts*. Durham: Duke University Press, 2002.
Anderson, Benedict, *Imagined Communities: Reflections on the Origin and Spread of Nationalism*. London: Verso, 2006.
Anderson, Linda, *Autobiography*. New York: Routledge, 2001.
Arnett, James, 'Colonizing, Decolonizing: Bad-Faith Liberalism and African Space Colonialism in Doris Lessing's Screenplay *The White Princess*', *Journal of Screenwriting*, 10:1 (2019): 81–95.
Arnett, James, 'Doris Lessing and the Ethical African Archive', *Tulsa Studies in Women's Literature*, 37:2 (2018): 435–44.
'Article the Second', *Treaty of Waitangi*, 1840, https://nzhistory.govt.nz/politics/treaty/read-the-treaty/english-text.
Ashcroft, Bill, 'Afterword: Travel and Power', in *Travel Writing, Form and Empire: The Poetics and Politics of Mobility*, ed. Julia Kuehn and Paul Smethurst. New York: Routledge, 2008, pp. 229–41.
Ashcroft, Bill, Gareth Griffiths and Helen Tiffin, *The Empire Writes Back: Theory and Practice in Post-Colonial Literatures*, 2nd edn. New York: Routledge, 2002.
Austin, Harry Ransom Center MS 15.5.
Austin, Harry Ransom Center MS 16.4.
Austin, Harry Ransom Center, Penelope Lively Papers, MS 11.6.
Bachelard, Gaston, *The Poetics of Space*, trans. Maria Jolas. Boston: Beacon Press, 1969.
Bailkin, Jordanna, *The Afterlife of Empire*. Berkeley: University of California Press, 2012.
Ballantyne, Tony, *Orientalism and Race: Aryanism in the British Empire*. Basingstoke: Palgrave, 2002.
Ballantyne, Tony, *Webs of Empire: Locating New Zealand's Colonial Past*. Vancouver: UCB Press, 2012.

Ballard, J. G., *Cocaine Nights*. London: Flamingo, 1997.
Ballard, J. G., *Concrete Island*. New York: Farrar, Straus, and Giroux.
Ballard, J. G., *Empire of the Sun*. London: Harper Perennial, 2006.
Ballard, J. G., *High-Rise*. London: Fourth Estate, 2016.
Ballard, J. G., *The Kindness of Women*. London: Harper Perennial, 2008.
Ballard, J. G., *Miracles of Life: Shanghai to Shepperton*. London: Harper Perennial, 2008.
Ballard, J. G., *A User's Guide to the Millennium: Essays and Reviews*. London: Flamingo, 1997.
Banner, Stuart, 'Conquest by Contract: Wealth Transfer and Land Market Structure in Colonial New Zealand', *Law & Society Review*, 34:1 (2000): 47–96.
Barber, Lynn, and J. G. Ballard, 'Alien At Home', *Sunday Review*, 15 September 1991, https://www.jgballard.ca/media/1991_sept15_independent_sunday_review.html.
Barghouti, Mourid, *I Saw Ramallah*, trans. Ahdaf Soueif. New York: American University in Cairo Press, 2000.
Barthes, Roland, *Roland Barthes*, trans. Richard Howard. New York: Noonday Press, 1977.
Baxter, Jeannette, *J. G. Ballard's Surrealist Imagination: Spectacular Authorship*. Farnham: Ashgate, 2009.
Baxter, John, *The Inner Man: The Life of J. G. Ballard*. London: Weidenfeld and Nicolson, 2011.
Bazin, Claire, *Janet Frame*. Tavistock: Northcote House, 2011.
Benstock, Shari, 'Authorising the Autobiographical', in *The Private Self: Theory and Practice of Women's Autobiographical Writings*, ed. Shari Benstock. Chapel Hill: University of North Carolina Press, 1988, pp. 7–33.
Bertelsen, Eve, 'Interview with Doris Lessing', in *Doris Lessing*, ed. Eve Bertelsen. Johannesburg: McGraw-Hill, 1985, pp. 93–120.
Bhabha, Homi K., *The Location of Culture*. Abingdon: Routledge, 2004.
Bhabha, Homi K., 'The World and the Home', *Social Text*, 31 (1992): 141–53.
Bhandar, Brenna, *Colonial Lives of Property: Land, Law, and Racial Regimes of Ownership*. Durham: Duke University Press, 2018.
Bickers, Robert, *Britain in China: Community, Culture and Colonialism 1900–1949*. Manchester: Manchester University Press, 1999.
Birch, Dinah, 'Growing Up', *London Review of Books*, 11:8 (1989), https://www.lrb.co.uk/the-paper/v11/n08/dinah-birch/growing-up.
Blixen, Karen, *Out of Africa*. London: Penguin, 2000.
Blomfield, Adrian, 'Radical South African Party Calls for Statue of Boer Leader Paul Kruger to Be Removed', *The Telegraph*, 20 May 2018, https://www.telegraph.co.uk/news/2018/05/20/radical-south-african-party-calls-statue-boer-leader-paul-kruger/.
Boehmer, Elleke, *Colonial and Postcolonial Literature: Migrant Metaphors*, 2nd edn. Oxford: Oxford University Press, 2005.
Boehmer, Elleke, ed., *Empire Writing: An Anthology of Colonial Literature 1870–1918*. Oxford: Oxford University Press, 2009.

Boehmer, Elleke, ed., *Stories of Women: Gender and Narrative in the Postcolonial Nation*. Manchester: Manchester University Press, 2005.

Boileau, Nicolas Pierre, 'Places of Being: Janet Frame's Autobiographical Space', *a/b: Auto/Biography Studies*, 22:2 (2007): 217–29.

Brazil, Kevin, David Sergeant and Tom Sperlinger, eds, *Doris Lessing and the Forming of History*. Edinburgh: Edinburgh University Press, 2016.

Brien, Donna Lee, 'Object Biography and Its Potential in Creative Writing', *New Writing: The International Journal for the Practice and Theory of Creative Writing*, 17:4 (2020): 377–90.

Brien, Donna Lee, and Kiera Lindsey, eds, *Speculative Biography: Experiments, Opportunities and Provocations*. New York: Routledge, 2022.

British Library, J. G. Ballard Papers, Add. MS 88938/2/1/7/4.

British Library, J. G. Ballard papers, Add MS 88938/2/1/6.

Brodzki, Bella, and Celeste Schenck, 'Introduction', in *Life/Lines: Theorising Women's Autobiography*, ed. Bella Brodzki and Celeste Schenck. Cornell: Cornell University Press, 1988, pp. 1–19.

Brown, Alexis, '*An Angel at My Table* (1990): Janet Frame, Jane Campion, and Authorial Control in the Auto/Biopic', *Journal of New Zealand Literature*, 34:1 (2016): 103–22.

Brown, Bill, *A Sense of Things: The Object Matter of American Literature*. Chicago: University of Chicago Press, 2003.

Burton, Antoinette, *Dwelling in the Archive: Women Writing House, Home and History in Late Colonial India*. Oxford: Oxford University Press, 2003.

Cairnie, Julie, 'Women and the Literature of Settlement and Plunder: Toward an Understanding of the Zimbabwean Land Crisis', *ESC: English Studies in Canada*, 33:1–2 (2007): 165–88.

Calder, Alex, *The Settler's Plot: How Stories Take Place in New Zealand*. Auckland: Auckland University Press, 2011.

Cannadine, David, *Ornamentalism: How the British Saw Their Empire*. London: Penguin, 2001.

Carby, Hazel V., *Imperial Intimacies: A Tale of Two Islands*. London: Verso, 2019.

Chandler, Raymond, *The Long Goodbye*. New York: Ballantine Books, 1971.

Chennells, Anthony, 'Doris Lessing and the Rhodesia Settler Novel', in *Doris Lessing*, ed. Eve Bertelsen. Johannesburg: McGraw-Hill, 1985, pp. 31–54.

Chennells, Anthony, 'Doris Lessing's Versions of Zimbabwe from *The Golden Notebook* to *Alfred and Emily*', *English Academy Review*, 32:2 (2015): 53–69.

Chikowero, Murenga Joseph, '"We Were Like Little Kings in Rhodesia": Rhodesian Discourse and Representations of Colonial Violence in *Kandaya* and *Don't Let's Go to the Dogs Tonight*', in *Strategies of Representation in Auto/Biography: Reconstructing and Remembering*, ed. Muchativugwa Hove and Kgomotso Masemola. Basingstoke: Palgrave Macmillan, 2014, pp. 116–42.

Coates Palgrave, Keith, *Trees of Southern Africa*. Cape Town: Penguin Random House, 1997.

Coetzee, J. M., *Stranger Shores: Essays 1986–1999*. London: Vintage, 2002.

Coetzee, J. M., *White Writing: On the Culture of Letters in South Africa*. London: Yale University Press, 1988.

'Coronavirus: UK to Have "World-Beating" Testing System', *BBC News*, 20 May 2020, https://www.bbc.co.uk/news/av/uk-politics-52745202.

Couser, G. Thomas, *Memoir: An Introduction*. Oxford: Oxford University Press, 2012.

Cronin, Jan, '"Encircling Tubes of Being": New Zealand as a Hypothetical Site in Janet Frame's *A State of Siege* (1966)', *Journal of New Zealand Literature*, 23:2 (2005): 79–91.

Cronin, Jan, *The Fame Function: An Inside-Out Guide to the Novels of Janet Frame*. Auckland: Auckland University Press, 2011.

Cusset, Catherine, 'The Limits of Autofiction', *Unpublished Conference Paper*, 2012, www.catherinecusset.co.uk/wp-content/uploads/2013/02/the-limits-of-autofiction.pdf.

Dalley, Jan, and Penelope Lively, 'Interview: Every Writer I Know Is a Hungry Reader', *Financial Times*, 22 June 2018, https://www.ft.com/content/962450a2-7499-11e8-b6ad-3823e4384287.

Darnell, Maxine, 'Attaining the Australian Dream: The Starr-Bowkett Way', *Labour History*, 91 (2006): 13–30.

Darwin, John, *Britain and Decolonisation: The Retreat from Empire in the Post-war World*. Basingstoke: Macmillan Press, 1988.

Dean, Andrew Dean, *Metafiction and the Postwar Novel: Foes, Ghosts, and Faces in the Water*. Oxford: Oxford University Press, 2021.

Dean, Andrew Dean, 'Reading an Autobiography: Michael King, Patrick Evans, and Janet Frame', *Journal of New Zealand Literature*, 29 (2011): 46–65.

Delrez, Marc, *Manifold Utopia: The Novels of Janet Frame*. Amsterdam: Rodopi, 2002.

DeLoughrey, Elizabeth M., *Roots and Routes: Navigating Caribbean and Pacific Island Literatures*. Honolulu: University of Hawai'i Press, 2007.

de Man, Paul, 'Autobiography as De-facement', *Modern Language Notes*, 94:5 (1979): 919–30.

De Mul, Sarah, 'Doris Lessing, Feminism and the Representation of Zimbabwe', *European Journal of Women's Studies*, 16:1 (2009): 33–51.

De Mul, Sarah, 'Zimbabwe and the Politics of the Everyday in Doris Lessing's *African Laughter*', in *Migratory Settings*, ed. Murat Aydemir and Alex Rotas. Amsterdam: Rodopi, 2008, pp. 139–56.

Diski, Jenny, *In Gratitude*. London: Bloomsbury, 2016.

Dix, Hywel, 'Introduction: Autofiction in English: The Story So Far', in *Autofiction in English*, ed. Hywel Dix. New York: Palgrave, 2018, pp. 1–23.

Dodson, Edward, 'Postimperial Englishness in the Contemporary White Canon', unpublished DPhil thesis, University of Oxford, 2017.

Doble, Josh, Liam J. Liburd and Emma Parker, eds, *British Culture After Empire: Race, Decolonisation, and Migration Since 1945*. Manchester: Manchester University Press, 2023.

Dorling, Danny, and Sally Tomlinson, *Rule Britannia: Brexit and the End of Empire*. London: Biteback, 2019.

Drayton, Richard, *Nature's Government: Science, Imperial Britain and the 'Improvement' of the World*. London: Yale University Press, 2000.

Dyer, Richard, *White: Essays on Race and Culture*, 2nd edn. New York: Routledge, 2017.

Eakin, Paul John, *Touching the World: Reference in Autobiography*. Princeton, NJ: Princeton University Press, 1992.

Edgerton, David, *The Rise and Fall of the British Nation*. London: Penguin, 2019.

Edmond, Rod, '"In Search of the Lost Tribe": Janet Frame's England', in *Other Britain: Other British: Contemporary Multicultural Fiction*, ed. A. Robert Lee. London: Pluto Press, 1995, pp. 161–74.

Eliot, T. S., *Selected Poems*. London: Faber and Faber, 2002.

Emecheta, Buchi, *Head Above Water*. London: Blackrose Press, 1986.

Esty, Jed, *A Shrinking Island: Modernism and National Culture in England*. Princeton, NJ: Princeton University Press, 2004.

Evans, Patrick, 'Dr Clutha's Book of the World: Janet Paterson Frame, 1924–2004', *Journal of New Zealand Literature*, 22 (2004): 15–30.

Evans, Patrick, 'The Case of the Disappearing Author', *Journal of New Zealand Literature*, 11 (1993): 11–20.

Fanon, Frantz, *Black Skin, White Masks*, trans. Richard Wilcox. New York: Grove Press, 2008).

Fanon, Frantz, *The Wretched of the Earth*, trans. Constance Farrington (London: Penguin, 2001.

Farrell, J. G., *The Singapore Grip*. London: Orion Books, 2010.

Feigel, Lara, *Free Woman: Life, Liberation and Doris Lessing*. London: Bloomsbury, 2018.

Flagel, Nadine, and Anastasia Kozak, 'Excavating the Self: Archeology and Life Writing in Penelope Lively's *Oleander, Jacaranda*', *a/b: Auto/Biography Studies*, 23:2 (2014): 245–63.

Foucault, Michel, *The Order of Things: An Archaeology of the Human Sciences*. London: Routledge, 2002.

Fowler, Corinne, 'We Need to Defend the Freedom to Research Our Histories in All Their Nuance', *Museums Association*, 16 February 2021, https://www.museums association.org/museums-journal/people/2021/02/qa-we-need-to-defend-the-free dom-to-research-our-histories-in-all-their-nuance/#.

Fournier, Lauren, *Autotheory as Feminist Practice in Art, Writing, and Criticism*. London: MIT Press, 2021.

Frame, Janet, *An Angel at My Table*, in *The Complete Autobiography*. London: Women's Press, 1990, pp. 147–287.

Frame, Janet, 'Beginnings', in *Beginnings: New Zealand Writers Tell How They Began Writing*, ed. Robin Dudding. Wellington: Oxford University Press, 1980, pp. 25–33.

Frame, Janet, 'Between My Father and the King', in *Between My Father and the King: New and Uncollected Stories*. Berkeley, CA: Counterpoint, 2013, pp. 10–12.

Frame, Janet, *The Carpathians*. New York: George Braziller, 1988.

Frame, Janet, *The Edge of the Alphabet*. New York: George Braziller, 1962.

Frame, Janet, *The Envoy from Mirror City*, in *The Complete Autobiography*. London: Women's Press, 1990, pp. 289–435.

Frame, Janet, *The Lagoon and Other Stories*. London: Bloomsbury, 1991.

Frame, Janet, *Owls Do Cry*. London: Virago, 2014.

Frame, Janet, *Scented Gardens for the Blind*. London: Women's Press, 1998.

Frame, Janet, *A State of Siege*. London: W. H. Allen, 1967.

Frame, Janet, *To the Is-Land*, in *The Complete Autobiography*. London: Women's Press, 1990, pp. 1–140.

Frame, Janet, *Towards Another Summer*. London: Virago, 2008.

Frame, Janet, *Yellow Flowers in the Antipodean Room*. New York: George Brazillier, 1969.

Francis, Samuel, *The Psychological Fictions of J.G. Ballard*. London: Bloomsbury, 2011.

Freud, Sigmund, 'The Uncanny', in *The Complete Psychological Works of Sigmund Freud, Volume XVII, An Infantile Neurosis and Other Works*, trans. James Strachey. London: Hogarth Press, 1955, pp. 219–53.

Fuentes-Vásquez, Carmen Luz, *Dangerous Writing: The Autobiographies of Willa Muir, Margaret Laurence and Janet Frame*. Amsterdam: Rodopi, 2013.

Fuller, Alexandra, *Don't Let's Go to the Dogs Tonight*. London: Picador, 2015.

Fuss, Diana, *The Sense of an Interior: Four Rooms and the Writers That Shaped Them*. Abingdon: Routledge, 2004.

Gallagher, Catherine, *Telling It Like It Wasn't: The Counterfactual Imagination in History and Fiction*. Chicago: University of Chicago Press, 2018.

Gasiorek, Andrzej, *J.G. Ballard*. Manchester: Manchester University Press, 2005.

Gelder, Ken, and Jane M. Jacobs, *Uncanny Australia: Sacredness and Identity in a Postcolonial Nation*. Melbourne: Melbourne University Publishing, 1994.

George, Rosemary Marangoly, *The Politics of Home: Postcolonial Relocations and Twentieth-Century Fiction*. Berkeley: University of California Press, 1999.

Gevisser, Mark, *Dispatcher: Lost and Found in Johannesburg*. London: Granta Books, 2015.

Gibbons, Peter, 'Non-Fiction', in *The Oxford History of New Zealand Literature in English*, ed. Terry Sturm, 2nd edn. Oxford: Oxford University Press, 1998, pp. 31–119.

Gide, André, *If It Die … An Autobiography*, trans. Dorothy Bussy. New York: Vintage Books, 2001.

Gildea, Robert, *Empires of the Mind: The Colonial Past and the Politics of the Present*. Cambridge: Cambridge University Press, 2019.

Gilroy, Beryl, *Black Teacher*. London: Cassel, 1976.

Gilroy, Paul, *After Empire: Melancholia or Convivial Culture?* Abingdon: Routledge, 2004.

Glover, William J., '"A Feeling of Absence from Old England": The Colonial Bungalow', *Home Cultures: The Journal of Architecture, Design, and Domestic Space*, 1:1 (2004): 61–82.

Goebel, Allison, *Gender and Land Reform: The Zimbabwe Experience*. London: McGill-Queen's University Press, 2005.

Gonzalez, Jennifer A., 'Autotopographies', in *Prosthetic Territories: Politics and Hypertechnologies*, ed. Gabriel Brahm Jr and Mark Driscoll. Oxford: Westview Press, 1995, pp. 133–47.

Gopal, Priyamvada, *Insurgent Empire: Anticolonial Resistance and British Dissent*. London: Verso, 2019.

Gove, Michael, 'All Pupils Will Learn Our Island Story', *Conservative Party Speeches*, 5 October 2010, https://conservative-speeches.sayit.mysociety.org/speech/601441.

Gregory, Derek, *The Colonial Present: Afghanistan, Palestine, Iraq*. Oxford: Wiley-Blackwell, 2004.

Grove, Richard, *Green Imperialism: Colonial Expansion, Tropical Island Edens and the Origins of Environmentalism, 1600–1860*. Cambridge: Cambridge University Press, 1995.

Hall, Catherine, and Sonya O. Rose, 'Introduction: Being at Home with the Empire', in *At Home with the Empire: Metropolitan Culture and the Imperial World*, ed. Catherine Hall and Sonya O. Rose. Cambridge: Cambridge University Press, 2011, pp. 1–31.

Hall, Stuart, with Bill Schwarz, *Familiar Stranger: A Life between Two Islands*. London: Penguin, 2018.

Harris, Cheryl, 'Whiteness as Property', *Harvard Law Review*, 106:8 (1993): 1707–91.

Hart, Matthew, *Extraterritorial: A Political Geography of Contemporary Fiction*. New York: Columbia University Press, 2020.

Hawke, G. R., *The Making of New Zealand: An Economic History*. Cambridge: Cambridge University Press, 1985.

Hayes, Patrick, *The Oxford History of Life-Writing, Volume 7, Postwar to Contemporary 1945–2020*. Oxford: Oxford University Press, 2022.

Heidegger, Martin, 'Building Dwelling Thinking', in *Basic Writings from Being and Time (1927) to the Talk of Thinking (1964)*, ed. D. F. Krell. New York: Routledge, 1993, pp. 347–63.

Helmreich, Anne, *The English Garden and National Identity: The Competing Styles of Garden Design 1870–1914*. Cambridge: Cambridge University Press, 2002.

Hirsch, Marianne, *Family Frames: Photography, Narrative and Postmemory*. Cambridge: Harvard University Press, 1997.

Hornung, Alfred and Ersntpeter Ruhe, eds, *Postcolonialism and Autobiography: Michelle Cliff, David Dabydeen, Opal Palmer Adisa*. Amsterdam: Rodopi, 1998.

Hough, Andrew, "Revealed: David Cameron's Favourite Childhood Book Is Our Island Story", *The Telegraph*, 29 October 2010, https://www.telegraph.co.uk/culture/books/booknews/8094333/Revealed-David-Camerons-favourite-childhood-book-is-Our-Island-Story.html.

Huddart, David, *Postcolonial Theory and Autobiography*. New York: Routledge, 2009.

Hughes, David McDermott, *Whiteness in Zimbabwe: Race, Landscape and the Problem of Belonging*. New York: Palgrave Macmillan, 2010.

Ignatiev, Noel, *How the Irish Became White*. New York: Routledge, 1995.

Innes, C. L., 'Authorising the Self: Postcolonial Autobiographical Writing', in *The Cambridge Introduction to Postcolonial Literatures in English*. Cambridge: Cambridge University Press, 2007, pp. 56–71.

Jackson, Isabella, *Shaping Modern Shanghai: Colonialism in China's Global City*. Cambridge: Cambridge University Press, 2018.

James, David, *Discrepant Solace: Contemporary Literature and the Work of Consolation*. Oxford: Oxford University Press, 2019.

Jones, Robert D., *Interiors of Empire: Objects, Space and Identity within the Indian Subcontinent, 1800–1947*. Manchester: Manchester University Press, 2007.

Kadar, Marlene, 'Coming to Terms: Life Writing – from Genre to Critical Practice', in *Essays on Life Writing: From Genre to Critical Practice*, ed. Marlene Kadar. Toronto: University of Toronto Press, 1992.

Kennedy, Dane, *Islands of White: Settler Society and Culture in Kenya and Southern Rhodesia, 1890–1939*. Durham: Duke University Press, 1987.

Keown, Michelle, *Pacific Islands Writing: The Postcolonial Literatures of Aotearoa/New Zealand and Oceania*. Oxford: Oxford University Press, 2007.

King, Michael, 'Janet Frame', *The Guardian*, 30 January 2004, https://www.theguardian.com.news/2004/jan/30/guardianobituaries.booksobituaries.

King, Michael, *The Penguin History of New Zealand*. London: Penguin, 2003.

King, Michael, *Wrestling With The Angel: The Life of Janet Frame*. London: Picador, 2001.

Kopytoff, Igor, 'The Cultural Biography of Things: Commoditization as Process', in *The Social Life of Things*, ed. Arjun Appadurai. Cambridge: Cambridge University Press, 1986, pp. 64–91.

Kuhn, Annette, *Family Secrets: Acts of Memory and Imagination*. London: Verso, 1995.

Lassner, Phyllis, *Colonial Strangers: Women Writing the End of the British Empire*. London: Rutgers University Press, 2004.

Law, Kate, *Gendering the Settler State: White Women, Race, Liberalism and Empire in Rhodesia 1950–1980*. New York: Routledge, 2016.

Lehtonen, Sanna, 'Writing Oneself into Someone Else's Story: Experiments with Identity and Speculative Life Writing in Twilight Fan Fiction', *Fafnir: Nordic Journal of Science Fiction and Fantasy Research*, 2:2 (2015): 7–18.

Lejeune, Philippe, *On Autobiography*, ed. Paul John Eakin, trans. Katherine Leary. Minneapolis: University of Minnesota Press, 1989.
Lessing, Doris, 'A Deep Darkness: A Review of *Out of Africa* by Karen Blixen', in *A Small Personal Voice: Essays, Reviews, Interviews*, ed. Paul Schlueter. New York: Alfred A Knopf, 1974, pp. 147–55.
Lessing, Doris, *African Laughter: Four Visits to Zimbabwe*. London: Flamingo, 1993.
Lessing, Doris, *Alfred and Emily*. London: Fourth Estate, 2008.
Lessing, Doris, *Going Home*. London: Pantha, 1984.
Lessing, Doris, 'Impertinent Daughters', *Granta*, 14 (1984), https://granta.com/impertinent-daughters/.
Lessing, Doris, *In Pursuit of the English: A Documentary*. London: Panther, 1980.
Lessing, Doris, 'My Mother's Life (Part Two), *Granta*, 17 (1985), https://granta.com/autobiography-part-two-my-mothers-life/.
Lessing, Doris, 'On Not Winning the Nobel Prize', 7 December 2007, https://www.nobelprize.org/prizes/literature/2007/lessing/25434-doris-lessing-nobel-lecture-2007/.
Lessing, Doris, *The Grass Is Singing*. Oxford: Heinemann, 1973.
Lessing, Doris, 'The Tragedy of Zimbabwe', in *Time Bites: Views and Reviews*. London: Harper Perennial, 2005, pp. 231–47.
Lessing, Doris, *The Wind Blows Away Our Words*. London: Picador, 1987.
Lessing, Doris, *Under My Skin: Volume One of My Autobiography, to 1949*. London: HarperCollins, 1994.
Lessing, Doris, *Walking in the Shade: Volume Two of My Autobiography, 1949–1962*. London: Fourth Estate, 2013.
Lively, Penelope, *According to Mark*. New York: Harper & Row, 1989.
Lively, Penelope, *Ammonites and Leaping Fish*. London: Fig Tree, 2013.
Lively, Penelope, *A House Unlocked*. London: Viking, 2001.
Lively, Penelope, 'Interview with the Author', 30 August 2017.
Lively, Penelope, 'Late Style', *BBC Radio 3*, 18 April 2017, http://www.bbc.co.uk/programmes/b08n2442.
Lively, Penelope, *Life in the Garden*. London: Fig Tree, 2017.
Lively, Penelope, *Making It Up*. London: Viking, 2005.
Lively, Penelope, *Moon Tiger*. London: Penguin, 2000.
Lively, Penelope, *Oleander, Jacaranda*. London: Penguin, 2006.
Lively, Penelope, *The Photograph*. London: Penguin, 2004.
Lively, Penelope, *The Presence of the Past: An Introduction to Landscape History*. London: Collins, 1976.
Lively, Penelope, 'The View from Elsewhere: Egypt', in *Discourses of Empire and Commonwealth*, ed. Alastair Niven and Sandra Robinson. Leiden: Brill Rodolpi, 2016, pp. 153–8.
Locke, John, *Second Treatise of Government and a Letter Concerning Toleration*, ed. Mark Goldie. Oxford: Oxford University Press, 2016.

Loomba, Ania, *Colonialism/Postcolonialism*. New York: Routledge, 1998.
Lord, Graham 'Child's View of African Empire' *The Times*, 28 May 1994.
Luckhurst, Roger, '*The Angle between Two Walls*': *The Fiction of J.G. Ballard*. Liverpool: Liverpool University Press, 1997.
Luckhurst, Roger, 'Petition, Repetition and "Autobiography": J. G. Ballard's *Empire of the Sun* and *The Kindness of Women*, *Contemporary Literature*, 35:4 (1994): 688–708.
Macdonald, Alistair, 'May Evoked Blitz Spirit to Show EU Brexit Progress', *Reuters*, 11 April 2019, https://uk.reuters.com/article/uk-britain-eu-blitz/may-evoked-blitz-spirit-to-show-eu-brexit-progress-idUKKCN1RN26Z.
MacKay, Marina, *Ian Watt: The Novel and the Wartime Critic*. Oxford: Oxford University Press, 2018.
Marshall, Henrietta Elizabeth, *Our Island Story: A History of Britain for Boys and Girls from the Romans to Queen Victoria*. London: Pheonix, 2005.
Marsh, Huw, 'Unlearning Empire: Penelope Lively's *Moon Tiger*', in *End of Empire and the English Novel since 1945*, ed. Rachael Gilmour and Bill Schwarz. Manchester: Manchester University Press, 2011, pp. 152–65.
McAllister, John, 'Knowing Native: Going Native: Cognitive Borderlines and the Sense of Belonging in Doris Lessing's *African Laughter* and Dan Jacobson's *The Electric Elephant*', in *Zimbabwean Transitions: Essays on Zimbabwean Literature in English, Ndebele and Shona*, ed. Mbongeni Z. Malaba and Geoffrey V. Davis. Amsterdam: Rodopi, 2007, pp. 25–38.
McClintock, Anne, *Imperial Leather: Race, Gender and Sexuality in the Colonial Context*. New York: Routledge, 1995.
McDonald, Keith, 'Days of Past Futures: Kazuo Ishiguro's *Never Let Me Go* as "Speculative Memoir"', *Biography*, 30:1 (2007): 74–83.
McGrath, Charles, '"A Writer Writes": Penelope Lively's Fiction Defies the Test of Time', *New York Times*, 4 May 2017, https://www.nytimes.com/2017/05/04/books/review/penelope-lively-profile-purple-swamp-hen.html.
McLeod, John, 'The Novel and the End of Empire', in *The Oxford History of the Novel in English, Volume Seven: British and Irish Fiction since 1940, Volume 7: British and Irish Fiction since 1940*, ed. Peter Boxall and Bryan Cheyette. Oxford: Oxford University Press, 2016, pp. 80–93.
McLeod, John, *Postcolonial London: Rewriting the Metropolis*. Abingdon: Routledge, 2004.
Mellor, Leo, *Reading the Ruins: Modernism, Bombsites and British Culture*. Cambridge: Cambridge University Press, 2011.
Mercer, Gina, 'A Simple Everyday Glass: The Autobiographies of Janet Frame', *Journal of New Zealand Literature*, 11 (1993): 41–8.
Mercer, Gina, *Janet Frame: Subversive Fictions*. Dunedin: Otago University Press, 1994.
Mignolo, Walter D., and Catherine E. Walsh, *On Decoloniality: Concepts, Analytics, Praxis*. Durham: Duke University Press, 2018.

Michell, Isabel, '"Turning the Stone of Being": Janet Frame's Migrant Poetic', in *Frameworks: Contemporary Criticism on Janet Frame*, ed. Jan Cronin and Simone Drichel. Amsterdam: Rodopi, 2009, pp. 107–35.

Mitchell, Peter. *Imperial Nostalgia: How the British Conquered Themselves*. Manchester: Manchester University Press, 2021.

Mitchell, Timothy, *Colonising Egypt*. Berkeley: University of California Press, 1991.

Mohanram, Radhika, *Imperial White: Race, Diaspora and the British Empire*. Minneapolis: University of Minnesota Press, 2007.

Moore-Gilbert, Bart, *Postcolonial Life-Writing: Culture, Politics and Self-Representation*. New York: Routledge, 2009.

Moore-Gilbert, Bart, *The Setting Sun: A Memoir of Empire and Family Secrets*. London: Verso, 2014.

Moran, Mary Hurley, *Penelope Lively*. New York: Twayne, 1993.

Morrison, Blake, 'The Righting of Lives', *The Guardian*, 17 May 2008, https://www.theguardian.com/books/2008/may/17/fiction.dorislessing.

Mungazi, Dickson A., *The Last Defenders of the Laager: Ian D. Smith and F. W. de Klerk*. London: Praeger, 1998.

Murray, Stuart, *Never a Soul at Home: New Zealand Literary Nationalism and the 1930s*. Victoria, New Zealand: Victoria University Press, 1998.

Niven, Alastair, and Sandra Robinson, *Discourses of Empire and Commonwealth*. Leiden: Brill Rodolpi, 2016.

Nuttall, Sarah, 'The Time Sea', *Wasafiri*, 36:2 (2021): 13–21.

Oettli-van Delden, Simone, *Surfaces of Strangeness: Janet Frame and the Rhetoric of Madness*. Wellington, New Zealand: Victoria University Press, 2003.

Olusoga, David, *Black and British: A Forgotten History*. London: Pan Books, 2017.

Olusoga, David, 'Historians Have Become Soft Targets in the Culture Wars. We Should Fight Back', *New Statesman*, 8 December 2021, https://www.newstatesman.com/culture/2021/12/historians-have-become-soft-targets-in-the-culture-wars-we-should-fight-back.

Opie, Iona, and Peter, 'Goldilocks and the Three Bears', in *Classic Fairy Tales*, compiled by Iona and Peter Opie. Oxford: Oxford University Press, 1980, pp. 260–3.

Orange, Claudia, *The Treaty of Waitangi*. Wellington: Bridget Williams Books, 1987.

Oró-Piqueras, Maricel, 'When the Personal and the Historical Collide: Reimagining Memory in Penelope Lively's *Making It Up*', *Life writing*, 14:1 (2017): 57–68.

O'Toole, Fintan, *Heroic Failure: Brexit and the Politics of Pain*. London: Head of Zeus, 2018.

Paddy, Ian, 'Empires of the Mind: Autobiography and Anti-Imperialism in the Work of J. G. Ballard', in *J.G. Ballard: Visions and Revisions*, ed. Jeannette Baxter and Rowland Wymer. London: Continuum, 2012, pp. 179–97.

Parker, Emma, "Doris Lessing's *Alfred and Emily:* Speculation in the Aftermath of Empire", *Critical Quarterly*, 63:1 (2021): 110–20.

Parker, Emma, 'Penelope Lively's Speculative Life Writing: A Discussion of *Making It Up* and *Ammonites and Leaping Fish*', *Moving Worlds: A Journal of Transcultural Writings*, 18:1 (2018): 63–78.

Paul, Kathleen, *Whitewashing Britain: Race and Citizenship in the Post-War Era*. Ithaca, NY: Cornell University Press, 1997.

'Penelope Lively's Life in Books', *BBC News*, 31 December 2011. https://www.bbc.co.uk/news/entertainment-arts-16362698.

'Penelope Lively Put Down Her Pen after a Life in Books', *The Times*, 16 May 2022, https://www.thetimes.co.uk/article/penelope-lively-puts-down-her-pen-after-a-life-in-books-m9qjqb375#:~:text=Dame%20Penelope%20Lively%20has%20vowed,time%20to%20%E2%80%9Cbow%20out%E2%80%9D.

Perrick, Penny, 'Taking the Tiger Lightly by the Tip of the Tail – This Year's Winner of the Best-Known Prize for Fiction', *Sunday Times*, 1 November 1987.

Phillips, Caryl, *Extravagant Strangers: A Literature of Belonging*. London: Faber & Faber, 1997.

Philips, Jock, and Terry Hearn, *Settlers: New Zealand Immigrants from England, Ireland and Scotland, 1800–1945*. Auckland: Auckland University Press, 2008.

Pilossof, Rory, *The Unbearable Whiteness of Being: Farmers' Voices from Zimbabwe*. Harare: Weaver Press, 2012.

Plato, 'Republic: VII', in *The Collected Dialogues of Plato*, ed. Edith Hamilton and Huntington Cairns, trans. Paul Shorey. Princeton, NJ: Princeton University Press, 1961, pp. 747–72.

Plotz, John, *Portable Property: Victorian Culture on the Move*. Woodstock: Princeton University Press, 2008.

Poletti, Anna, *Stories of the Self: Life Writing After the Book*. New York: New York University Press, 2020.

Porter, Bernard, *The Absent-Minded Imperialists*. Oxford: Oxford University Press, 2004.

Pratt, Mary Louise, *Imperial Eyes: Travel Writing and Transculturation*, 2nd edn. New York: Routledge, 2008.

Prawer Jhabvala, Ruth, *My Nine Lives: Chapters of a Possible Past*. London: John Murray, 2004.

Priestland, David, et al., 'Michael Gove's New Curriculum: What the Experts Say', *The Guardian*, 12 February 2012, https://www.theguardian.com/commentisfree/2013/feb/12/round-table-draft-national-curriculum.

Prendergast, Christopher, *Counterfactuals: Paths of the Might Have Been*. London: Bloomsbury, 2019.

Prosser, Jay, *Light in the Dark Room: Photography and Loss*. Minneapolis: University of Minnesota Press, 2005.

Proust, Marcel, *Remembrance of Things Past: 1*, trans. C. K. Scott Moncrieff and Terence Kilmartin. Harmondsworth: Penguin, 1983.

Rasch, Astrid, 'Introduction', *Life Writing After Empire*. New York: Routledge, 2018, pp. 1–6.
Rasch, Astrid, 'Postcolonial Nostalgia: The Ambiguities of White Memoirs of Zimbabwe', *History & Memory*, 30:2 (2018): 147–80.
Robinson, Roger 'New Zealand', in *The Commonwealth Novel Since 1960*, ed. Bruce King. Basingstoke: Macmillan, 1991, 105–20.
Rogers, Douglas, *The Last Resort: A Memoir of Zimbabwe*. London: Short Books, 2010.
Rossi, Umberto, 'Mind Is the Battlefield: Reading Ballard's "Life Trilogy" as War Literature', in *J. G. Ballard: Contemporary Critical Perspectives*, ed. Jeannette Baxter. London: Continuum, 2008, pp. 66–78.
Rubenstein, Roberta, *Home Matters: Longing and Belonging, Nostalgia and Mourning in Women's Fiction*. New York: Palgrave, 2001.
Rubenstein, Roberta, *Literary Half-Lives: Doris Lessing, Clancy Sigal and Roman à Clef*. New York: Palgrave, 2014.
Ruskin, John, 'Conclusion to Inaugural Lecture (1870)', in *Empire Writing: An Anthology of Colonial Literature 1870–1918*, ed. Elleke Boehmer. Oxford: Oxford University Press, 2009, pp. 16–20.
Ryan, James R., *Picturing Empire: Photography and the Visualisation of the British Empire*. London: Reaktion Books, 1997.
Sage, Lorna, *Doris Lessing*. London: Methuen, 1983.
Said, Edward, *Culture and Imperialism*. London: Chatto & Windus, 1993.
Said, Edward, *On Late Style: Literature Against the Grain*. London: Bloomsbury, 2006.
Said, Edward, *Out of Place: A Memoir*. London: Granta, 2000.
Said, Edward, *Reflections on Exile and Other Essays*. Cambridge, MA: Harvard University Press, 2000.
Salmond, Anne, *Tears of Rangi: Experiments Across Worlds*. Auckland: Auckland University Press, 2017.
Sarabando, Andreia, '"The Dreadful Mass Neighbourhood of Objects" in the Fiction of Janet Frame', *Journal of Postcolonial Writing*, 51:5 (2015): 603–14.
Saunders, Max, *Self Impression: Life-Writing, Autobiografiction, and the Forms of Modern Literature*. Oxford: Oxford University Press, 2013.
Schofield, Camilla, *Enoch Powell and the Making of Postcolonial Britain*. Cambridge: Cambridge University Press, 2013.
Scholes, Lucy, and Penelope Lively, 'The Art of Fiction No. 241', *Paris Review*, 226 (2018), https://www.theparisreview.org/interviews/7209/the-art-of-fiction-no-241-penelope-lively.
Schwarz, Bill, '"The Only White Man in There": The Re-Racialisation of England, 1956–1968', *Race & Class*, 38:1 (1996): 65–78.
Schwarz, Bill, *The White Man's World (Memories of Empire)*. Oxford: Oxford University Press, 2011.
Schwarz, Bill, 'Wild Power: The Aftershocks Of Decolonisation and Black Power', in *Global White Nationalism: From Apartheid to Trump*, ed. Daniel Geary, Camilla

Schofield and Jennifer Sutton. Manchester: Manchester University Press, 2020, pp. 71–105.

Sellers, Simon, and Dan O'Hara, eds, *Extreme Metaphors: Interviews with J.G. Ballard, 1967-2008*. London: Fourth Estate, 2012.

Shilliam, Robbie, *Race and the Undeserving Poor: From Abolition to Brexit*. Newcastle: Agenda, 2018.

Small, Helen, *The Long Life*. Oxford: Oxford University Press, 2007.

Smith, Sidonie, and Julia Watson, eds, *De/colonizing the Subject: The Politics of Gender in Women's Autobiography*. Minneapolis: University of Minnesota Press, 1992.

Smith, Sidonie, and Julia Watson, eds, 'Introduction: Situating Subjectivity in Women's Autobiographical Practices', in *Women, Autobiography, Theory: A Reader*. Madison: University of Wisconsin Press, 1998, pp. 3–56.

Smith, Sidonie, and Julia Watson, eds, *Reading Autobiography: A Guide for Interpreting Life Narratives*, 2nd edn. Minneapolis: University of Minnesota Press, 2010.

Sontag, Susan, *On Photography*. London: Penguin, 2002.

Soukhani, Henghameh, 'Empire, Race, and the Autotheoretical Impulse', *Moving Worlds: A Journal of Transcultural Writing*, 20:2 (2021): 21–36.

Southey, Robert, 'The Story of the Three Bears', in *Classic Fairy Tales*, compiled by Iona and Peter Opie. Oxford: Oxford University Press, 1980, pp. 264–9.

Squire, J. C., *If It Had Happened Otherwise*. London: Longman, 1931.

Stead, Henry, "Comrade Doris": Lessing's Correspondence with the Foreign Commission of the Board of Soviet Writers in the 1950s', *Critical Quarterly*, 63:1 (2021): 35–47.

Steel, Flora Annie, and Grace Gardiner, *The Complete Indian Housekeeper and Cook*. Oxford: Oxford University Press, 2010.

Stoler, Ann Laura, *Carnal Knowledge and Imperial Power: Race and the Intimate in Colonial Rule*. Berkeley: University of California Press, 2010.

Stoler, Ann Laura, 'The Rot Remains: From Ruins to Ruination', in *Imperial Debris: On Ruins and Ruination*, ed. Ann Laura Stoler. Durham: Duke University Press, 2013, pp. 1–38.

Stonebridge, Lyndsey, *Placeless People: Writing, Rights, and Refugees*. Oxford: Oxford University Press, 2018.

Stonor Saunders, Frances, 'The Suitcase', *London Review of Books*, 42:15 (2020), https://www.lrb.co.uk/the-paper/v42/n15/frances-stonor-saunders/the-suitcase.

Strongman, Luke, *The Booker Prize and the Legacy of Empire*. Amsterdam: Rodopi, 2002.

Suleri, Sara, *Meatless Days*. Chicago: University of Chicago Press, 1989.

Taylor, Jenny, 'Memory and Desire on *Going Home*: The Deconstruction of a Colonial Radical', in *Doris Lessing*, ed. Eve Bertelsen. Johannesburg: McGraw-Hill, 1985, pp. 55–63.

Tuck, E., and K. W. Yang, 'Decolonisation Is Not a Metaphor', *Decolonisation: Indigeneity, Education & Society*, 1:1 (2012): 1–40.

Vidler, Anthony, *The Architectural Uncanny: Essays in the Modern Unhomely*. Cambridge, MA: MIT Press, 1992.

Ward, Stuart, 'Introduction', in *British Culture and the End of Empire*. Manchester: Manchester University Press, 2001, pp. 1–21.

Ware, Vron, *Beyond the Pale: White Women, Racism and History*. London: Verso, 1992.

wa Thiong'o, Ngũgĩ, *Decolonising the Mind: The Politics of Language in African Literature*. London: Heinemann Educational, 1986.

Walder, Dennis, *Postcolonial Nostalgias: Writing, Representation and Memory*. New York: Routledge, 2011.

Watkins, Susan, *Doris Lessing*. Manchester: Manchester University Press, 2010.

Watkins, Susan, 'Remembering Home: Nation and Identity in the Recent Writings of Doris Lessing', *Feminist Review*, 85 (2007): 97–115.

Watkins, Susan, 'Second World Life Writing: Doris Lessing's *Under My Skin*', *Journal of Southern African Studies*, 42:1 (2016): 137–48.

Watkins, Susan, '"Summoning Your Youth at Will": Memory, Time and Ageing in the Work of Penelope Lively, Margaret Atwood and Doris Lessing', *Frontiers: A Journal of Women Studies*, 34:2 (2013): 222–44.

Webb, W. L., 'Favourites Fail to Make Booker Short List', *The Guardian*, 24 September 1987.

Webb, W. L., 'Lively Leaps Off with 15,000 Pounds Booker Prize', *The Guardian*, 30 October 1987.

Wellington, Alexander, Turnbull Library, MS-Papers-9153-18.

Wevers, Lydia, 'Self Possession: "Things" and Janet's Frame's Autobiography', in *Frameworks: Contemporary Criticism on Janet Frame*, ed. Jan Cronin and Simone Drichel. Amsterdam: Rodopi, 2009, pp. 51–67.

Whitlock, Gillian, *Postcolonial Life Narratives: Testimonial Transactions*. Oxford: Oxford University Press, 2015.

Whitlock, Gillian, *Soft Weapons: Autobiography in Transit*. Chicago: University of Chicago Press, 2007.

Whitlock, Gillian, *The Intimate Empire: Reading Women's Autobiography*. London: Cassell, 2000.

Whittle, Matthew, *Post-War Literature and the 'End of Empire'*. New York: Palgrave, 2016.

Wills, Clair, *Lovers and Strangers: An Immigrant History of Post-War Britain*. London: Penguin, 2017.

Wilson, D. Harlan, *J.G. Ballard*. Urbana: University of Illinois Press, 2017.

Wood, Michael, *The Road to Delphi: The Life and Afterlife of Oracles*. New York: Farrar, Straus and Girouz, 2003.

Woolf, Virginia, 'A Sketch of the Past', in *Moments of Being: Unpublished Autobiographical Writings*. London: Grafton, 1986, pp. 71–160.

Wymer, Rowland, 'Ballard's Story of O: "The Voices of Time" and the Quest for (Non) Identity', in *J.G. Ballard: Visions and Revisions*, ed. Jeannette Baxter and Rowland Wyler. London: Continuum, 2012, pp. 19–34.

Young, Robert, J. C., *Postcolonialism: An Historical Introduction*. Oxford: Blackwell, 2001.

Index

Ahmed, Sara 18–19, 32, 40, 157–8, 162, 169
Anderson, Benedict 12, 119
Aotearoa/New Zealand (*see also* Māori) 1, 14–18, 21, 89, 122–4, 128–37, 141–6, 150, 172, 174
   Dunedin 131–40, 142–3, 170
   Oamaru 128, 132, 137, 171
   Otago 128, 140–2
   Pākehā culture 123–4, 127, 135–6, 139–40, 142
   racism in 128, 146
   Treaty of Waitangi (1840) 136, 140
autobiography (*see also* life writing) 1, 3, 8–14, 29, 42, 61, 85–7, 98, 122, 129, 134–53, 157, 160, 163, 174, 177
autofiction 43–5, 85, 177

Bachelard, Gaston, 16, 154, 156, 168, 170, 172–3
Ballard, J. G. 2–8, 13–24, 45, 57–90, 97, 112, 127–8, 147, 152, 156–63, 166–70, 174–7
   31a Amherst Avenue, 15, 23, 57–80, 83–9, 97
   Arrival in Britain 2–3, 76, 87
   Cocaine Nights 69
   Concrete Island 66, 71
   Empire of the Sun 13, 19, 59–79, 156–63, 170, 176
   High-Rise 69
   The Kindness of Women 2, 59–62, 75–86
   Miracles of Life 3, 59–70, 75–9, 83–7, 176
   swimming pools, 59, 62, 65–6, 69–73, 85
Banks, Joseph 30
Barghouti, Mourid, 155
Barthes, Roland 154–6, 166, 168, 172–3
Bhabha, Homi K. 57, 72, 89
Bhandar, Brenna 124, 139, 142

biography (*see also* life writing) 9, 43, 121, 156
Blixen, Karen 103
Britain
   contemporary 21–4, 27, 29, 43, 55, 148, 170
   heroic failure 78
   interwar 2
   metropole 6, 8, 22–3, 62, 122, 143, 150, 175
   monarch 122, 128, 131–4, 159, 170–2
   post-war 1–7, 20, 27, 52–4, 87, 144–7, 149–50, 173, 175–6
   racism in 6, 144–6, 148, 150
British
   isolationism 22–3
   Nationality Act (1948) 144, 175
   National Health Service 146–7
   national identity 48–9, 54–5, 78, 148, 158–9, 167
British Empire 1, 4, 60, 65–6, 70, 86, 91, 93, 97, 123, 128, 143–4, 167, 173, 177
   histories of 6, 30, 53–5
   memories of 20–3, 27, 55, 144, 148–9, 176–7
Brown, Bill 156–7

Cairo 3, 15, 19, 26, 28–43, 46–50, 54, 60, 108, 170
   Gezira Sporting Club, the 36, 39, 50
   Zamalek Island 47–8
Cameron, David 55
Campion, Jane 122
China (*see also* Shanghai) 14, 57, 59, 88
   Chinese communism 87
Churchill, Winston 2, 4
Coetzee, J. M. 93, 135
colonialism 18, 33, 36, 88, 97, 120, 124–5, 127, 139, 144, 152
   afterlives of 4–5, 7, 23, 61, 143, 177
   as a network 14, 22, 53, 128, 135, 158

legacies in Britain 7, 21–4, 27, 29, 55, 87, 127, 144–50, 174–7
neo-colonialism 69, 139, 173–4
possession of land 33–5, 104, 123, 136, 138–9, 142
colonial
   cartographies 5, 41, 108–9, 128, 131, 162
   contact zones 33–4
   domesticity 16–19, 22–3, 27–8, 33–6, 47, 51, 67–8, 72, 74, 88, 111, 133–4, 158, 168, 173, 176
   education 3, 6, 23, 30, 53, 122, 128, 146, 159
   frontiers 6, 11, 17, 28, 30, 40, 88, 98, 100, 106, 127, 163, 175
   gardens 18, 23, 30–5, 40, 54, 63, 168
   identity 19, 22–3, 30, 67, 81, 84, 87–9, 127, 158, 164, 166–9, 175
   uncanny 6, 15, 60–3, 68, 74, 162, 175
   violence 65, 72, 75, 98, 134, 144, 176
Commander of the British Empire (CBE) 20, 91, 93
commonwealth, the 143–4, 146
counterfactuals 28, 41–52, 54, 95, 164
Cronin, Jan 131, 136–7, 151

de Waal, Edmund 154–5
decolonisation 18, 21, 24, 42, 47, 50, 60–2, 103, 147, 166, 168, 170
   histories of 4–8, 81, 85–9, 127, 144, 173–5
   theories of 102–3, 124, 127
Dunedin 131–43, 170

Egypt (*see also* Cairo) 3, 14–15, 18–20, 26–54, 168–73
   British Protectorate 3, 30
   desert, the 19–20, 35, 39, 46, 53
Emecheta, Buchi 6, 143
Empires of the home 15–20, 22–3, 67–8, 74–5, 88–9, 158, 166–9
Englishness 36, 48, 81
exhibitions
   British Empire Exhibition (Wembley, 1924–5) 96
   South Seas Exhibition (Dunedin, 1925–6) 128
   World Exhibition (Paris, 1889) 38

Fanon, Frantz 11, 27–8, 32, 39, 47, 51
Farrell, J. G. 59
Feigel, Lara 97, 107, 118
feminism 9–10, 13
First World War, the 3, 72, 74, 93, 96, 119, 122, 132–4, 164
Frame, Janet 1–8, 13–24, 45, 60, 118, 121–52, 157, 166–77
   arrival in Britain 1, 127, 134, 143–4, 172
   An Angel at My Table 13, 121–2, 124–7, 137–43, 151, 171
   Between My Father and the King 132–4
   criticism of home ownership 15, 21, 89, 93, 123–5, 127, 136–42
   The Carpathians 130, 136
   The Edge of the Alphabet 122
   The Envoy from Mirror City 1–2, 122, 124–5, 127, 135, 139–52, 172
   experiences of poverty 15, 23, 121, 124, 129, 138, 140, 167, 171
   hospitalisation 121–4, 135–6, 139, 142, 151, 171–2, 176
   journey to Britain 1–4, 6, 16, 122, 127, 135
   Owls Do Cry 136, 142
   Scented Gardens for the Blind 134
   A State of Siege 124
   To the Is-Land 15, 23, 122–5, 127–31, 134–6, 138, 167, 170
   Towards Another Summer 125–6
   Yellow Flowers in the Antipodean Room 149
Freud, Sigmund 15, 60–2, 68–70, 72, 74, 82, 89, 162
   unheimlich 15, 21, 60–2, 73, 80, 82, 85–6, 89, 162, 175

Gallagher, Catherine 41, 46, 51
Gevisser, Mark 91–2
Gilroy, Beryl 6, 143
Gilroy, Paul (*see also* post-imperial melancholia) 55, 144, 148–9
green imperialism 30, 33, 63

Hall, Stuart 6–7, 12
Hall, Catherine and Sonya O. Rose 22–3, 29
Heart of Darkness (1899) 84
Heidegger, Martin 16

Index

India (*see also* Partition) 4, 18, 65, 85, 144
  Anglo-Indians 167

King, Michael 130, 132, 141, 151
Kuhn, Annette 40

Lejeune, Philippe 10, 126
Lessing, Doris 1–8, 14–24, 42–5, 48, 80, 88, 91, 120, 127–8, 142, 147, 152, 156–8, 162–70, 173–7
  African Laughter 5, 15, 92–8, 107–17, 119
  Alfred and Emily 5, 42–5, 93–5, 97, 104, 116–20, 164–6, 170
  arrival in Britain 1–5, 96, 157
  communist sympathies 94, 107, 176
  Going Home 5, 91–2, 94, 97–108, 110, 113–16, 163–4
  prohibited immigrant 94, 107, 115
  The Grass is Singing 65, 101, 157, 164
  The Wind Blows Away Our Words 67
  Under My Skin 17, 48, 93–6, 103, 111, 116–18, 163, 165
  Walking in the Shade 2, 93, 98
life writing (*see also* autobiography, autofiction, biography, memoir, travel writing)
  as distinct literary genre, 8–10, 14, 177
  autobiographical space 121, 126
  postcolonial Autotheory 11–13
  postcolonial life writing 8, 10–14
  speculative life writing 26, 28, 41–9, 51, 93, 116, 119, 164–5, 174
Lively, Penelope 2–8, 13–55, 60, 63, 80, 97, 127–8, 147, 149, 152, 157–8, 164–77
  According to Mark 26
  A House Unlocked 26–7, 42
  Ammonites and Leaping Fish 26–7
  Arrival in Britain 3–5, 27, 53
  Booker prize 25
  Life in the Garden 26–7, 31, 52–3, 144, 147–9
  Making It Up 13, 26–8, 41–51, 54, 164–5
  Moon Tiger 25, 29
  Oleander, Jacaranda 3, 15, 19, 26–42, 46, 48–54, 63, 149, 167, 169–72
  The Photograph 26
London 14, 23, 48, 51–5, 81, 96, 98, 108, 112, 125, 135, 142–53, 170, 172–4

Buckingham Palace 159
Blitz, the 2–3, 21, 36, 51–4, 122, 144, 147–9
imperial metropole 1–8, 77, 122, 127
racism in 6, 144–6, 148, 150
St Paul's Cathedral 36, 51–4, 149
Lunghua Civilian Assembly Centre 2, 15, 60–2, 74–87, 89, 97, 112, 156, 158–63

Māori (*see also* Aotearoa/New Zealand) 124, 128, 130, 139–41, 146
  Land rights 123–5, 136, 139–40, 146
Marshall, Elizabeth Henrietta 55
  Our Island Story 55–6
masculinity 47, 65, 122
Massey, Doreen 20
Mau Mau uprising, the 4, 92
McClintock, Anne 18, 28, 130–1
memoir (*see also* life writing) 2–19, 24–9, 35–7, 40–6, 48, 52–3, 89, 91–100, 102–13, 118–20, 127, 164–5
  travel memoir 92–8, 102, 104, 106–9, 113, 116, 120, 174–5
Moore-Gilbert, Bart 10–12
Mugabe, Robert 97–8, 103

nostalgia 12, 20–2, 54, 97–8

objects 16, 71–2, 82, 127, 131–5, 150, 153–75
  autotopographies 156, 160–1, 166
  furniture 23, 28, 46, 66–7, 70, 73, 84–5, 131–4, 136, 152–8, 166–8, 171–5
  heirlooms 16, 20, 24, 133–4, 156–8, 173
  luggage [trunks, suitcases, bags] 104, 156–70, 173
  photograph albums 20, 28, 35, 39–40, 157, 169

Palestine 3, 47, 49, 53
Partition of India (1947) 4, 12, 144
Phillips, Caryl 28
photography 20, 28, 35–40, 48, 52–3, 156–61, 164, 169, 171–3
Plato 82–5
  Allegory of the Cave 82–3, 85
postcolonial studies 8, 10–14, 28, 61, 122, 124, 127
post-imperial

Britain 21, 29, 78, 87, 124, 159, 176
identity 7, 60
life writing 8, 16, 45, 126, 156, 158
literature 13
melancholia (*see also* Paul Gilroy) 5, 127, 144, 148, 152
uncanny 60, 80, 85, 89, 162
Prawer Jhabvala, Ruth 42, 44
Prendergast, Christopher 41–2, 51
Prosser, Jay, 36, 39

racial segregation 39, 47, 50, 88, 91–2, 96, 106, 111, 168, 175–6
Rhodes, Cecil 33, 106, 108
Ruskin, John 33

Said, Edward 11–13, 18, 34–5, 44, 139, 155
Salmond, Anne 123, 125, 141
Sargeson, Frank 142
Schwarz, Bill 7–8, 175
science fiction 79
Second World War, the 2, 4, 27, 36, 52, 59–61, 72, 85–9, 93, 146–50, 170
　allied powers 46, 63, 162
　axis powers 41, 46, 60
　bombing of Hiroshima and Nagasaki 76
servants 19, 32–4, 40, 57, 63, 67–8, 88, 168
　nannies 23, 30, 34–5, 47, 49, 57, 71, 168
Shanghai
　Cathedral School 23, 159
　French Concession 57, 63, 70, 88
　International Settlement 3, 14–15, 18, 57–76, 80–9, 112, 160–2
　Japanese invasion of 57, 60, 63, 70, 73, 85–6

Singapore 59, 69, 81, 88, 161
Sontag, Susan 40
South Africa 1, 11, 47, 49–50, 91–2, 106
　apartheid era, 50, 91–2, 97, 106
　Cape Town 1, 49–51
Southern Rhodesia (*see also* Zimbabwe) 2, 14, 18, 48, 88, 91–111, 115–20, 163–6
　farming 88, 96, 98, 101–3, 108, 114–16
　Lake Kariba 106, 108
　Land Apportionment Act 94
Steel, Flora Annie 17
Stoler, Ann Laura 5, 7, 19–20, 67–8, 74–5
　interior frontiers 20, 51, 67–8, 74
Stonor Saunders, Frances 154–5
Suez Canal, the 32, 50
Suez Crisis, the 4, 50, 144, 150

thing theory 156–7, 166
travel writing (*see also* life writing) 92–5, 98, 104, 109, 113–16, 141–2, 174, 177

Vidler, Anthony 61–2, 74, 82

Ware, Vron 65
Whiteness 8, 13, 15, 18–19, 28, 32, 40, 48, 88–9, 144–6, 150, 157, 162, 172, 175
Whitlock, Gillian 10–14, 38, 94, 105
Wills, Clair, 4, 174
Woolf, Virginia, 8–9

Zimbabwe (*see also* Southern Rhodesia) 2, 92, 94, 98, 103, 107–19
　Independence (1980) 4, 93–4, 107–8, 174
　Land Reform 98, 103

www.ingramcontent.com/pod-product-compliance
Lightning Source LLC
Chambersburg PA
CBHW052116300426
44116CD00010D/1685